BLACK AMERICA SERIES

GWINNETT COUNTY GEORGIA

BLACK AMERICA SERIES

GWINNETT COUNTY GEORGIA

Jennifer E. Cheeks-Collins

ARCADIA PUBLISHING

ISBN 978-0-7385-1405-5

Published by Arcadia Publishing
Charleston, South Carolina

Printed in the United States of America

Library of Congress Catalog Card Number: 2001094876

For all general information contact Arcadia Publishing at:
Telephone 843-853-2070
Fax 843-853-0044
E-Mail sales@arcadiapublishing.com
For customer service and orders:
Toll-Free 1-888-313-2665

Visit us on the Internet at www.arcadiapublishing.com

Contents

ACKNOWLEDGMENTS

I would like to first thank the African-American citizens of Gwinnett County for being such wonderful people. You made this adventure a joy. There is so much greatness in the life of the African-American community in Gwinnett County. This book only touches the tip of a very dominating and powerful force that exists within the community. Thank you for inviting me into your homes, your lives, and your history.

I give endless thanks to Katie White and the Arcadia Publishing team. My vision for this county and the African-American community is starting to unfold and become a reality. Special thanks goes to the Pleasant Hill Baptist Church family. You have embraced me with such open arms.

I give multitudes of appreciation to the following people: Beauty Baldwin, Clara Collins, Michael Douglas, Julia Dunham, Rufus Dunnigan, Thomas and Dorethia Livsey, Dorothy Maxey, Josephine Maxey, Eron and Susan Moore, Hattie Peters, Percy Scott, Timothy and Ruth Summerour, Julia Williams, Iri Williams, and Thelma R. Yarbough. I thank you all for allowing me to share your family histories. The Georgia Department of Archives and History and the Gwinnett Historical Society were excellent resources in accessing historic photos for this project.

I thank God for putting certain people in my life—people that give me support and inspire me to move forward. I thank Joseph and Gail Basar, Tiana A. Cheeks-Budgewater, Lee and Joyce Collins, Sharon Collins, Adwin and Angela Gray, Yolanda Jackson, LaShonda Johnson, James and Thelma Myers and family, and Shundra Summers. I sincerely appreciate the love you all give individually. Thanks again!

To my parents—I thank you for the gift of life. Mom, you are a light that shines so brilliantly in my life. You have given me strength, courage, and wisdom through your profound teachings. I thank you for raising me to be a God-fearing individual. My life is like a well-nourished flower; you took care of me and now I have begun to blossom. I know your rewards are great in a place beyond the skies. I love you, Mother. Dad, I thank you for all the lessons I learned from you in life.

To my husband, Keith—I love you more than you will ever know. This book would have not been possible without your technical expertise. I thank God for putting you in my life. You have given your full and total support to this book and to me. Your love is special and will always be cherished.

Finally, I would like to acknowledge the victims, their families, and friends who were affected by the terrorist attacks on America in New York, Washington, D.C., and Pennsylvania on September 11, 2001. You will never be forgotten. May God grant you peace.

Lord, I thank you for all your greatness . . .

——Jennifer E. Cheeks-Collins

INTRODUCTION

We realize that our future lies chiefly in our own hands. We know that neither institutions nor friends can make a race stand unless it has strength in its own foundation. In order to succeed it must practice the virtues of self-reliance, self-respect, industry, perseverance, and economy.
——Paul Robeson

The county of Gwinnett was founded in 1818; Creek and Cherokee Indians first occupied the area. Gwinnett County was named for Button Gwinnett, one of the three Georgia signers of the Declaration of Independence. Few African slaves made up the population of Gwinnett in the early 1820 census. As the slave trade increased, more slaves were brought into the county. However, the numbers are low in comparison to other Georgia counties. With this said, there have been Africans in the area since there has been a European presence.

Very little is documented about the history of Africans and African Americans in Gwinnett. Slave records, sharecropper's logs, and church and cemetery records are a rare find in this county. History books based on Gwinnett fail to acknowledge the rich and long-standing history of African Americans. My findings of the African-American community of Gwinnett were overwhelmingly vast. The community is filled with people from all walks of life. We have surely missed a valuable lesson through the lack of documentation of African-American history in Gwinnett.

There are many African-American residents I did not have the opportunity to interview while doing research for this book. I only wish I had a chance to hear your stories of days long ago in Gwinnett. I wish I could have included all the contributions African Americans have made to the county. It is definitely a new day in Gwinnett, compared to 175 years ago. I salute all persons past and present that helped make this county what it is today.

The pages within this book are meant to display the life of African Americans in the county. These people are all remarkable, and they tell their story through pictures. The foundation of the community is religion, and the African-American citizens in this area are well grounded in the church. I was unable to obtain a photo from every historically black church in the county. I would like to recognize the following, which are not pictured within this book: Mt. Carmel Baptist Church, Mt. Zion Methodist Church, New Bethel A.M.E. Church, O'Kelley Chapel Baptist Church, and Union Baptist Church.

I challenge all African-American citizens from Gwinnett to research your history and preserve it; the world needs to know about the great people of Gwinnett! This book takes the reader from the early days of the county through the present, and I hope you, the reader, will get a sense of the rich history of our African-American community. There are still many untold stories that need a listening ear, so I encourage you to preserve your own family's history.

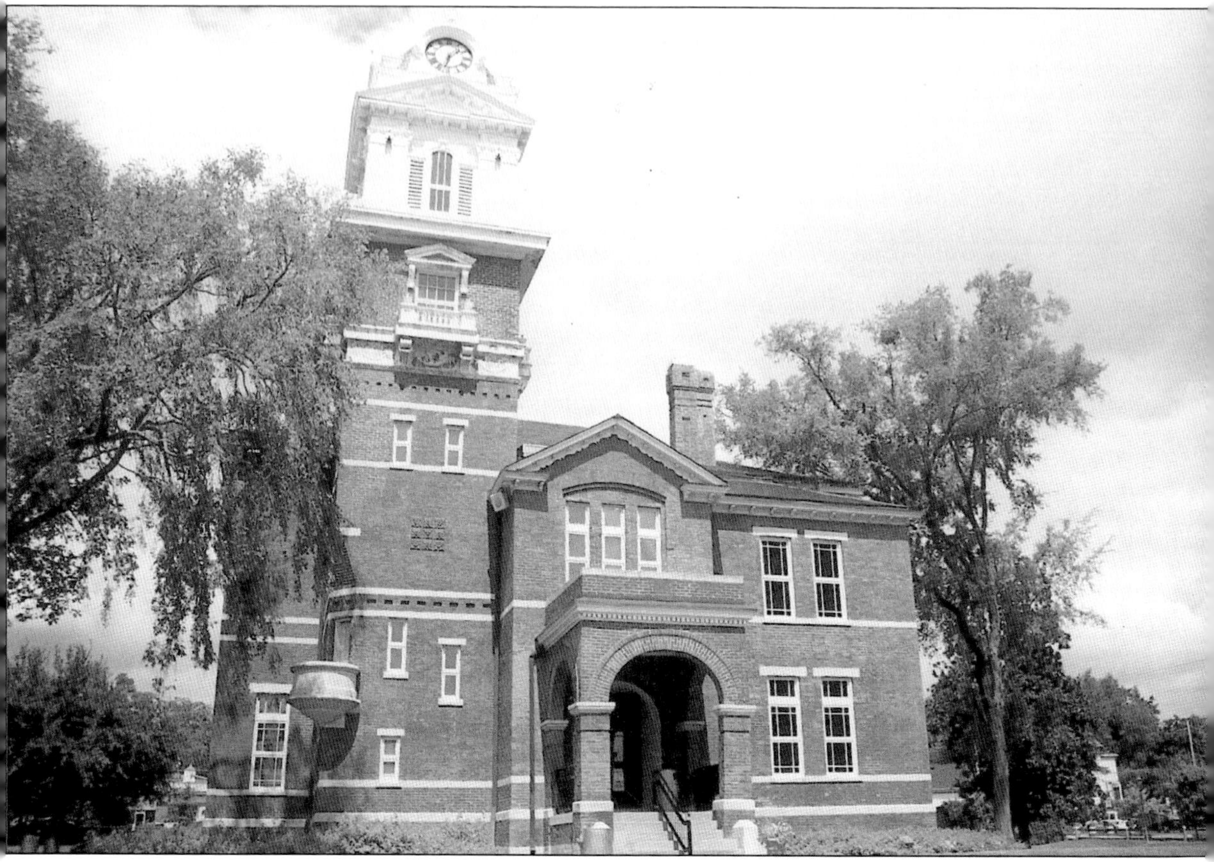

The Old Historic Gwinnett County Courthouse was built in 1885 and is listed on the National Register of Historic Places. Gwinnett County was named after Button Gwinnett, father of the State Constitution and a signer of the Declaration of Independence. Two years after the founding of Gwinnett County, Elisha Winn was charged by the state to locate a county seat. Government administration, official elections, and court were being held in his home and barn before government buildings were constructed. On March 14, 1821, Winn paid $200 for 250 acres of land in Lawrenceville and designed the street system including the Courthouse Square. The first courthouse on the square burned in 1871. A second building was hastily constructed, and dismantled a few years later. The present building was constructed by E.G. Lind. The new building was operating by 1885. Two major renovations took place over the past century. The first was in 1908, when the four-story clock tower was added. The second was in 1935 as part of the WPA projects instituted by Franklin Delano Roosevelt. The building is still standing today, although no official government business takes place there.

One

Early Days

The secret to success is to learn to accept the impossible, to do without the indispensable, and to bear the intolerable.
——Nelson Mandela

The early days in Gwinnett County for African Americans were those of farming and domestic labor. Hard work was standard for all races. Every class of people had a defined place in the early years, and the "place" of African Americans was normally that of slavery. After emancipation many freed slaves moved to Northern states and Canada in search of a better life. Ex-slaves who remained in Gwinnett built the African-American community that still exists today.

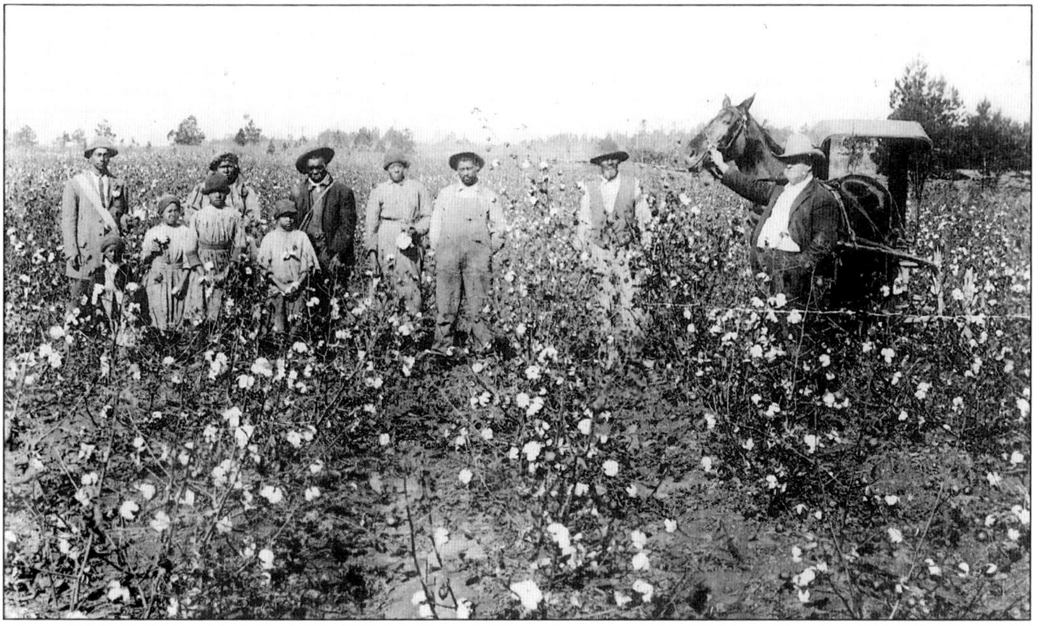

Black sharecroppers and an overseer work in a cotton field in Gwinnett County in 1912. (Courtesy of Georgia Department of Archives and History.)

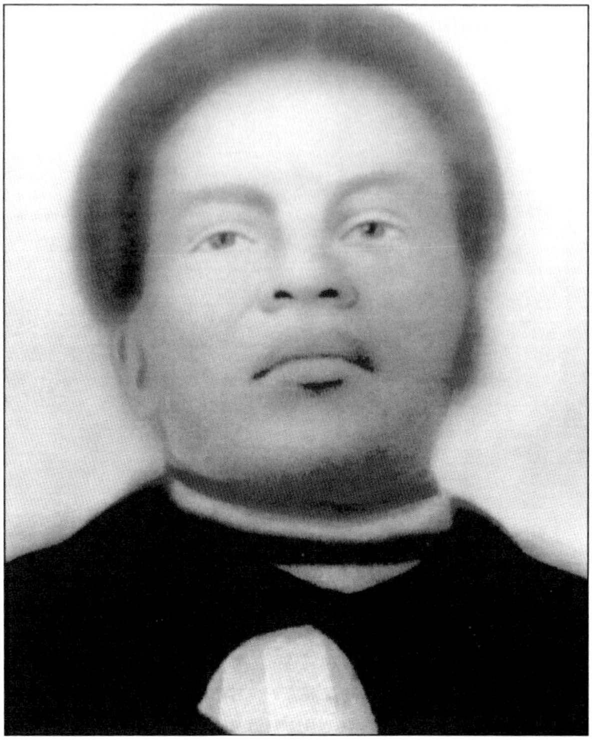

Amelia Peeks, the wife of Felix Peeks (pictured below), is seen here in the 1800s. Mr. and Mrs. Peeks raised five children in Dacula, Georgia. (Courtesy of Thomas Livsey.)

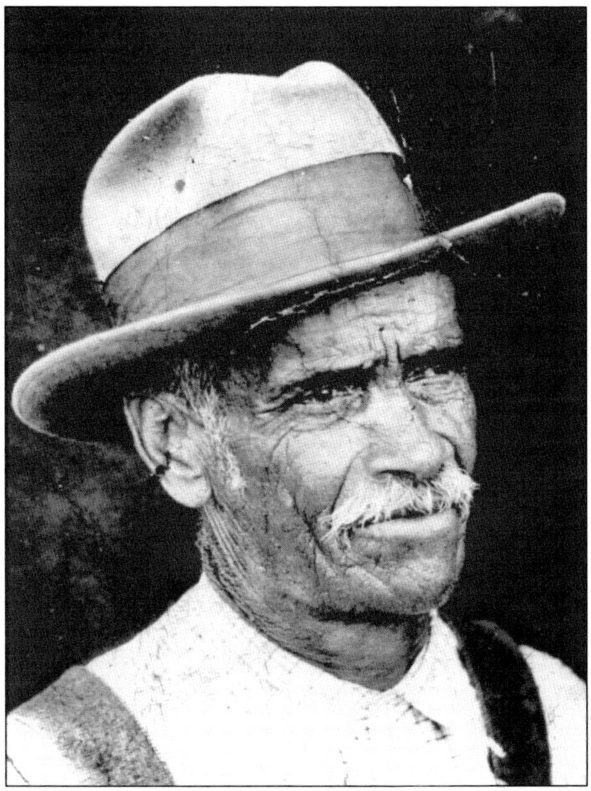

Felix Peeks is pictured in the 1900s. Mr. Peeks farmed in the Dacula area for most of his life. (Courtesy of Thomas Livsey.)

Ex-slaves Laura Gholston and Madison "Mat" Gholston were elders in the community and two of the founding members of the Loving Aid Society. The society was founded by ex-slaves to ensure their families proper Christian burials. (Courtesy of the Gwinnett Historical Society.)

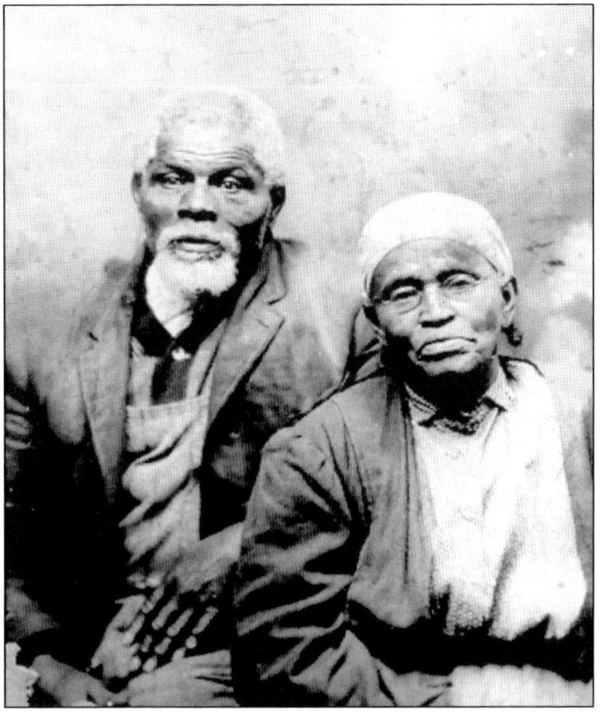

This former slave couple from Gwinnett became employed by John B. Lankford after slavery. (Courtesy of Georgia Department of Archives and History.)

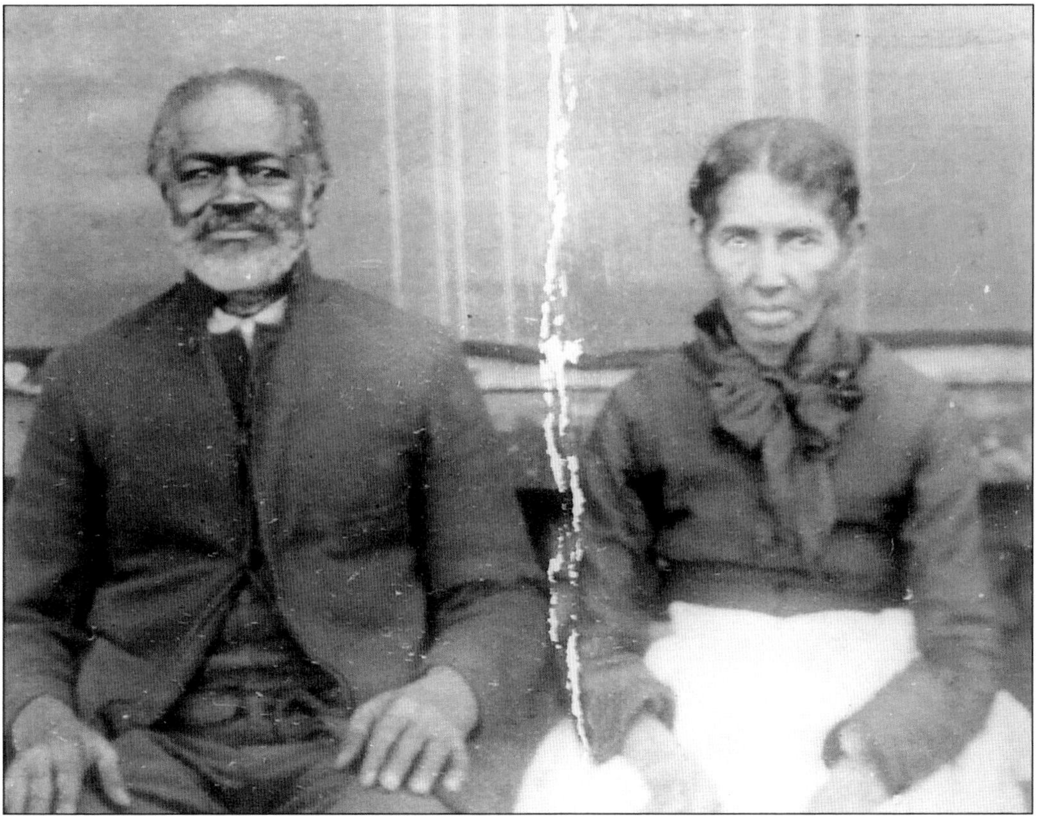

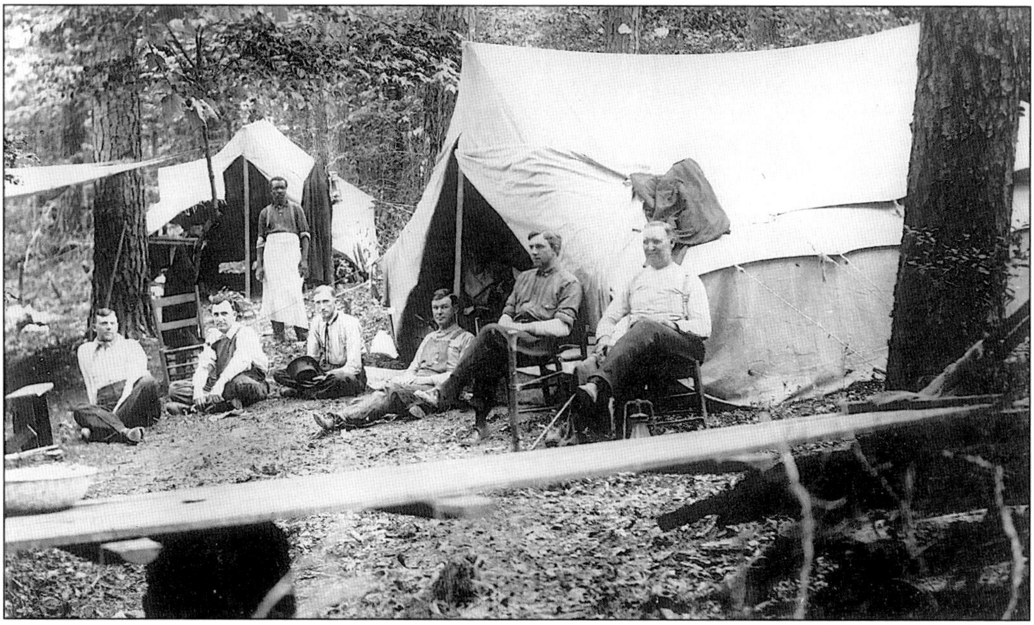

Campers from Buford gather in front of their campground on the Chattahoochee River. Seated from left to right are "Wid" Shadburn, W.C. Walter Drake, John Sewell, G. Hamilton, Frank Light, and John Deaton. The cook is "Hutch" Thomas, standing in the background, *c.* 1915. (Courtesy of Georgia Department of Archives and History.)

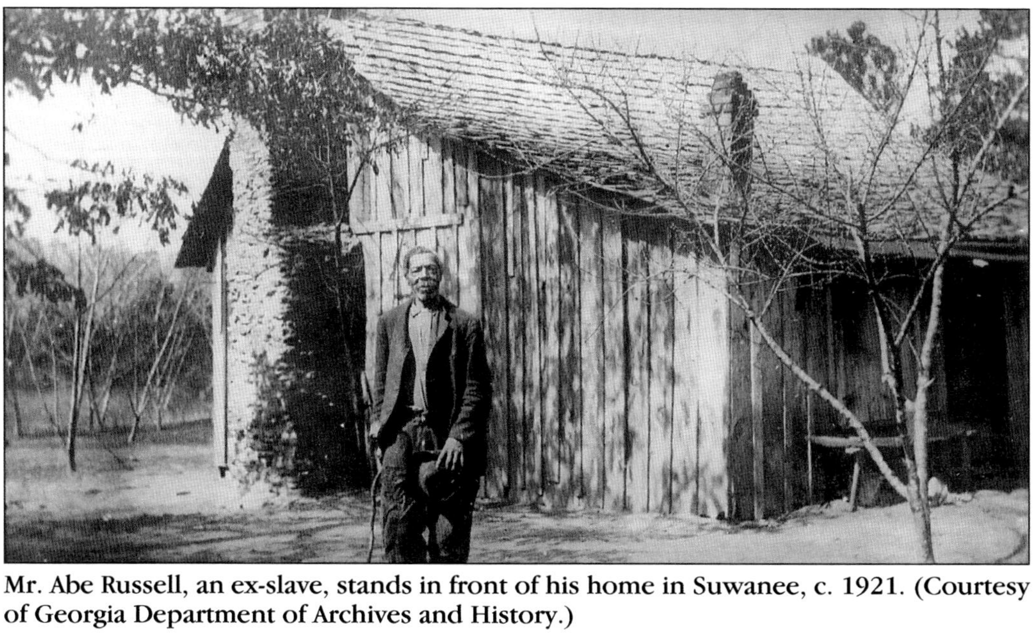

Mr. Abe Russell, an ex-slave, stands in front of his home in Suwanee, c. 1921. (Courtesy of Georgia Department of Archives and History.)

Morena Livsey is pictured with sons Hiram Livsey (standing) and baby boy Livsey in Dacula, c. 1912. This photo is seen on the back cover of the book. Mrs. Livsey's infant son died shortly after this picture was taken. (Courtesy of Thomas Livsey.)

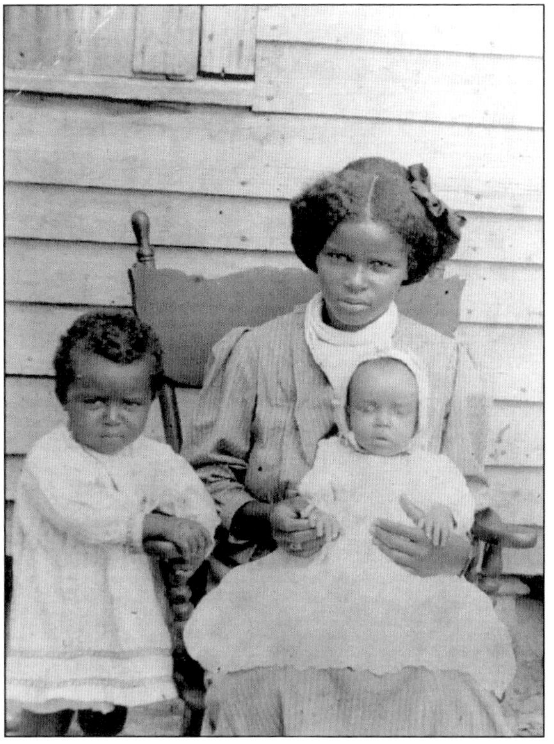

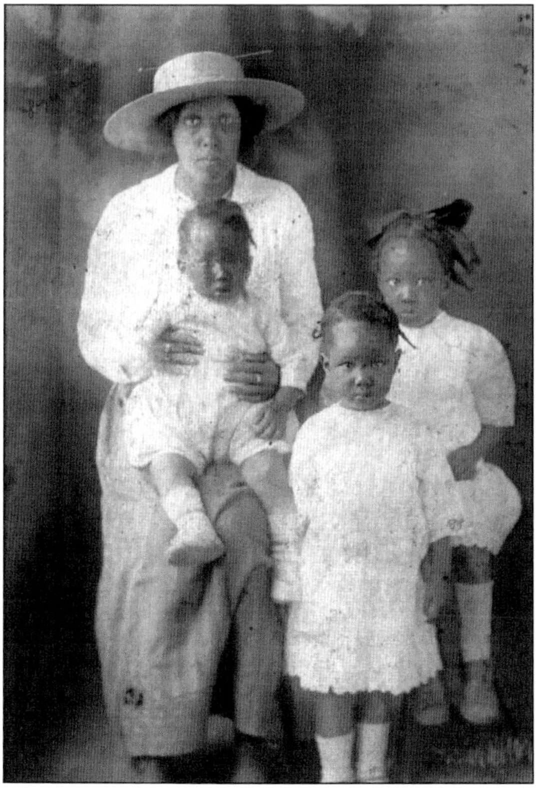

Eliza Cain is seen with her young children in the early 1900s in Dacula. (Courtesy of Ruth Summerour.)

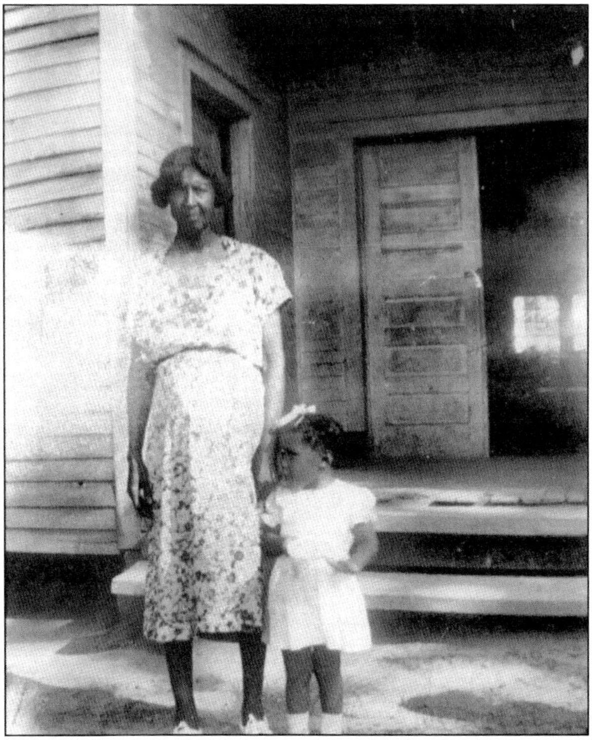

Savannah Sims and granddaughter Shirley stand in front of their home in Dacula in the early 1900s. (Courtesy of Ruth Summerour.)

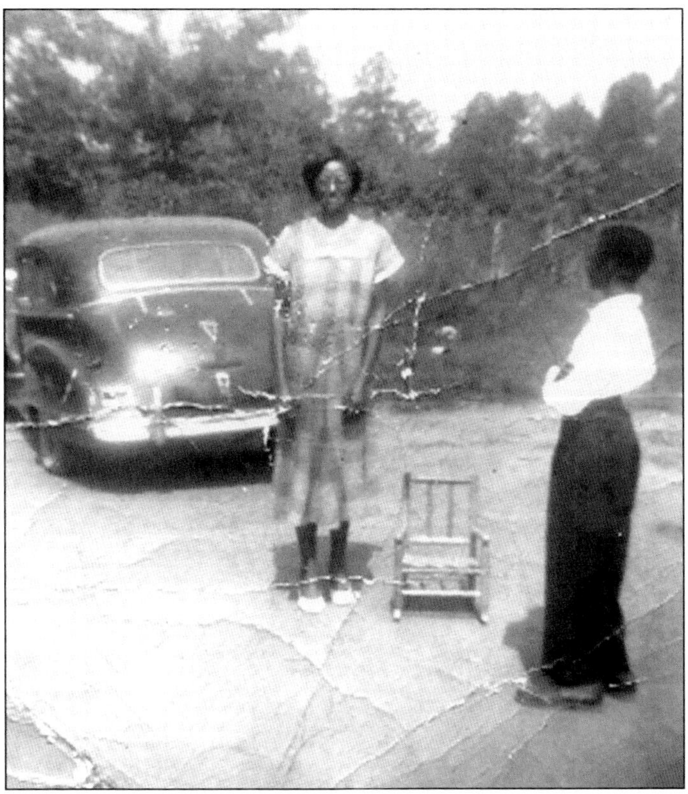

Eddie Mahaffey and her son William are pictured in Dacula in the 1950s. Mrs. Mahaffey farmed to support her family. (Courtesy of Eron and Susan Moore.)

The Lott family is seen in the 1940s. From left to right are Henry Lott, Ollie Gholston Lott, and Marion Lott. Henry was an employee of the Gwinnett County school system for over 25 years; Ollie stayed home and raised 7 children. (Courtesy of Dorothy Maxey.)

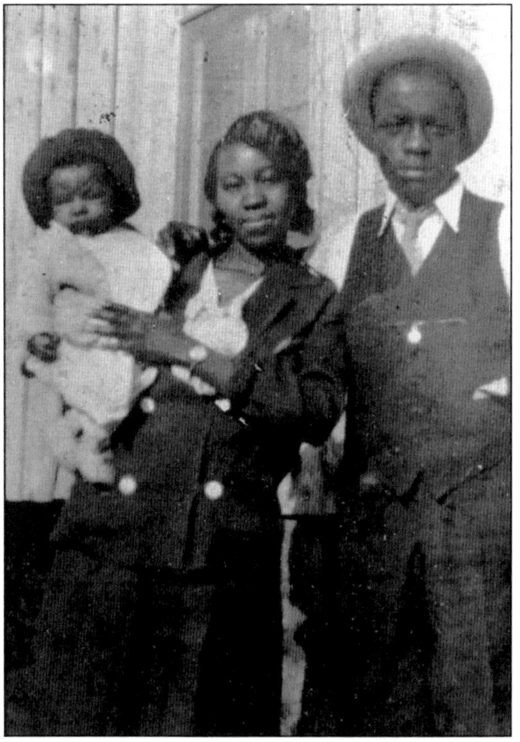

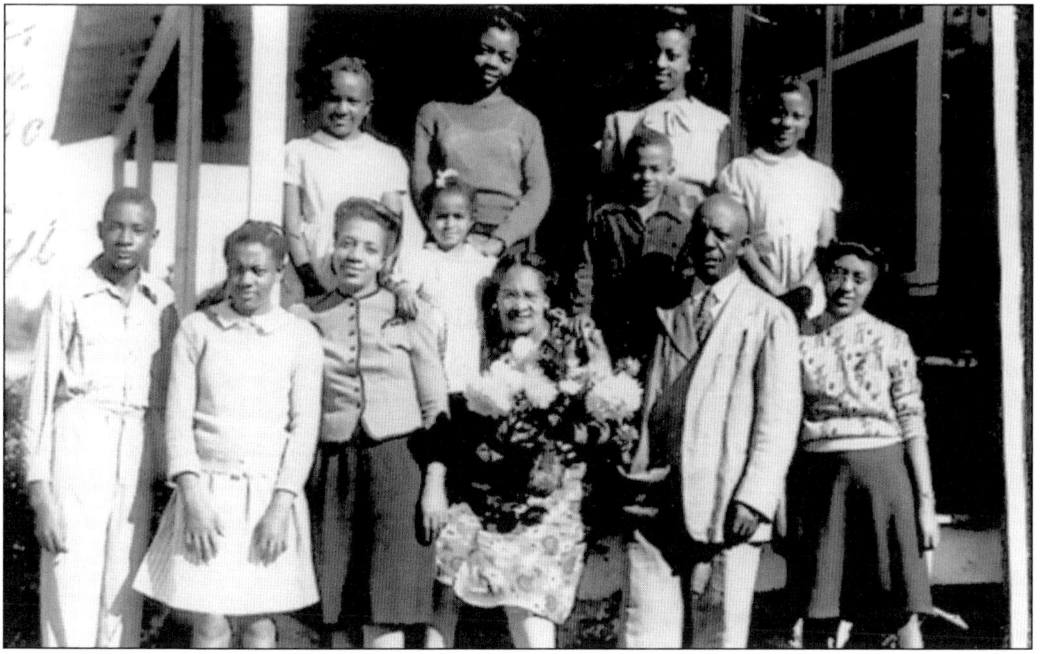

The Scales family from Gwinnett is pictured *c.* 1940. Seen from left to right are Willie Scales, Agnis Scales, Macy Scales, Mary Scales, two unidentified, Lula Scales, Tom Scales, Minnie Scales, Christine Scales (on top) and the two in back are unidentified. (Courtesy of Thomas Livsey.)

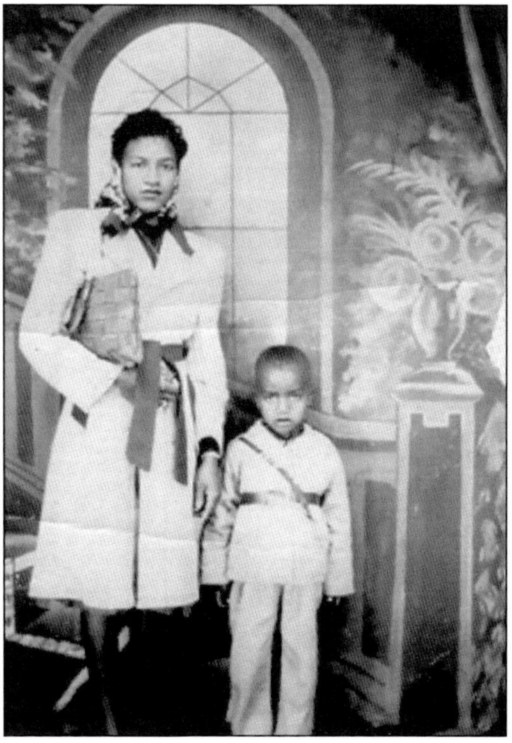

Bobby Echols is seen here with his mother Alice Maxey. Alice Maxey still lives in Lawrenceville at the age of 81. (Courtesy of the Gwinnett County Historical Society.)

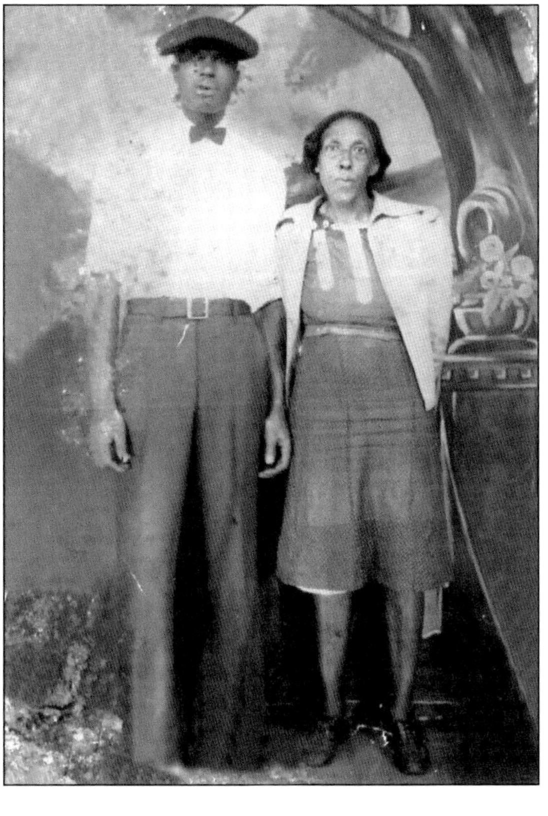

Eliza Cain poses for a photograph with her son-in-law Redemious "Reddy" Maddox. (Courtesy of Ruth Summerour.)

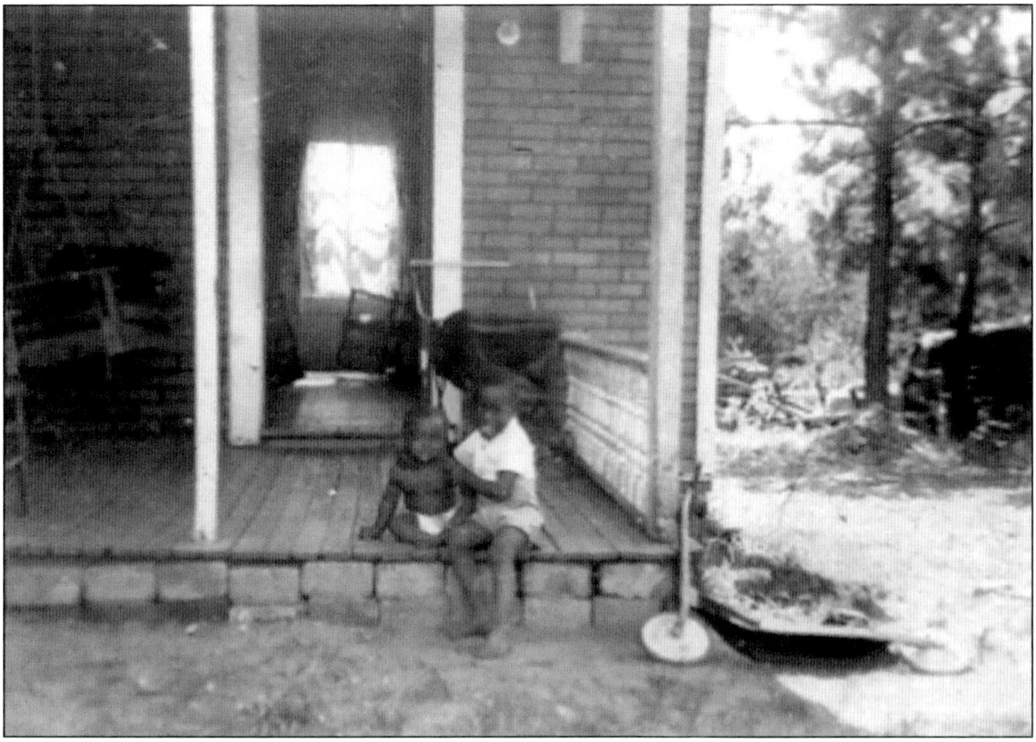

Johnny and Terry Maxey play on the front porch of their Honeysuckle Street home in Lawrenceville in 1948. (Courtesy of Dorothy Maxey.)

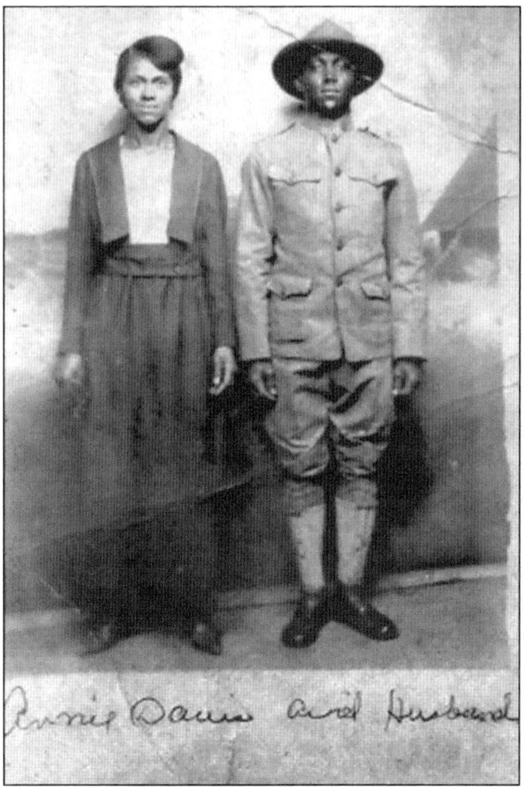

Annie Davis is pictured with her husband in Lawrenceville in the early 1900s. (Courtesy of Gwinnett Historical Society.)

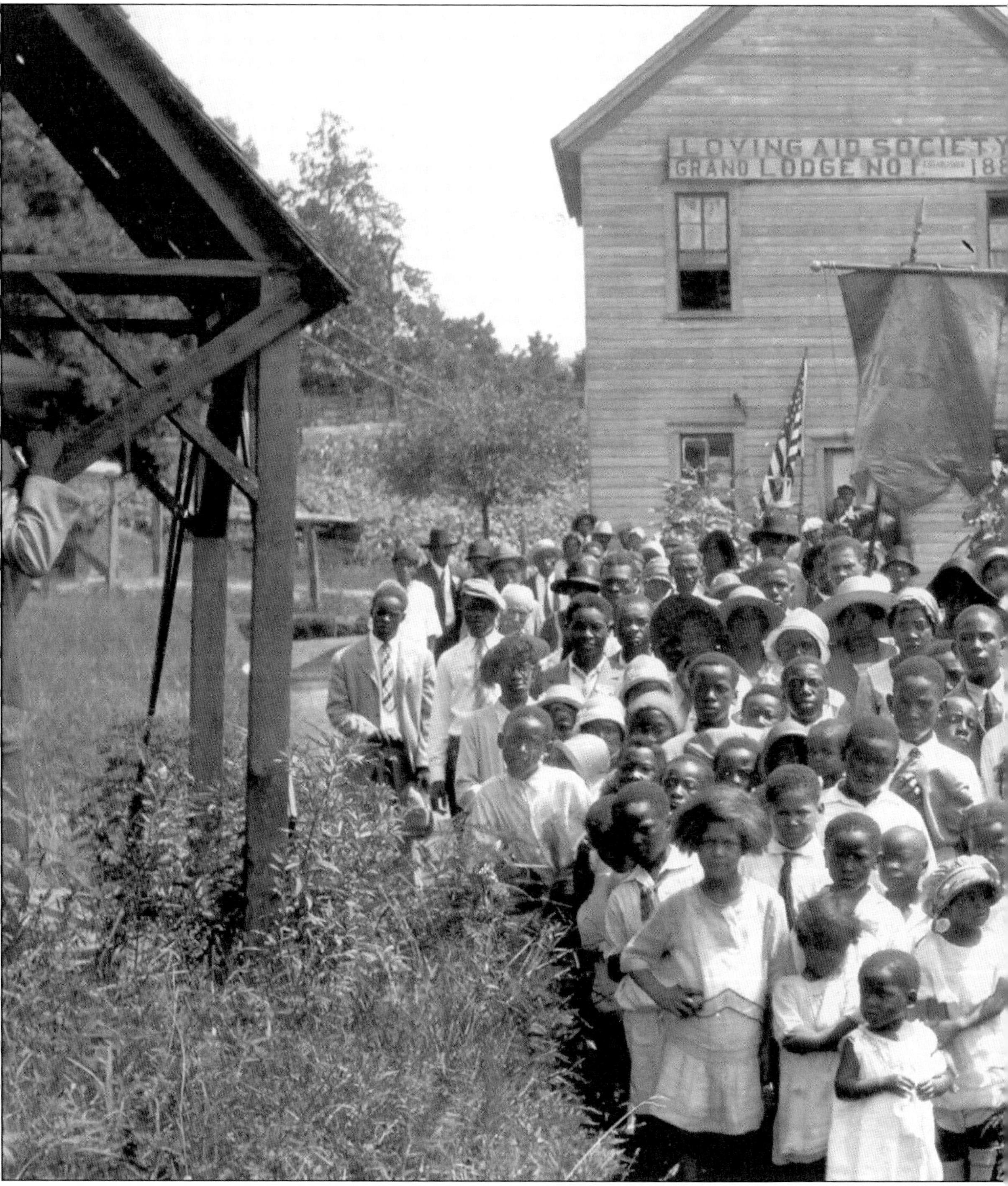

The Loving Aid Society was organized to give a form of burial insurance to ex-slaves and people of color. The society performed numerous community service acts. This group picture of some of the members was taken in the 1920s. Each June the society would have an annual "Turn Out" where the members would come together to feast and

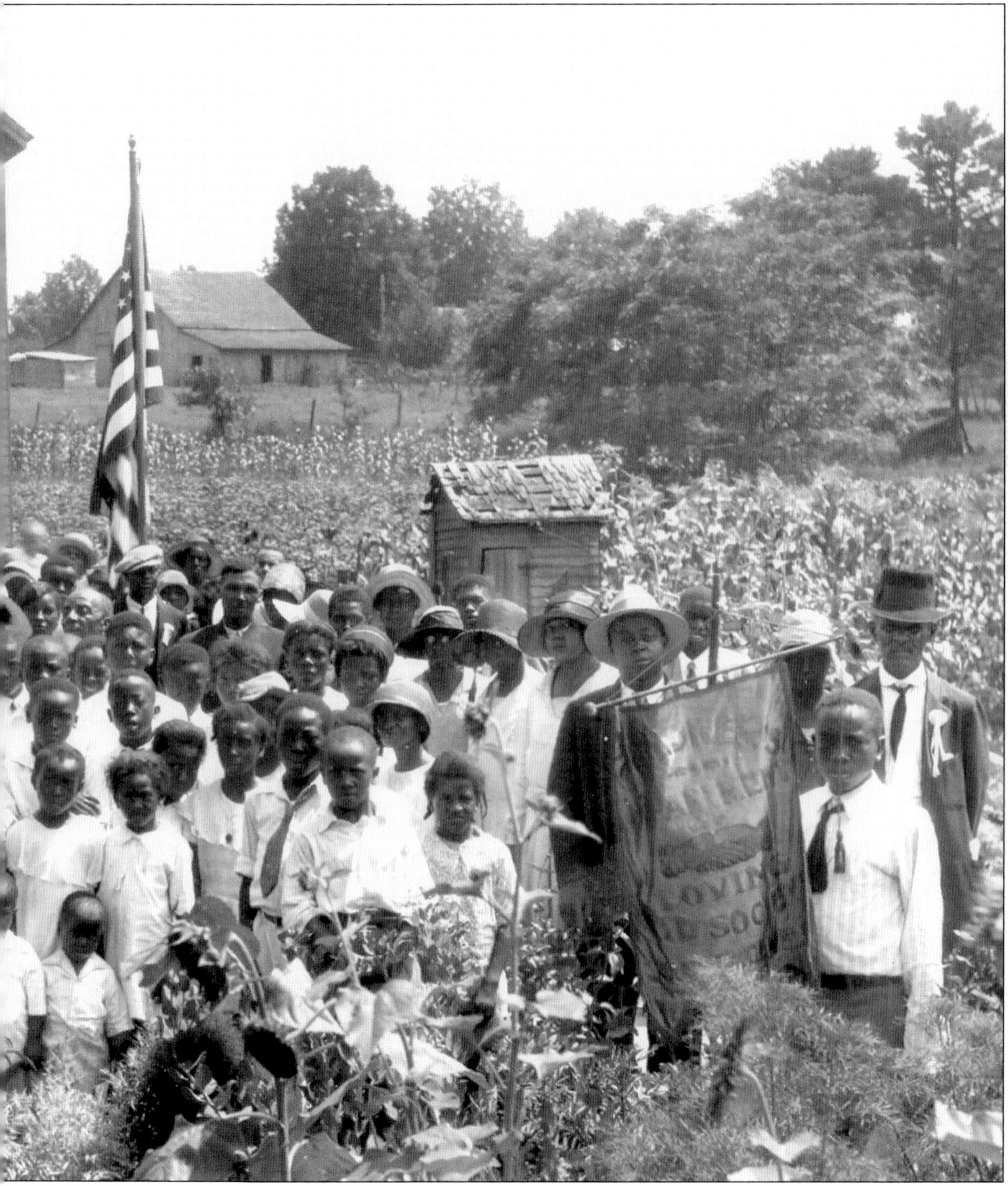

socialize. The building has been torn down and a more modern structure now stands in its place. This photo can also be seen on the front cover of the book. (Courtesy of Timothy Summerour.)

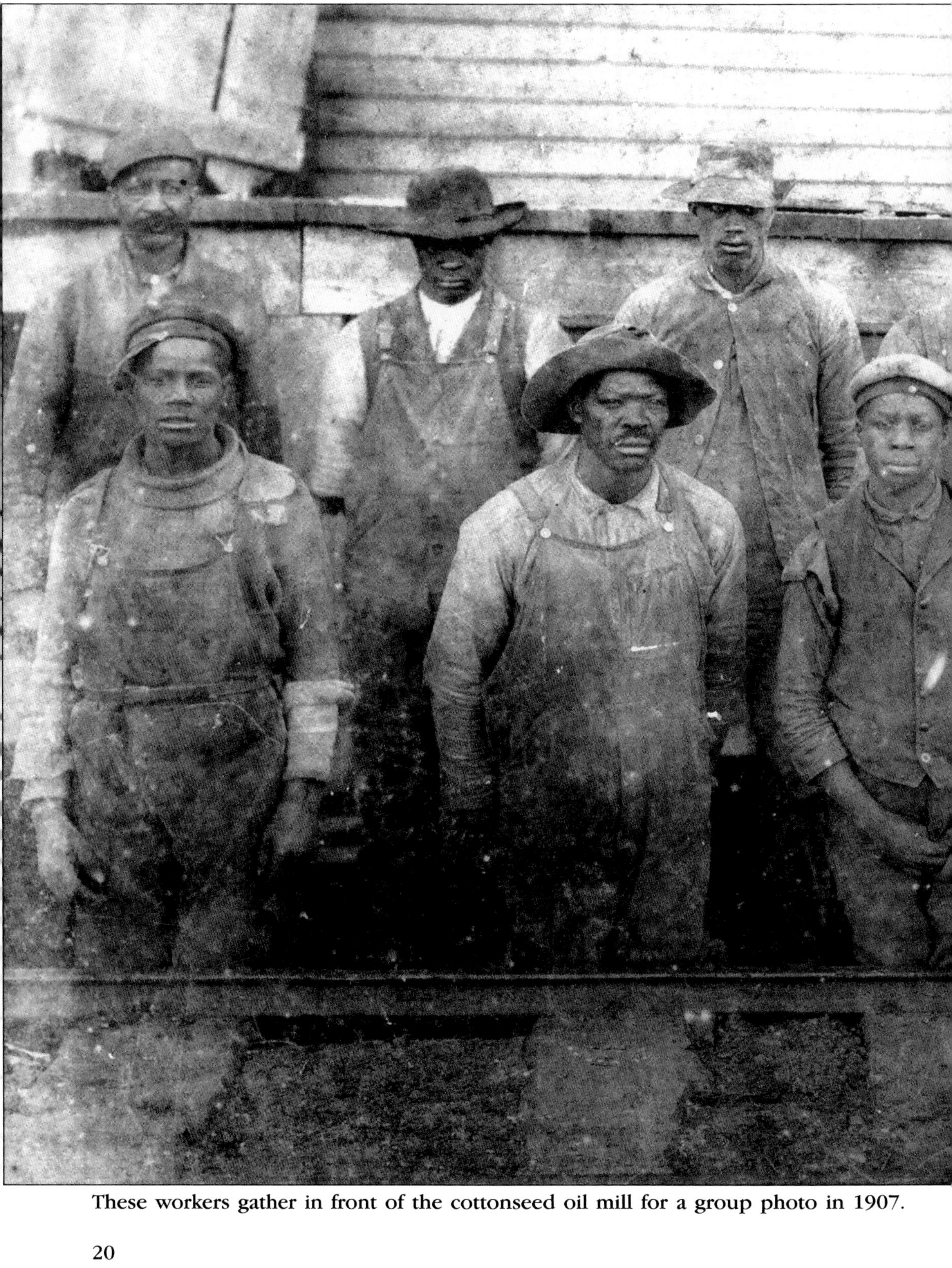

These workers gather in front of the cottonseed oil mill for a group photo in 1907.

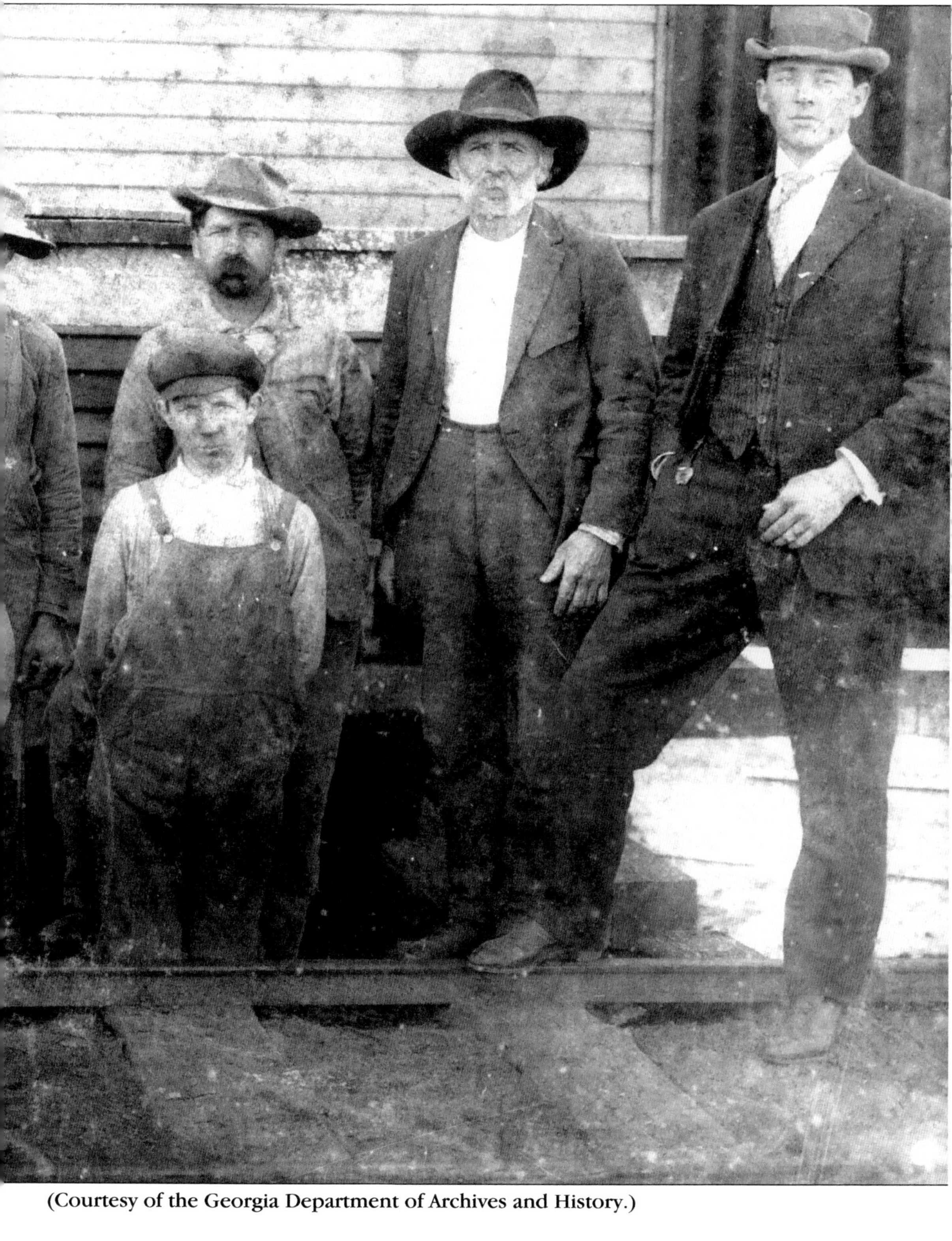

(Courtesy of the Georgia Department of Archives and History.)

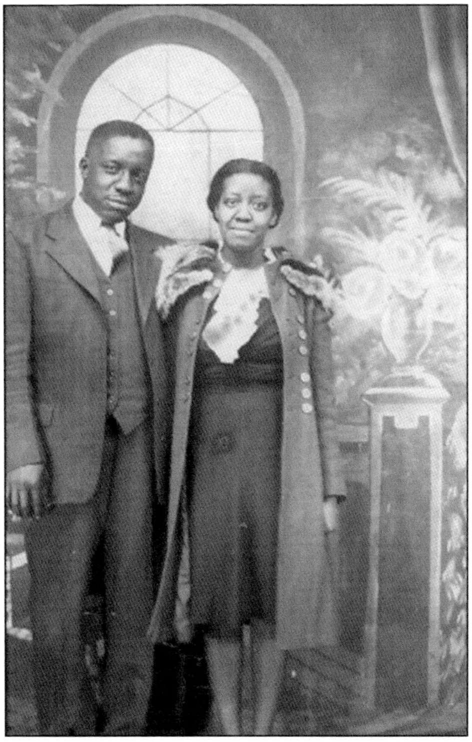

Rev. Henry Lott and wife Annie Lott are seen in the 1940s. They were married for over 25 years. (Courtesy of Dorothy Maxey.)

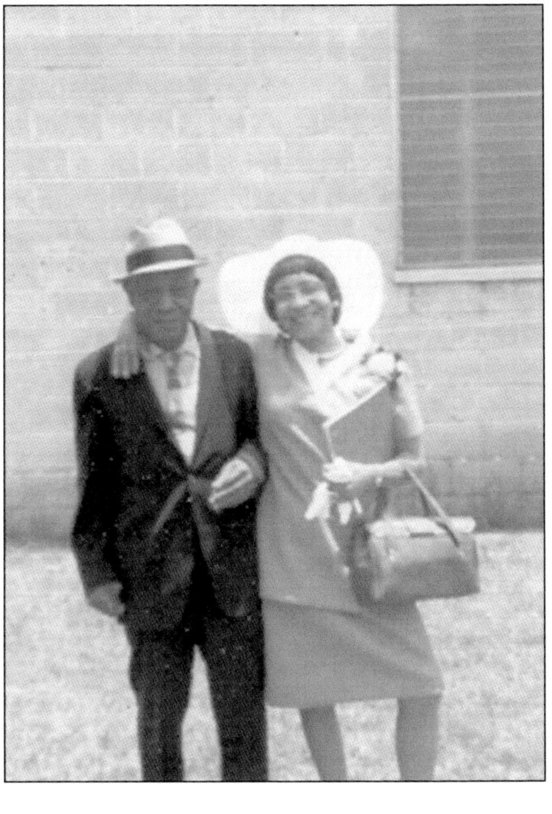

Clifford Maxey Sr. and Lena Maxey are pictured in 1960 outside the Pleasant Hill Baptist Church in Lawrenceville. Mrs. Lena Maxey currently resides in Lawrenceville at the age of 92. (Courtesy of Dorothy Maxey.)

Clifford Maxey Jr. poses with his niece Margaret Lott in 1946. Mr. Maxey had recently returned from World War II when this photo was taken. (Courtesy of Dorothy Maxey.)

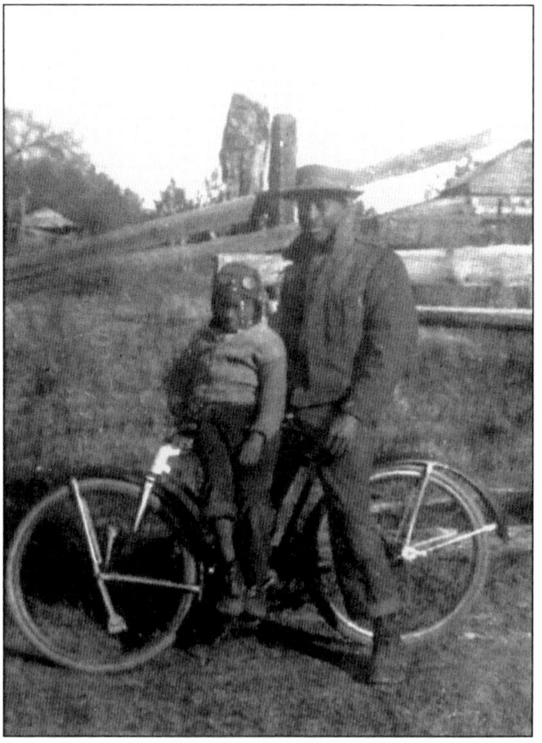

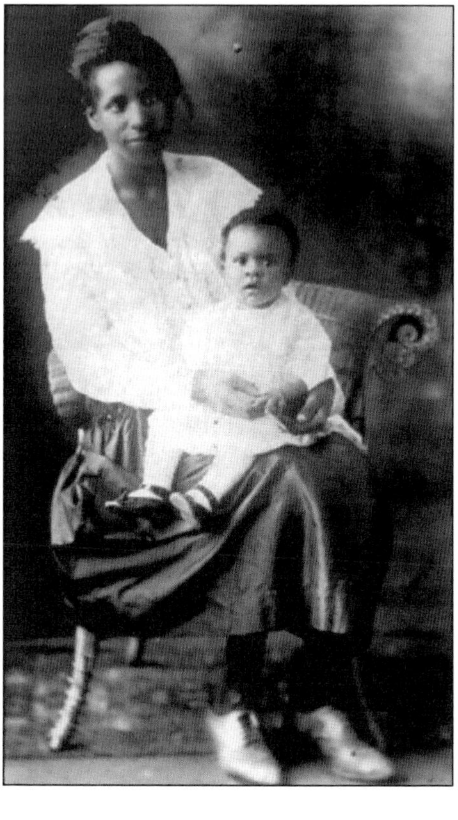

Willa Bryant holds her baby girl Alice for this photo taken in 1919. Alice, who is now Alice Maxey, resides in Lawrenceville at the age of 82. (Courtesy of Gwinnett Historical Society.)

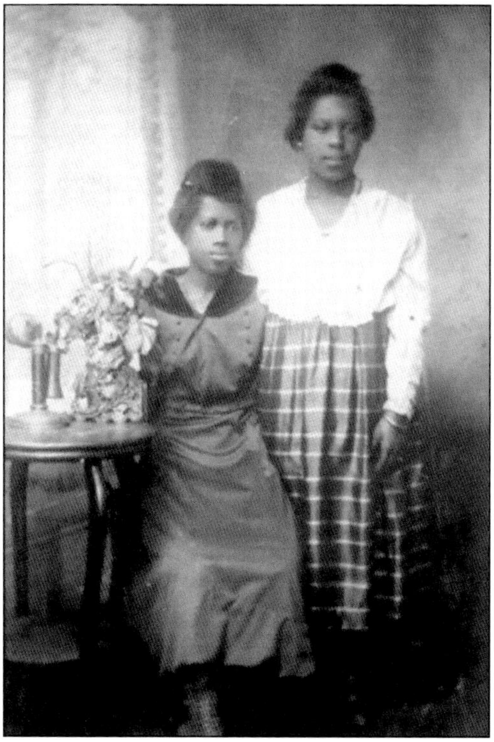

Ossie and Rubena Rodgers of Gwinnett County are the subject of this photograph. Rubena was an educator at Pleasant Hill Baptist Church and Mt. Calvary Methodist Church in Gwinnett County. (Courtesy of the Gwinnett Historical Society.)

From left to right, Clara Collins, Effie Parish, and Earl Collins pose for a Sunday photo in Lawrenceville, *c.* 1965. (Courtesy of Clara Collins.)

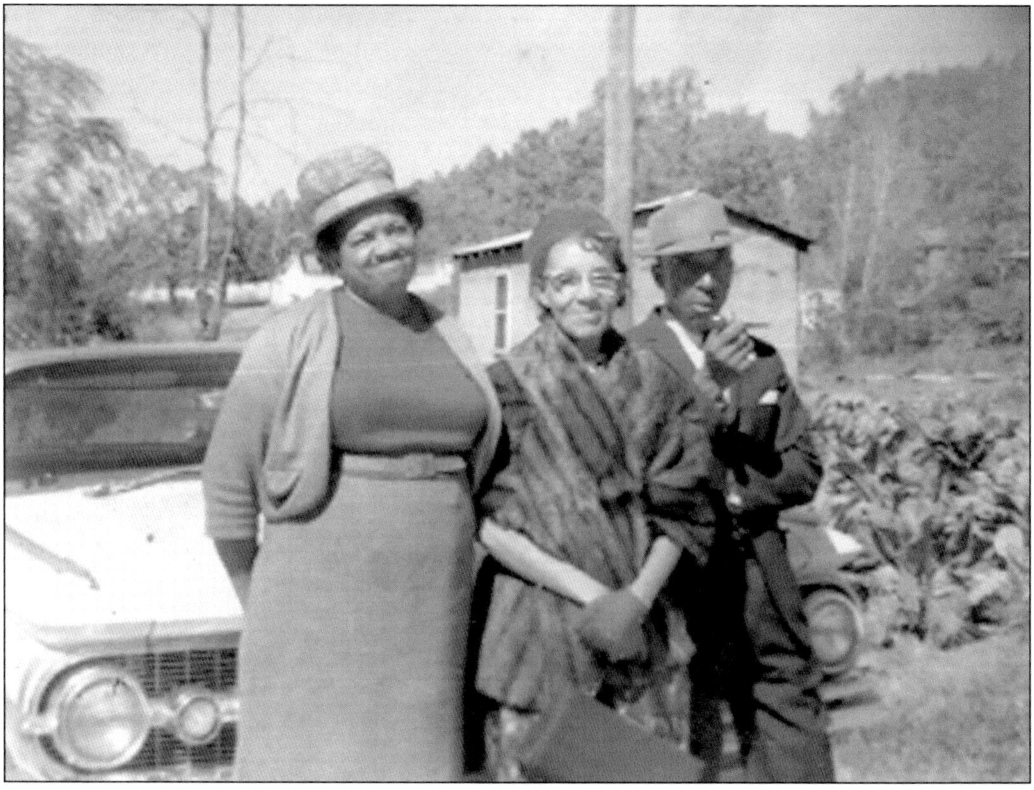

Mack and Mary Haygood are photographed in front of their home on Neal Boulevard in Lawrenceville in the 1950s. Mack worked as a shoe repairman and Mary was a housewife. They were the grandparents of T.S. Summerour. (Courtesy of Josephine Maxey.)

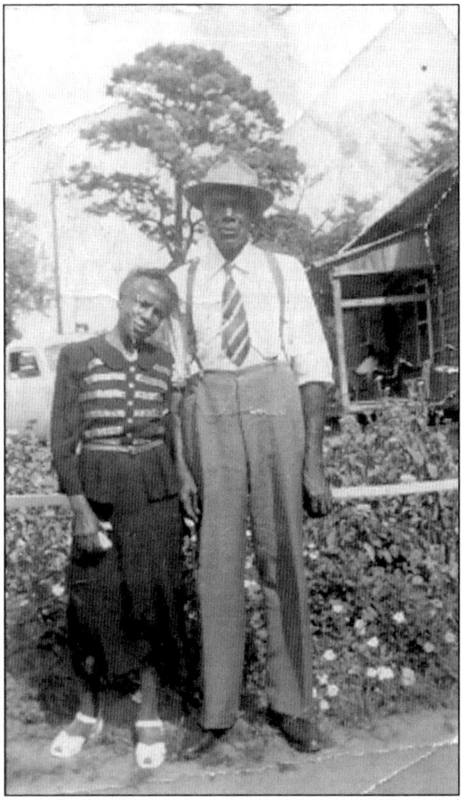

From left to right, Robert Gholston, Carrene Maxey, Carolyn Maxey, and an unidentified man pose for this April 1960 photo. (Courtesy of Dorothy Maxey.)

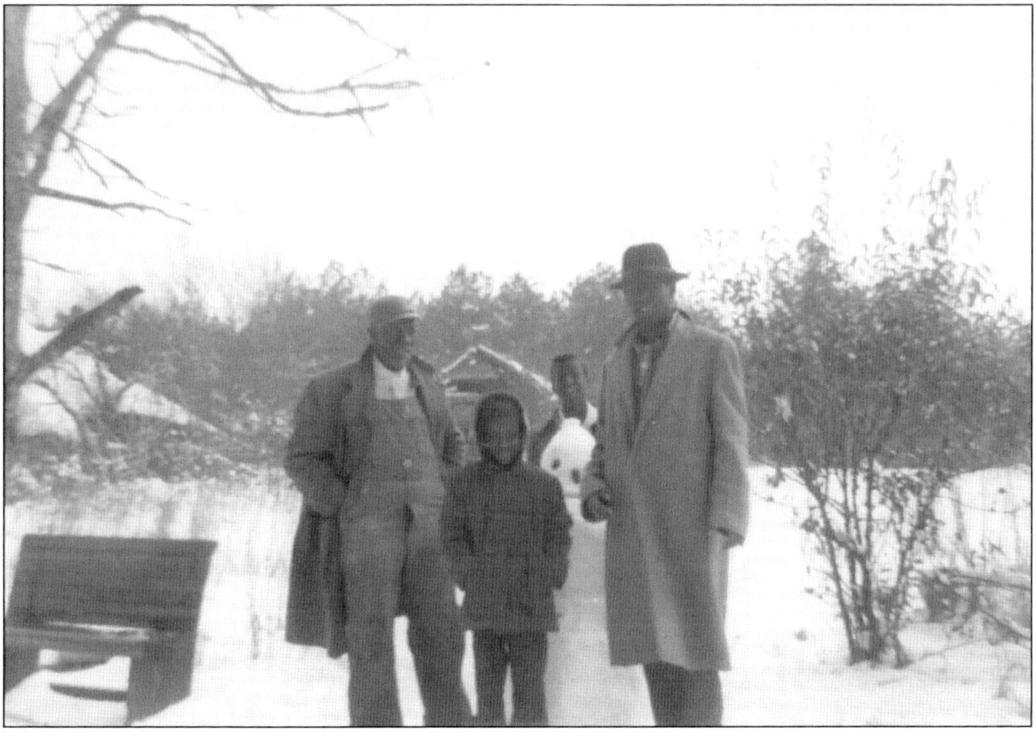

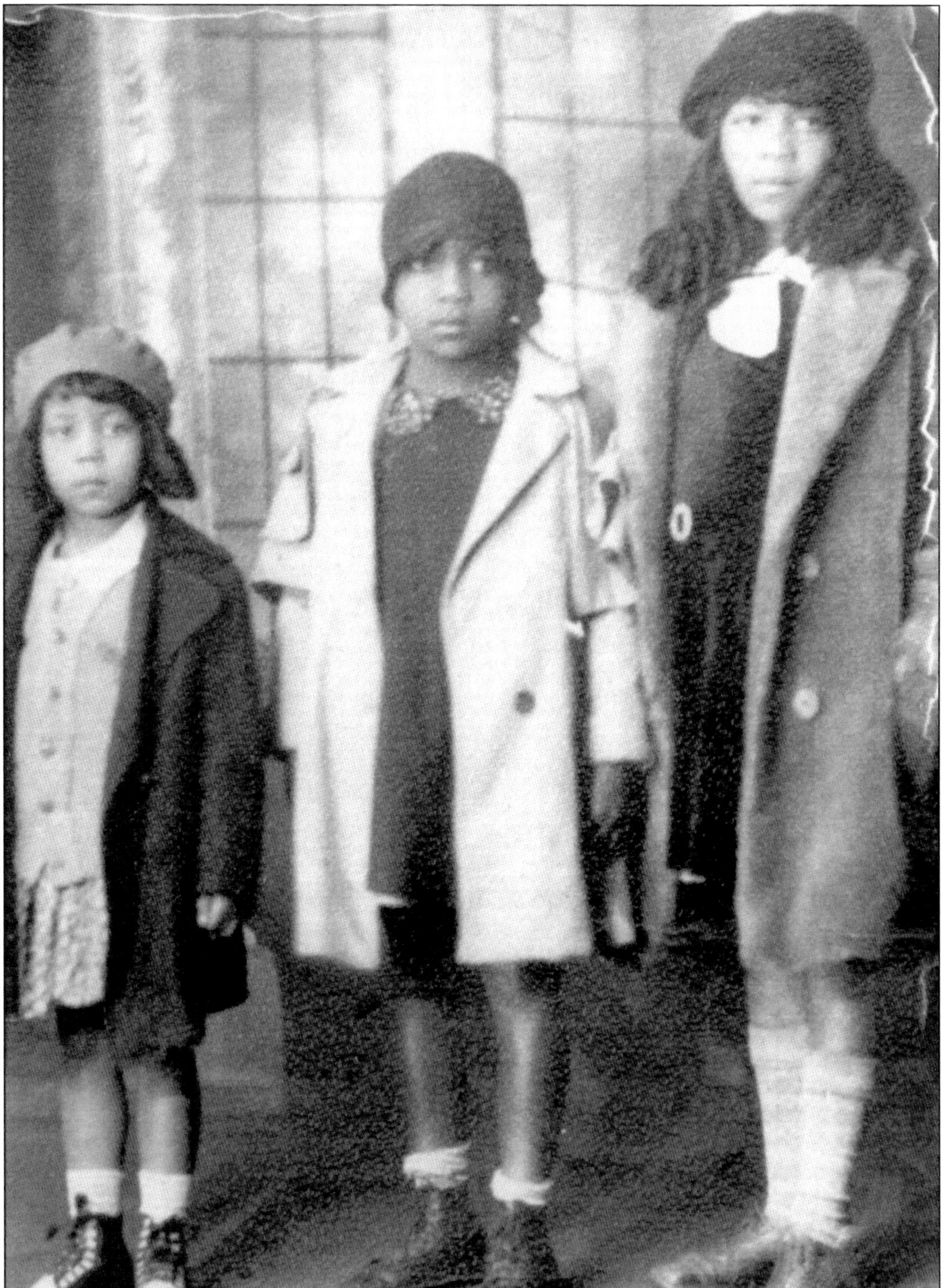

Three Thompson sisters pose for a photo in the 1940s. Seen from left to right are Annie Thompson, Betty Thompson, and Florence Thompson. (Courtesy of Rufus Dunnigan.)

The Gholston sisters are pictured in 1912. From left to right are Georgia, Julia, and Laura. Georgia is deceased and Julia and Laura both live in Lawrenceville. (Courtesy of Julia Dunham).

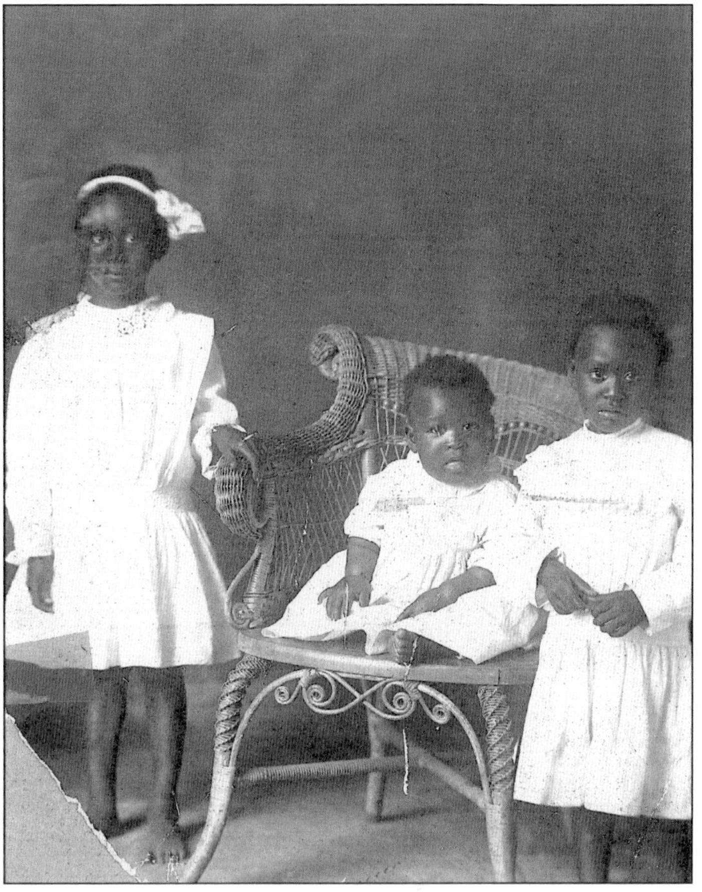

This picture of the Hudson family of Gloster was taken in the 1800s. From left to right are (front row) Jesse Hudson; his daughter Jessie (kneeling); and wife Mariah Hudson; (back row) M. Hudson (cousin); A. Hudson (son); M. Hudson (daughter); Otis Hudson (son); Bertha Hudson (daughter); Georgia Hudson (daughter); and Ella Hudson (daughter). The family farmed to make a living. (Courtesy of Julia Dunham.)

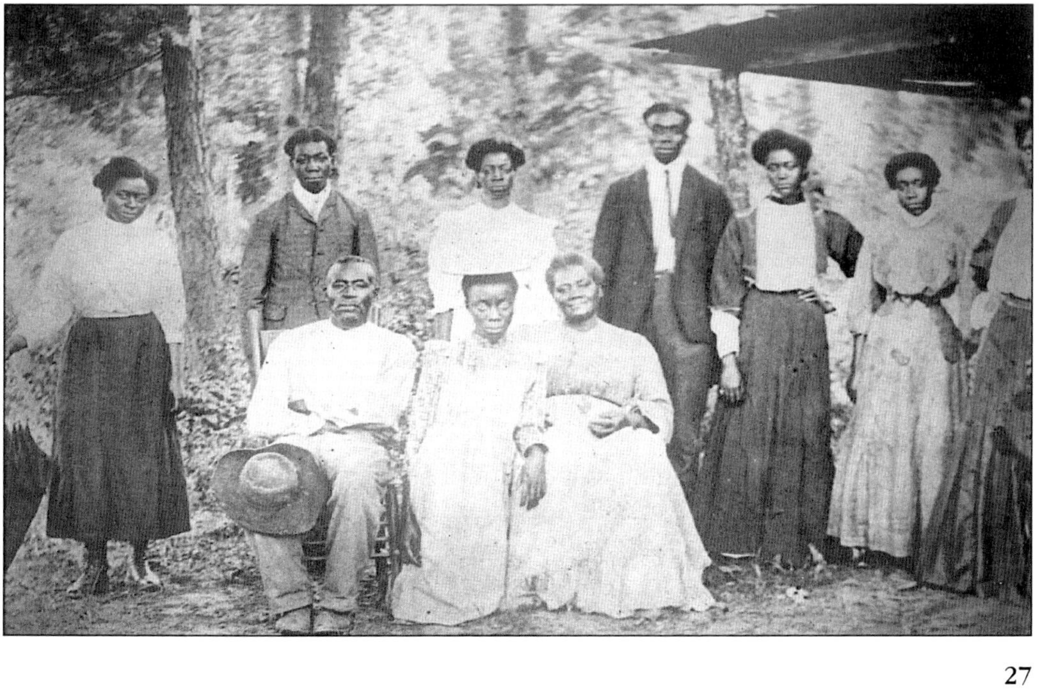

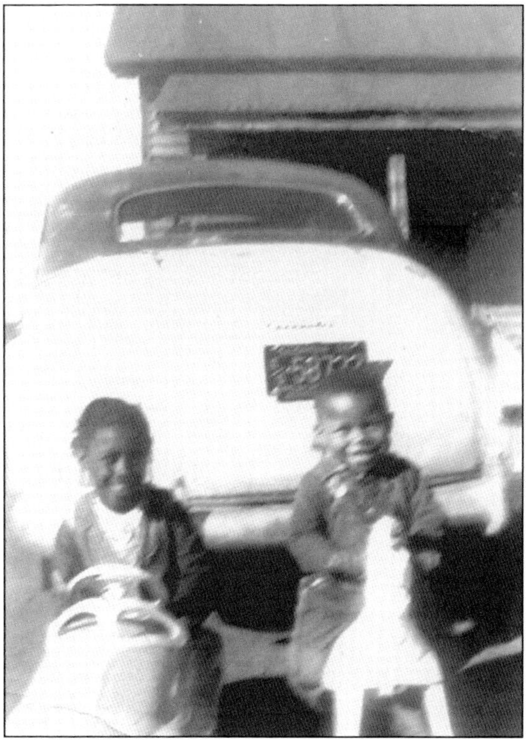

Gail and Anthony Hutchins are pictured at Christmas in the 1950s. They resided in Dacula with their parents Clifford and Geneva Hutchins. (Courtesy of Eron and Susan Moore.)

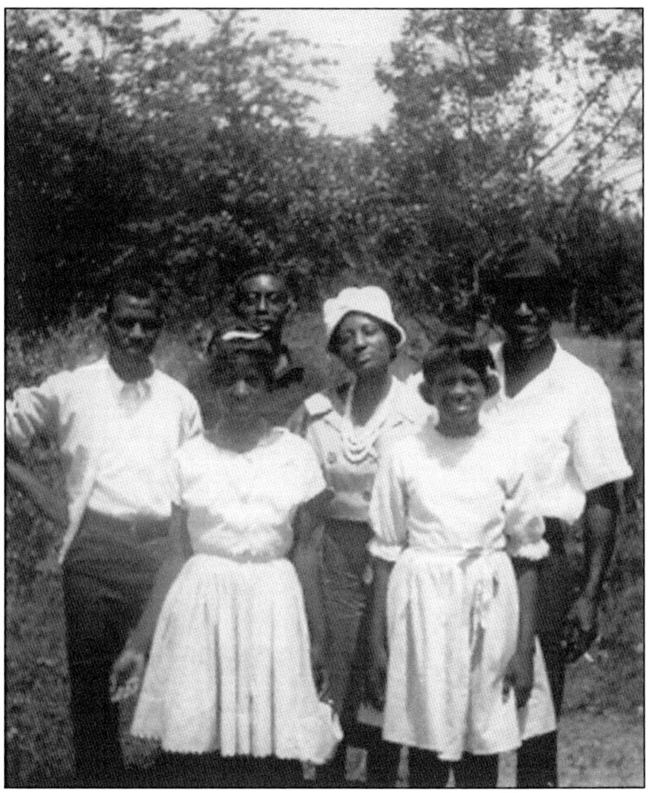

This Maxey family photo was taken in Lawrenceville on a Sunday afternoon in the 1960s. (Courtesy of Dorothy Maxey.)

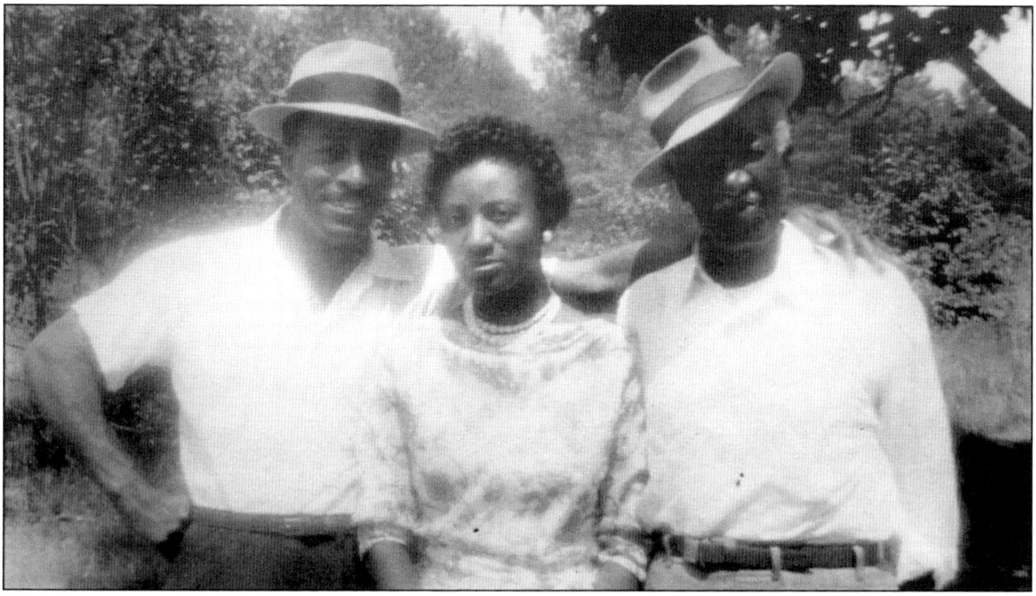

Pictured from left to right in 1962 are Clifford Maxey Jr., Dorothy Maxey, and Robert Gholston Sr. (Courtesy of Dorothy Maxey.)

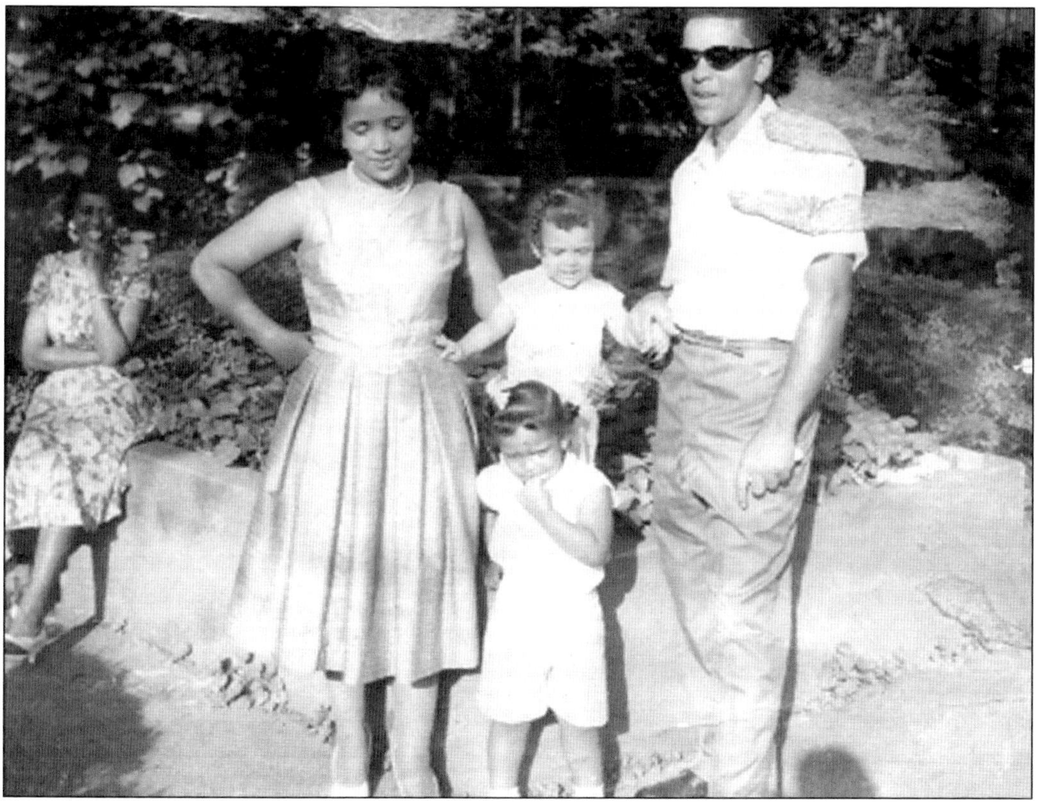

Dorethia and Thomas Livsey are pictured with their daughters Sheryl and Yolanda. The family was visiting Alvia Hall, pictured in the background. (Courtesy of Thomas Livsey.)

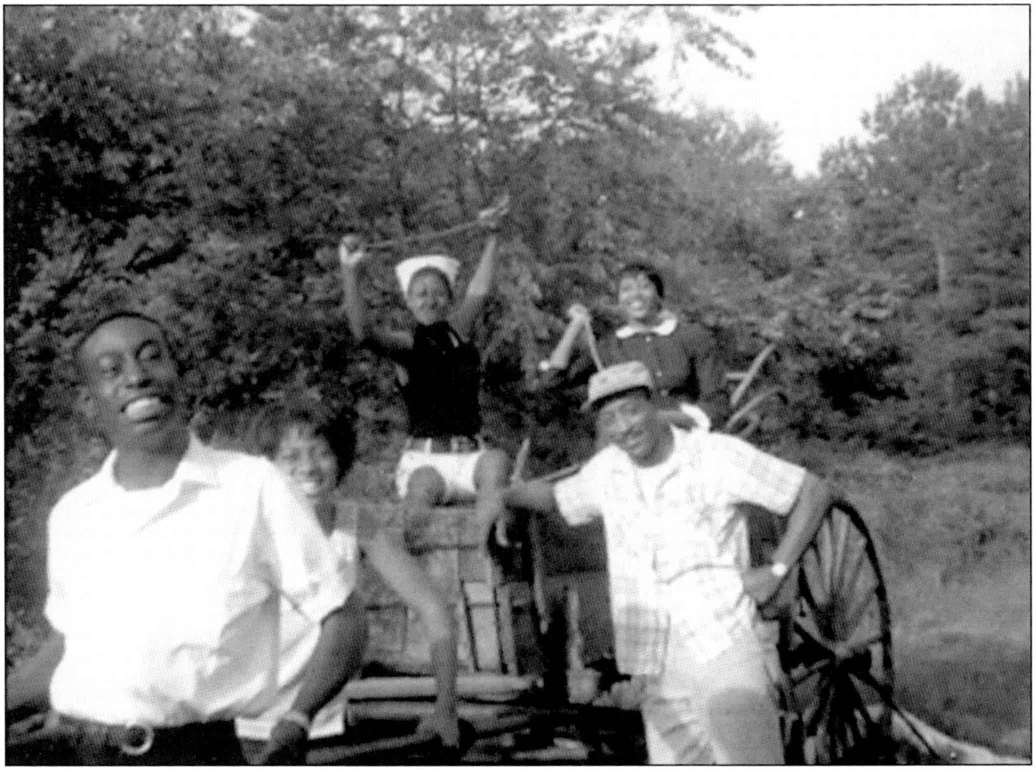

In June of 1967, Terry Maxey, Carolyn Maxey, Carrene Maxey, Annie Maxey, and Cliff Maxey Jr. pose with a wagon over 100 years old. (Courtesy of Dorothy Maxey.)

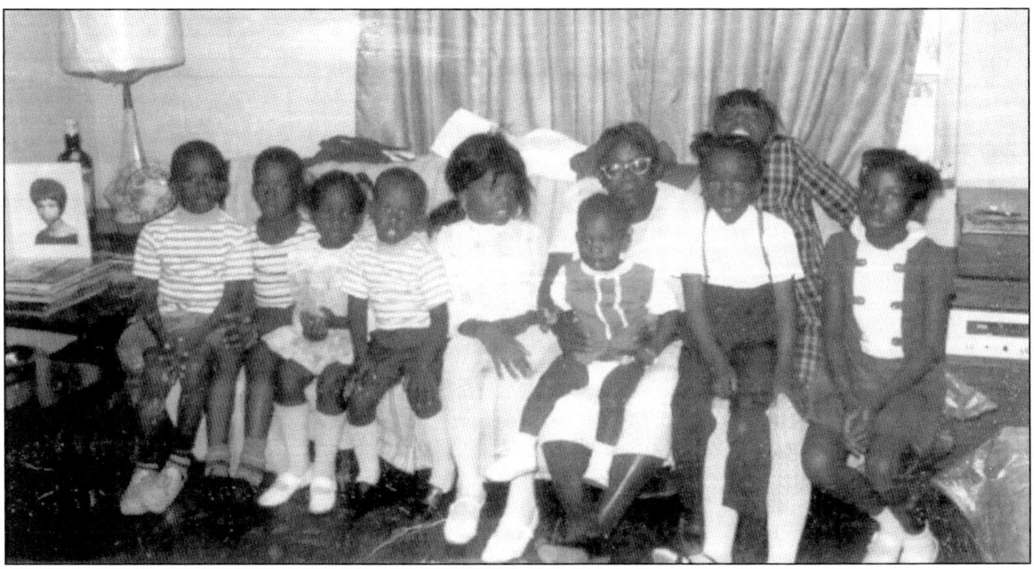

A proud grandmother poses with her grandchildren. Seen from left to right are (front row) Frankie Daniel, Don Daniel, Donna Faye Hosch, Dewight Daniel, Melanie Patillo, Monique King, Perry Hosch,and Sharon Hosch; (back row) Etta Mae Hosch and Sheila Hosch. (Courtesy of Thelma R. Yarbough.)

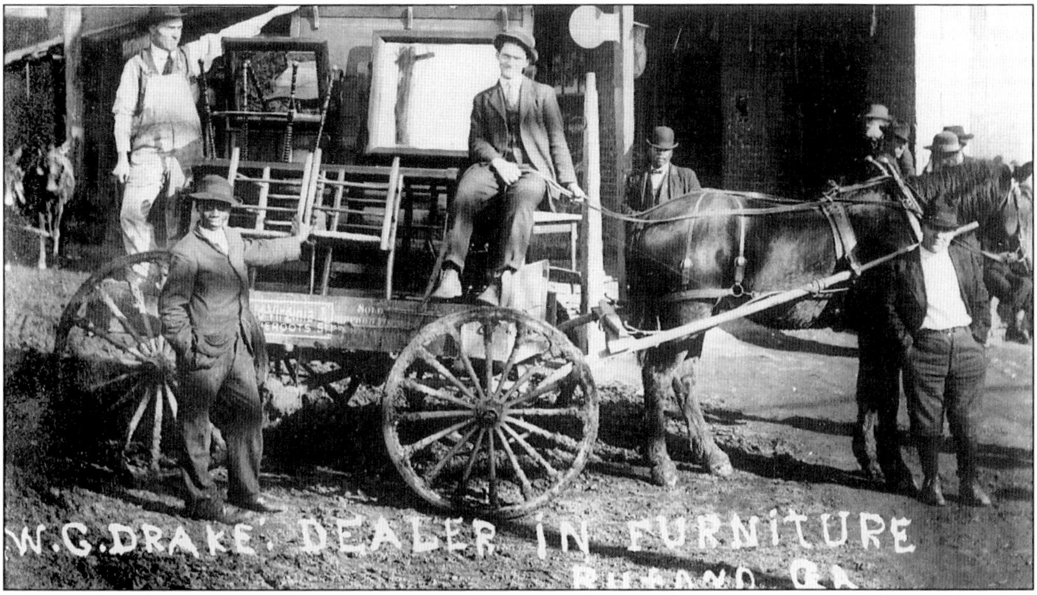

A young black man working at the Drake Furniture Company in the 1900s stands proudly in front of the furniture delivery wagon. (Courtesy of Georgia Department of Archives and History.)

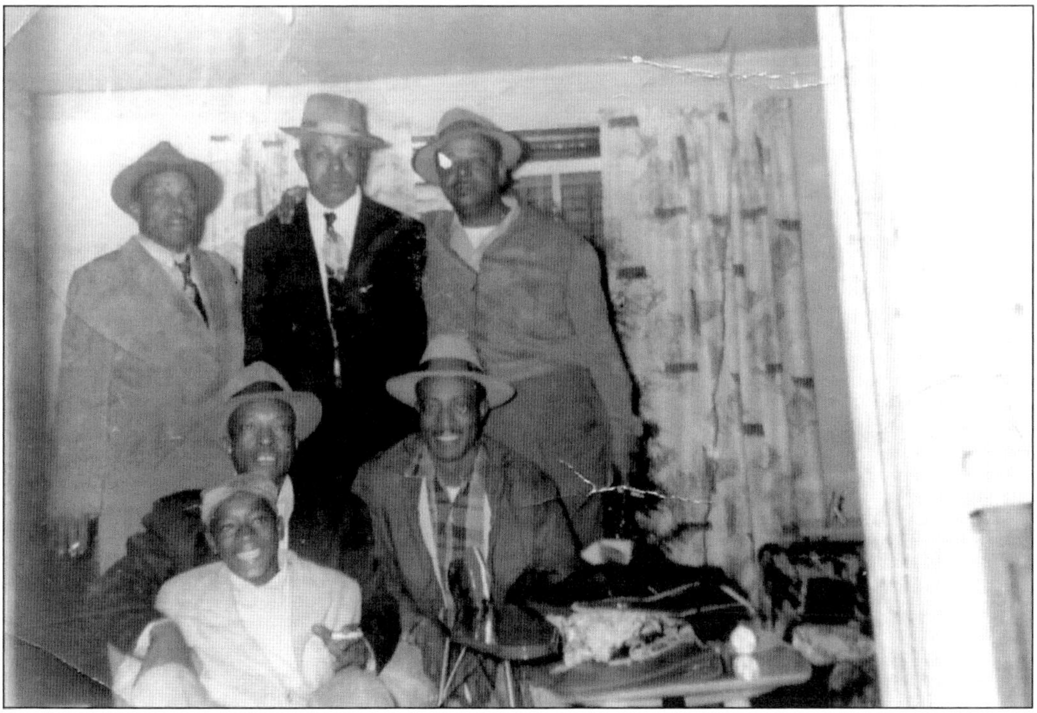

These men knew how to have a good time! Seen from left to right are (front row) unidentified, Alvin "Sam" Maxey, and Cliff Maxey Jr; (back row) "Junior" Dailey, M.C. Haygood, and Tom King . They are pictured in the 1960s. (Courtesy of Dorothy Maxey.)

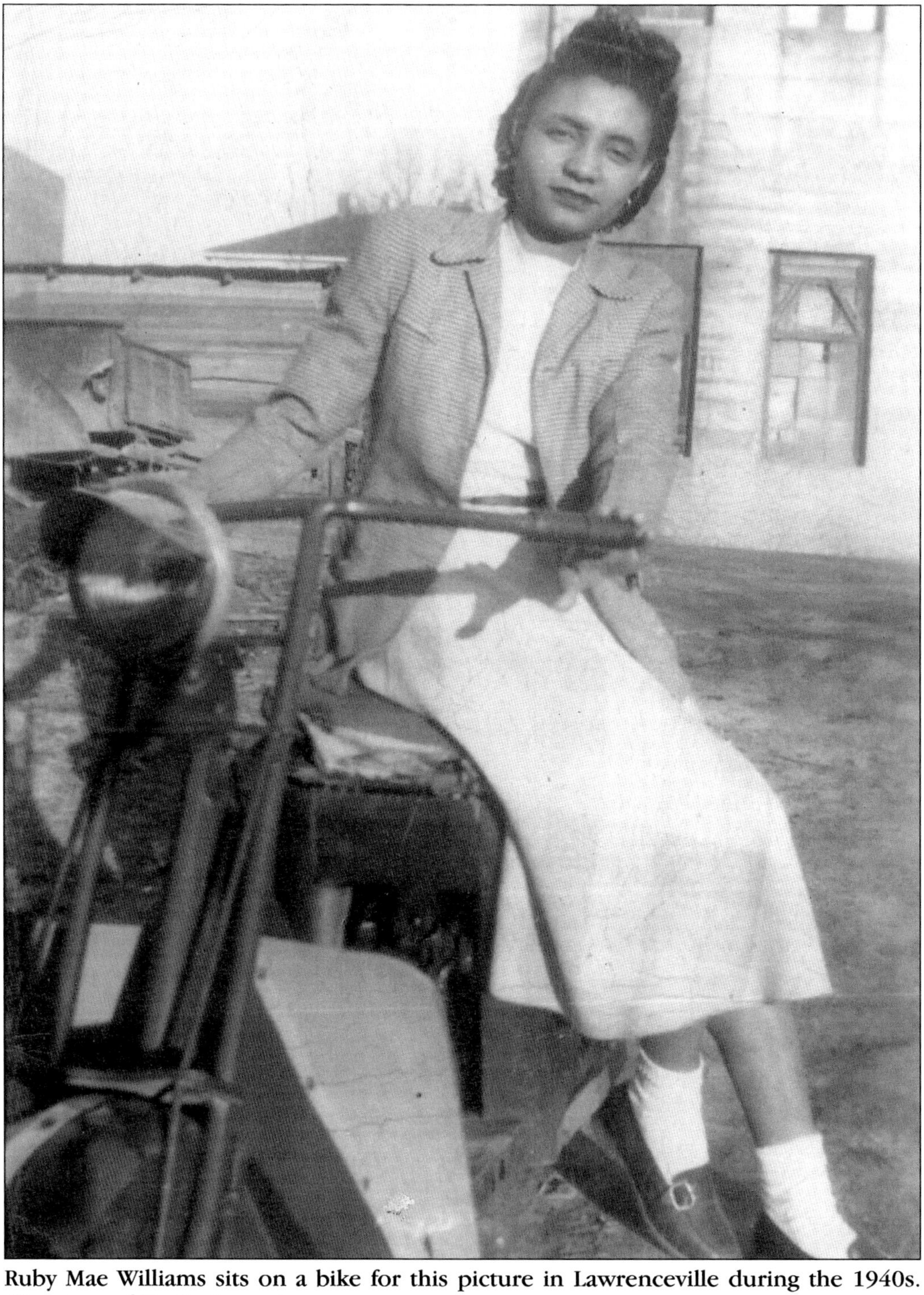

Ruby Mae Williams sits on a bike for this picture in Lawrenceville during the 1940s. (Courtesy of Hattie Peters.)

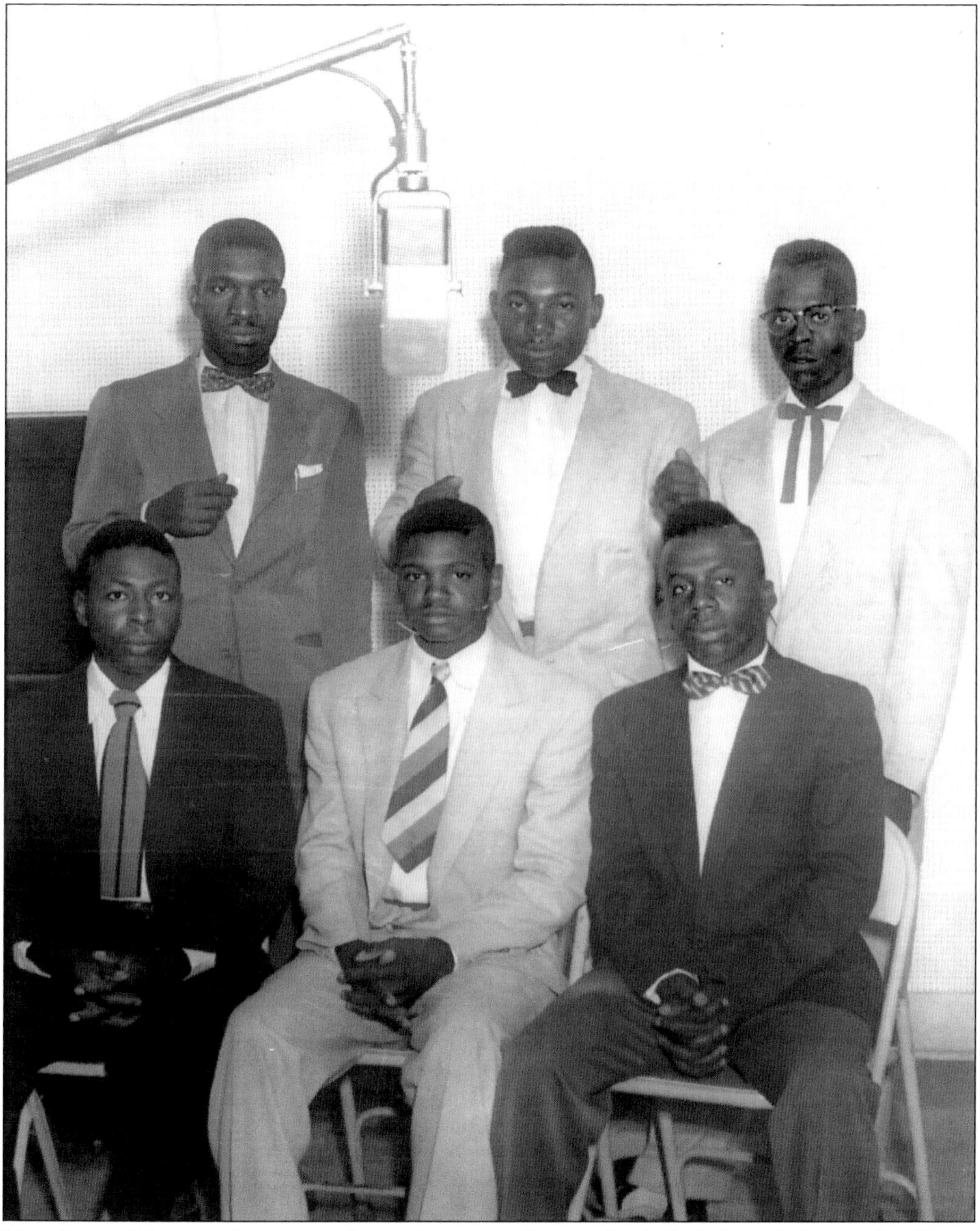

Members of this singing group from Gwinnett County included, from left to right, (front row) Ellis Kemp, L.D. Jones, and Ernest Yarbough Jr.; (back row) John Brown, Willie Hutchins, and Carlton Yarbough. (Courtesy of Thelma Yarbough.)

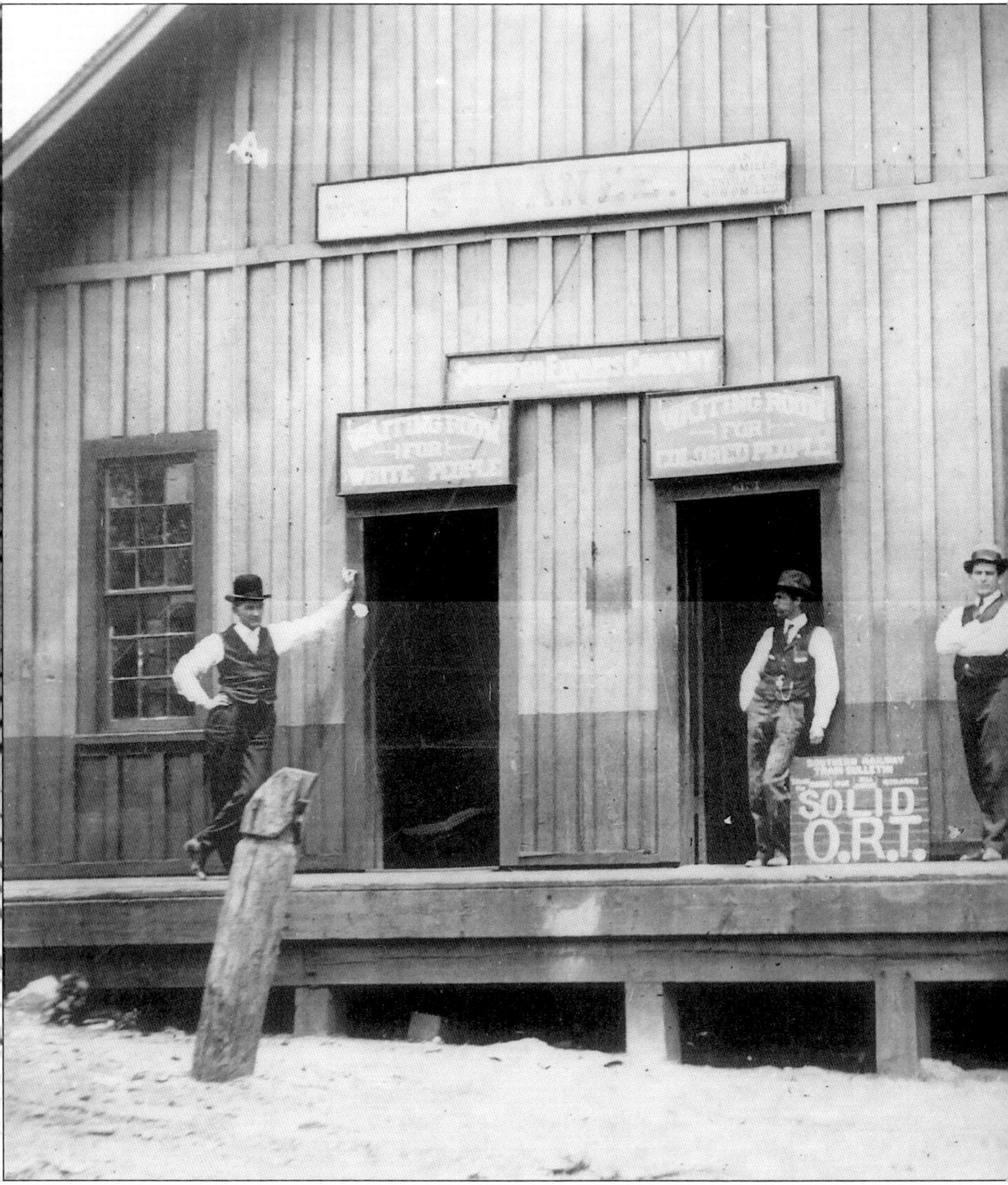

These men are standing in front of the train depot in Suwanee. Notice the "separate but equal" accommodations for "White" and "Colored" passengers. This depot served

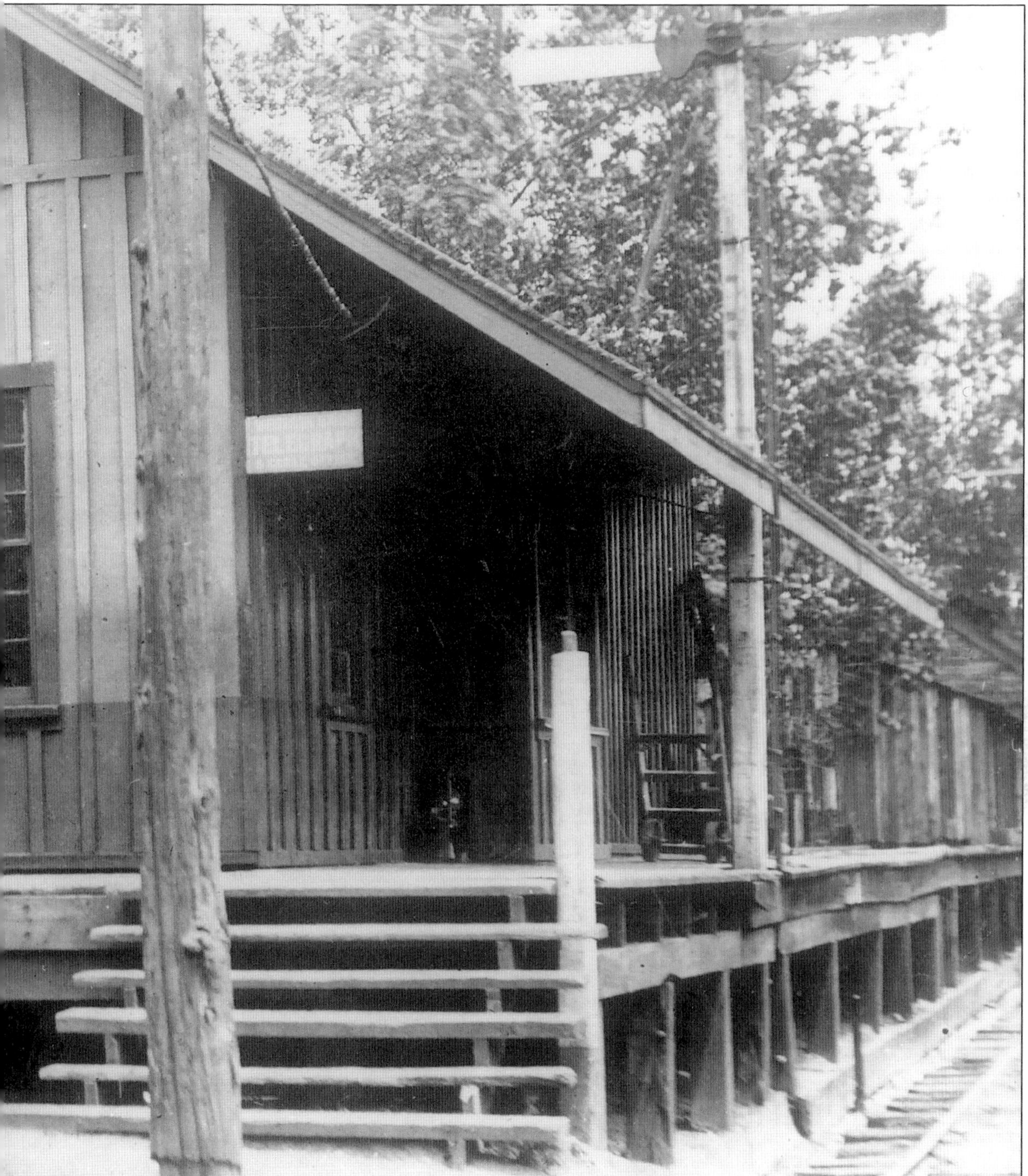

railroad connections between Suwanee and Lawrenceville until the early 1920s. (Courtesy of Georgia Department of Archives and History.)

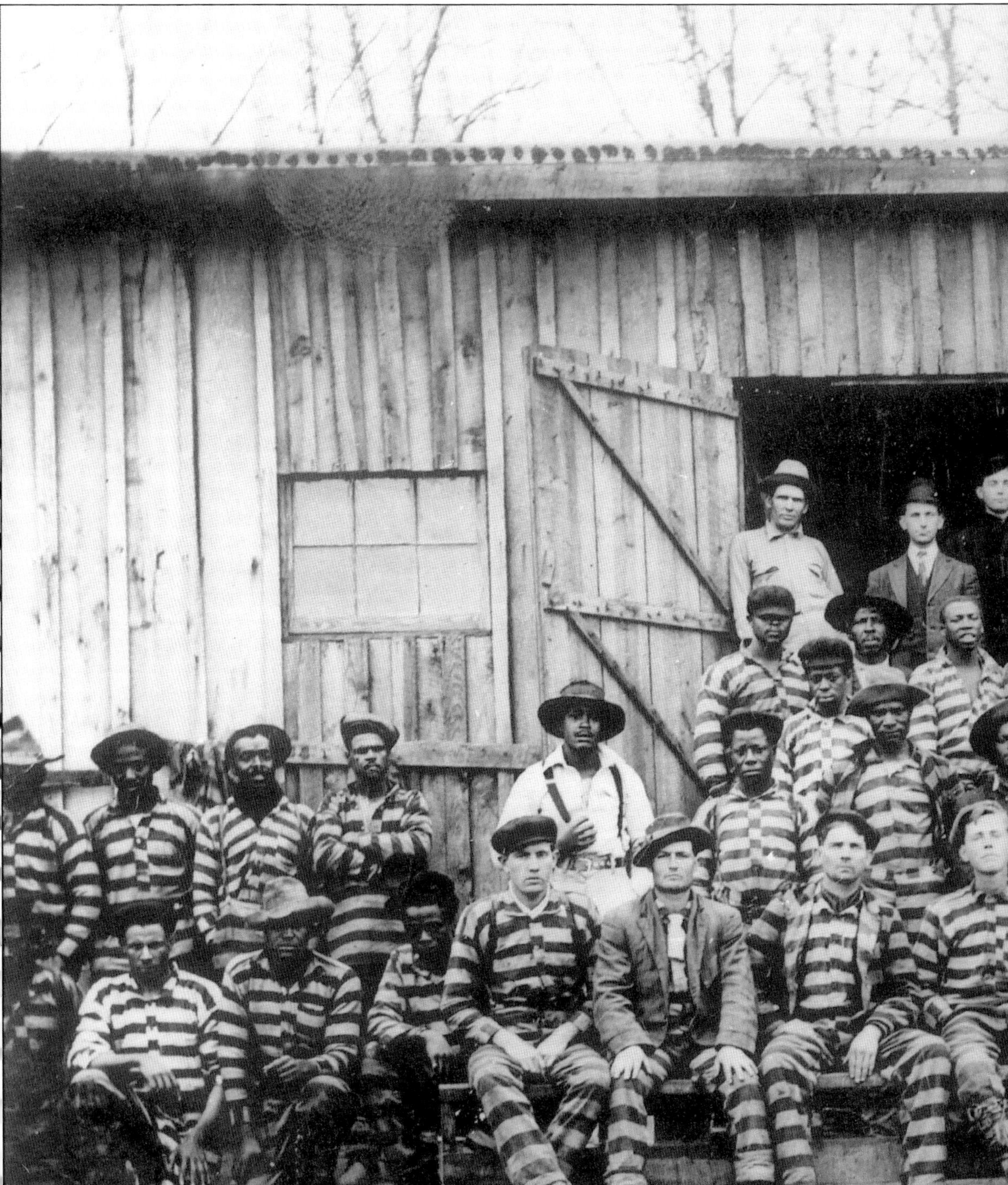

Convicts in Gwinnett County gather to take a group photo *c.* 1920. (Courtesy of

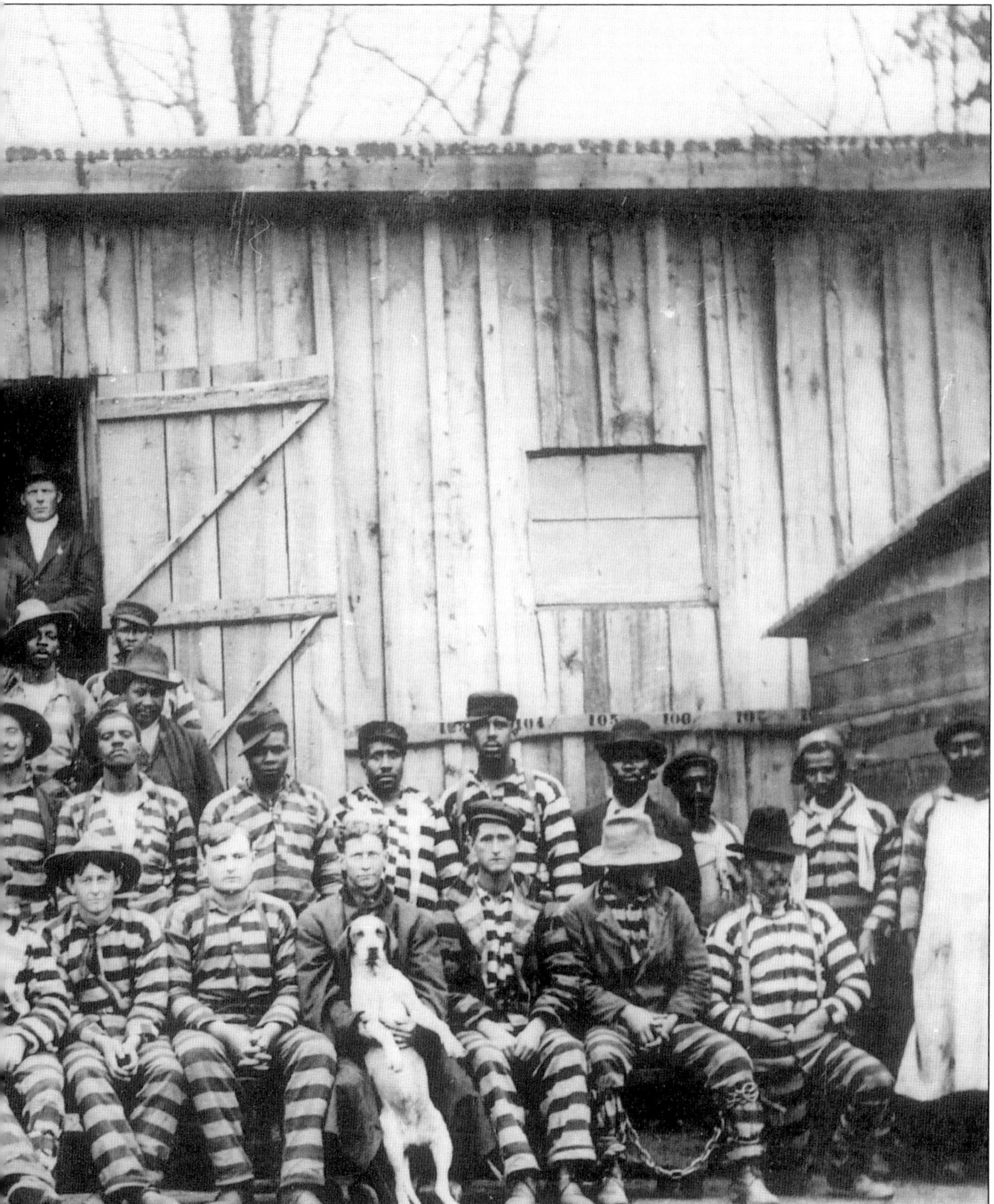

Georgia Department of Archives and History.)

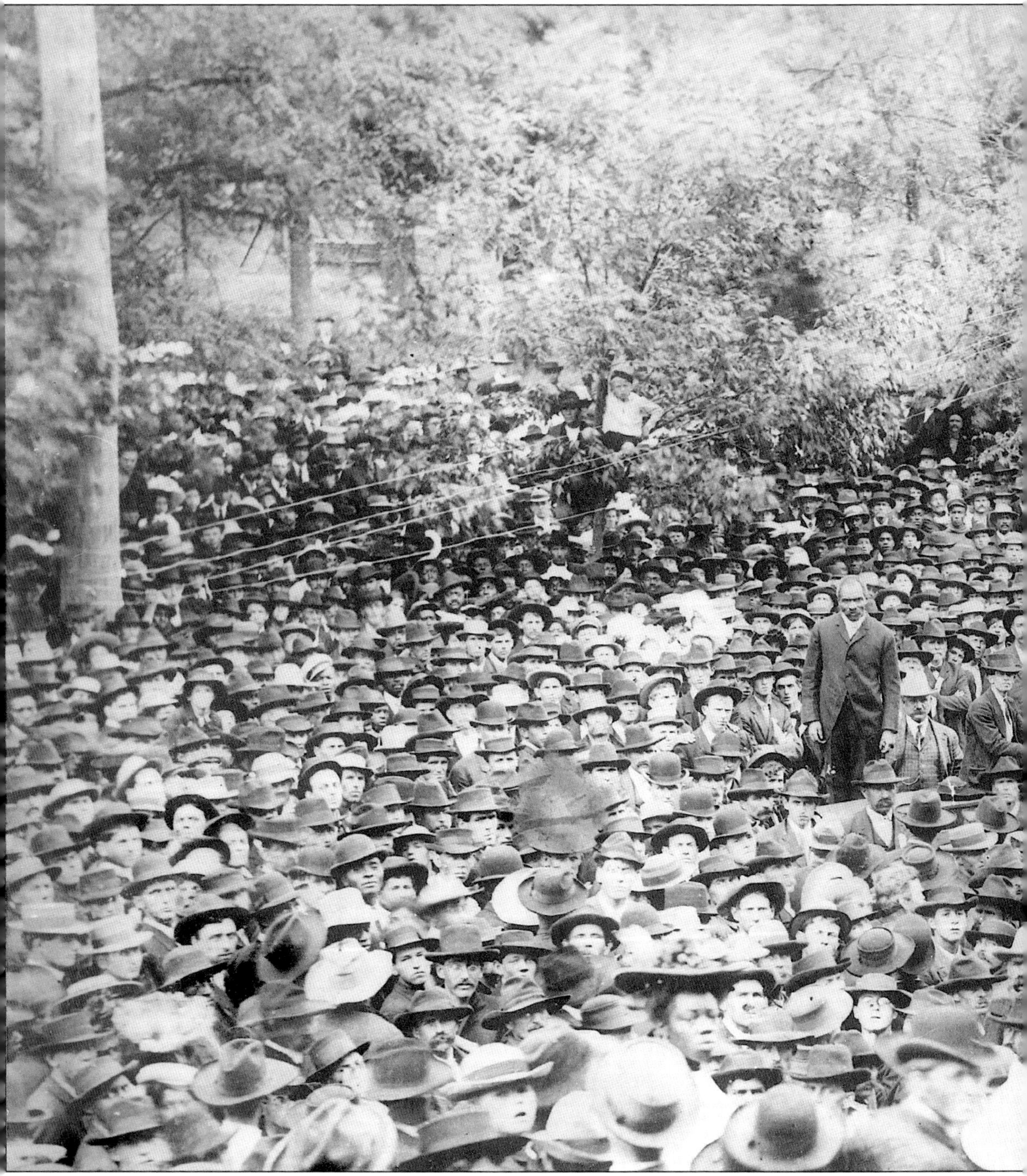

A photograph taken in Lawrenceville on May 8, 1908 depicts a crowd gathered to witness the public hanging of Henry Campbell. He was tried and convicted of murdering Ella Hudson and her daughter. Campbell is the man standing on a raised

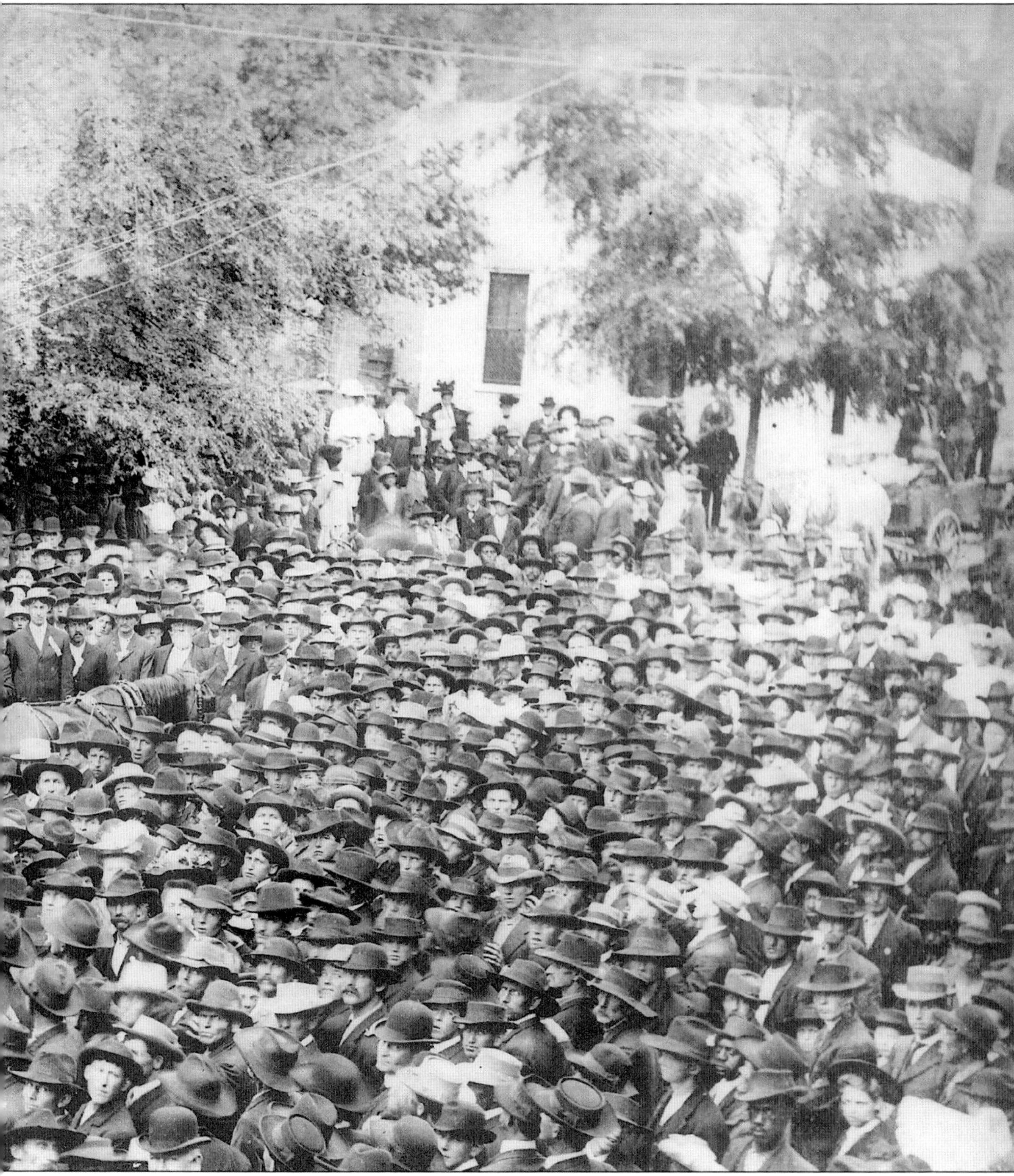

platform in the center of the crowd. (Courtesy of Georgia Department of Archives and History.)

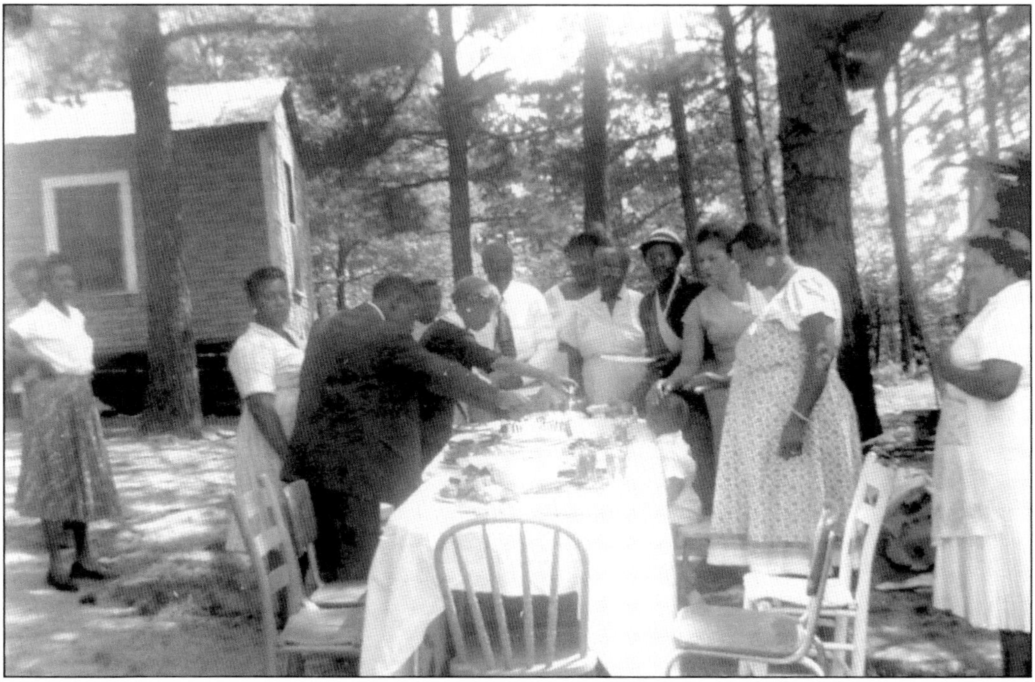

A May 1960 birthday party for Robert Gholston took place at Rhodes Jordan Park in Lawrenceville. Mr. Gholston told his family not to go to any trouble for his birthdays, but every year the family gave him a party. (Courtesy of Dorothy Maxey.)

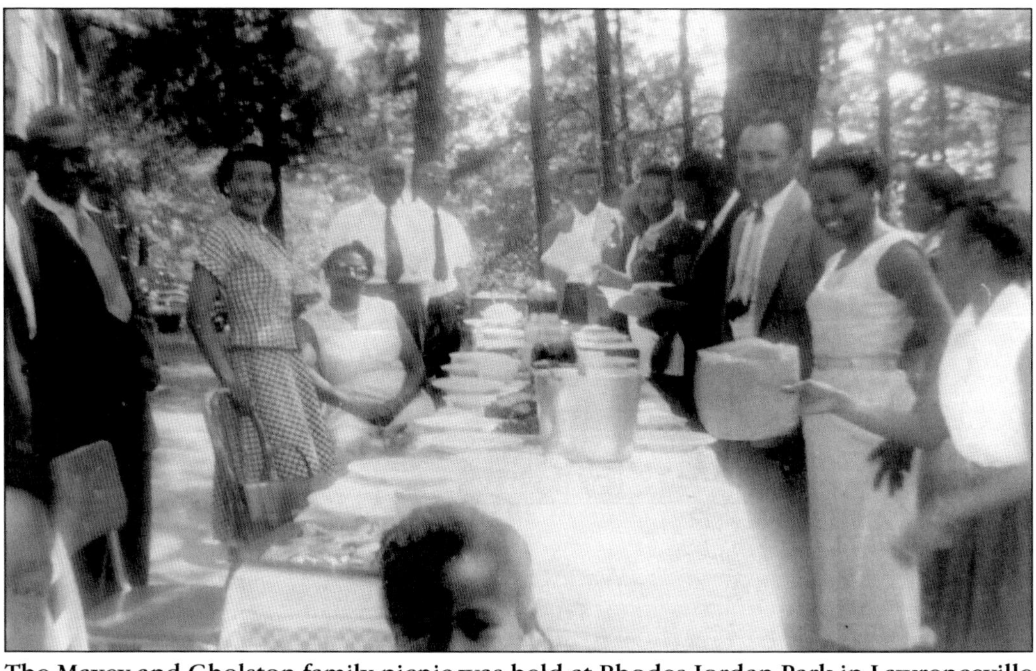

The Maxey and Gholston family picnic was held at Rhodes Jordan Park in Lawrenceville in the 1960s. The two families married into each other's families and the picnics became part of their regular gatherings. (Courtesy of Dorothy Maxey.)

Three Gholston sisters pose for this picture taken in the late 1940s. All three sisters were born and raised in Lawrenceville. Pictured from left to right are Julia, Georgia, and Laura. (Courtesy of Julia Dunham.)

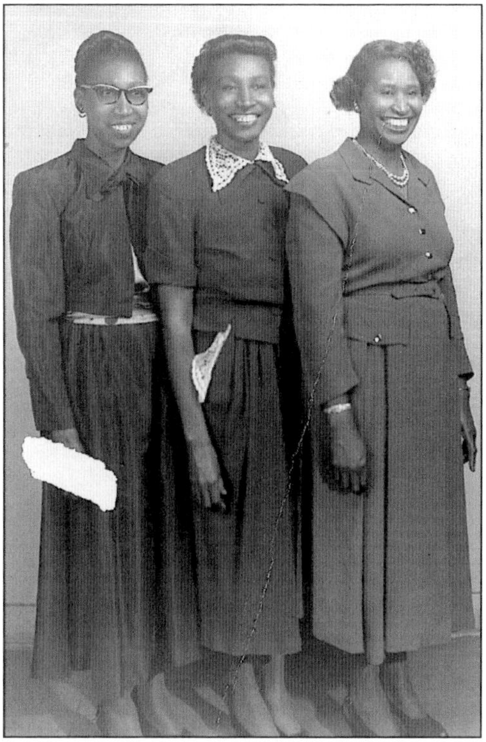

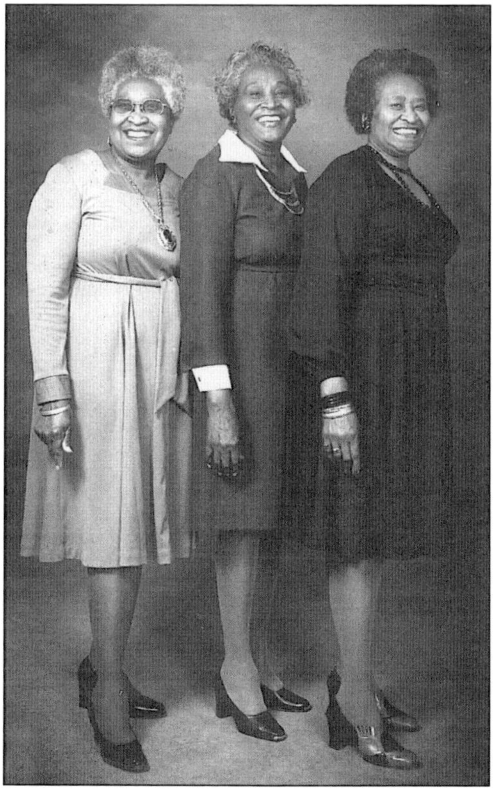

The Gholston sisters are pictured here 30 years later in the 1970s. Pictured from left to right are Julia, Georgia, and Laura; Georgia is now deceased. (Courtesy of Julia Dunham.)

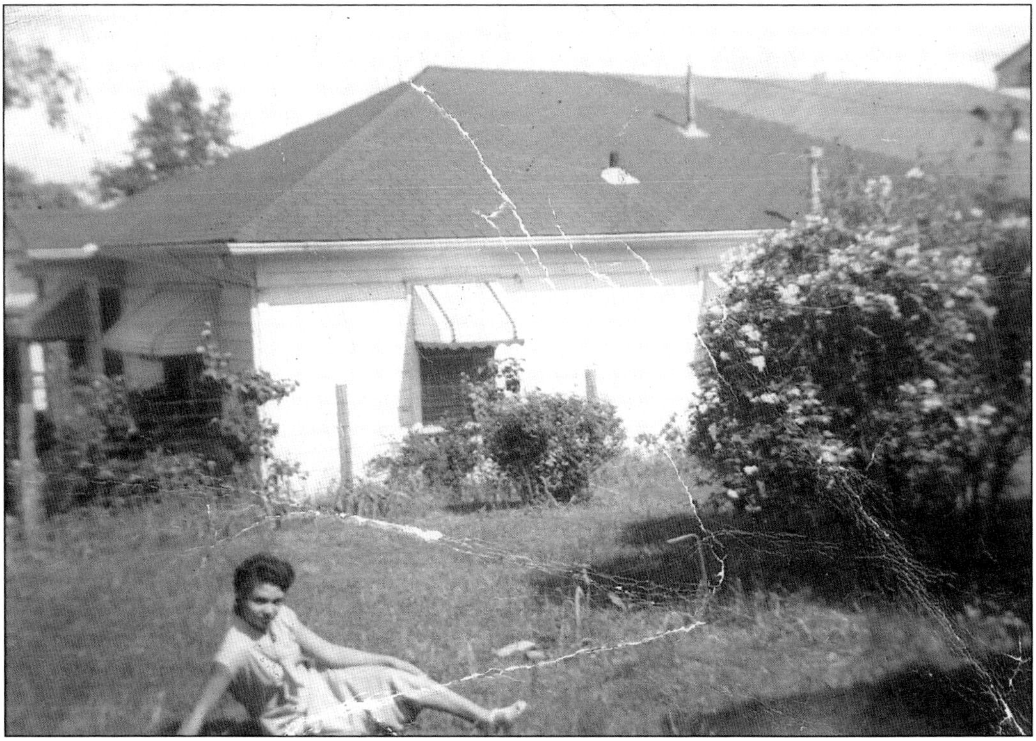

Ruby Mae Williams sits in the yard for this picture taken in Lawrenceville in the 1950s. (Courtesy of Hattie Peters.)

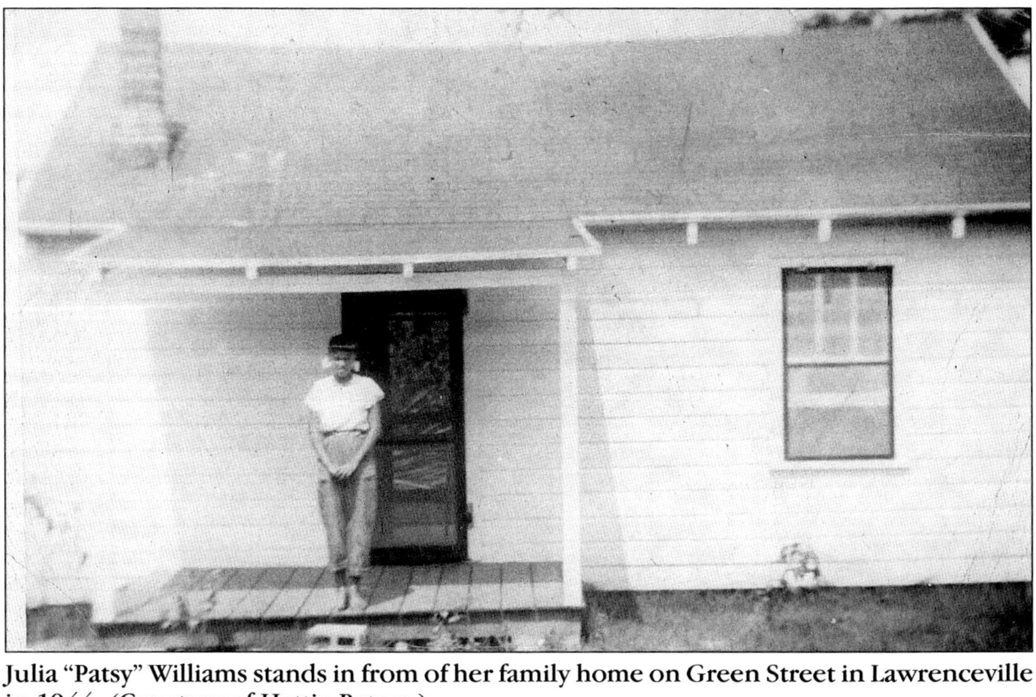

Julia "Patsy" Williams stands in from of her family home on Green Street in Lawrenceville in 1944. (Courtesy of Hattie Peters.)

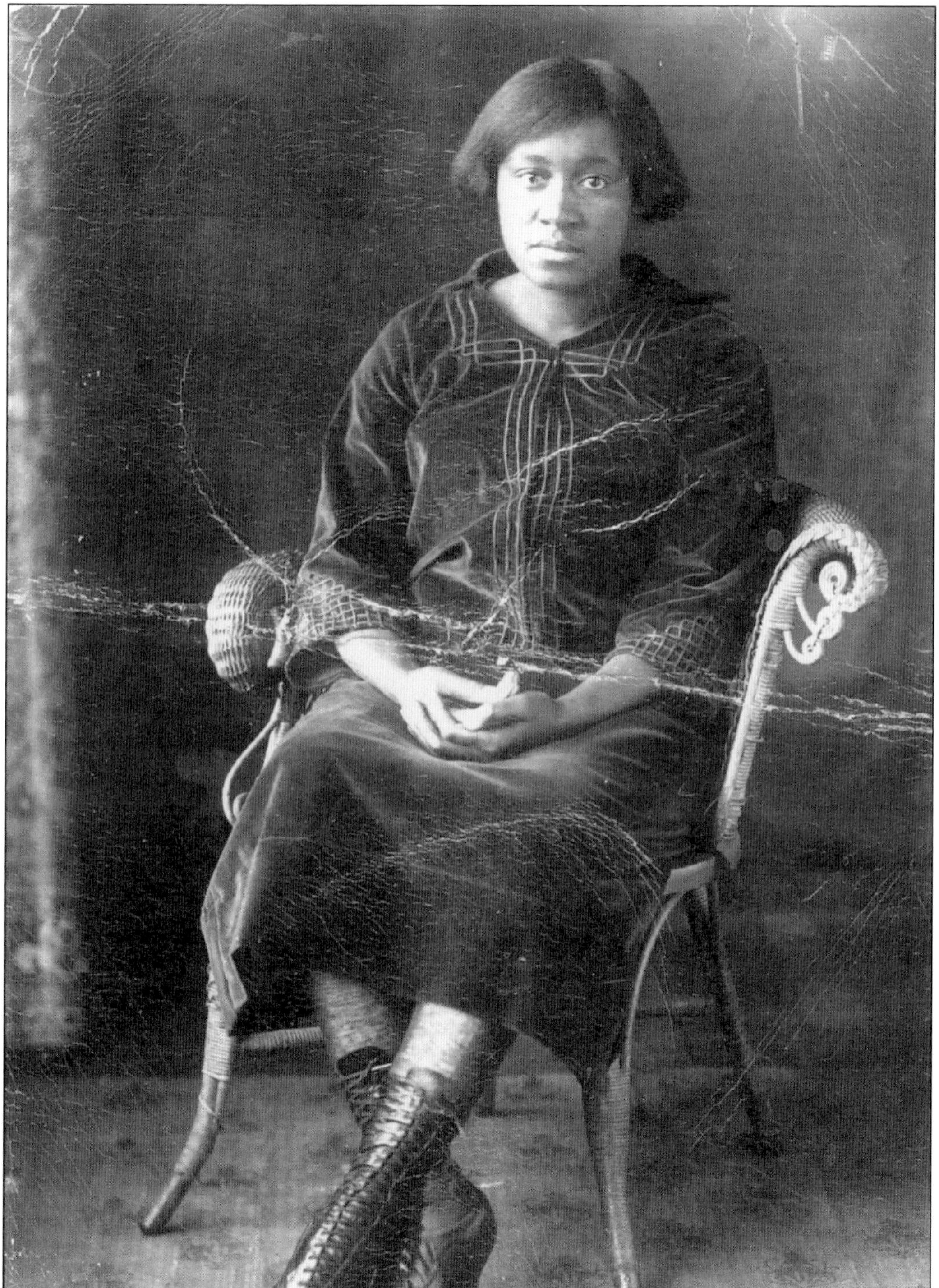

Dela Powell sits for this picture taken during the 1930s. She was a member of Pleasant Hill Baptist Church in Lawrenceville for over 50 years. (Courtesy of Hattie Williams.)

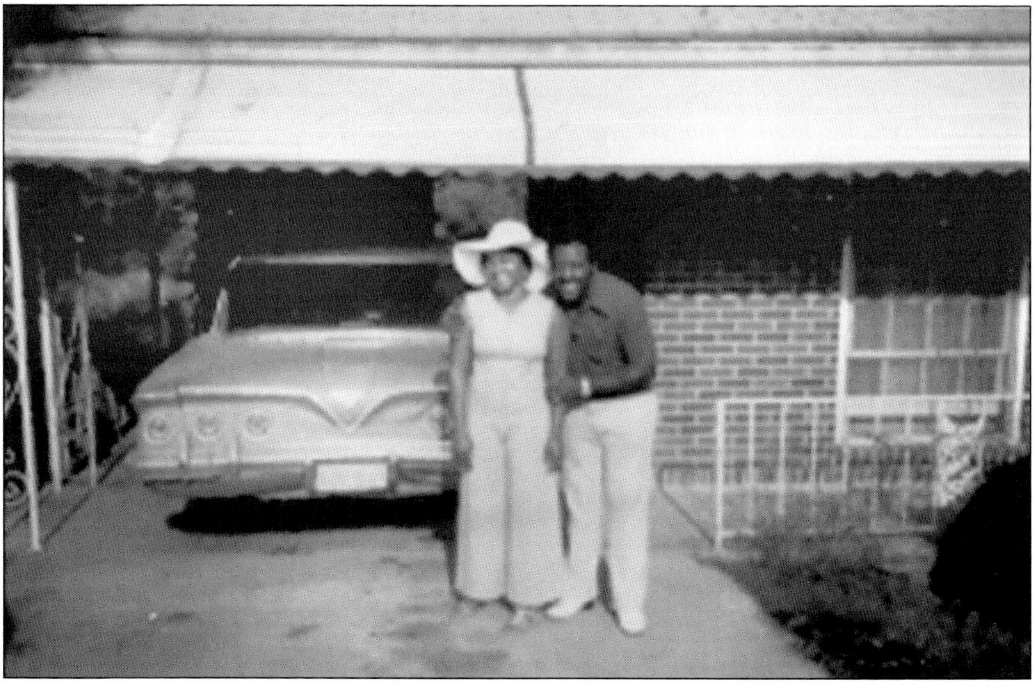

Ruth and Timothy Summerour are seen in Lawrenceville in the 1970s. (Courtesy of Ruth Summerour.)

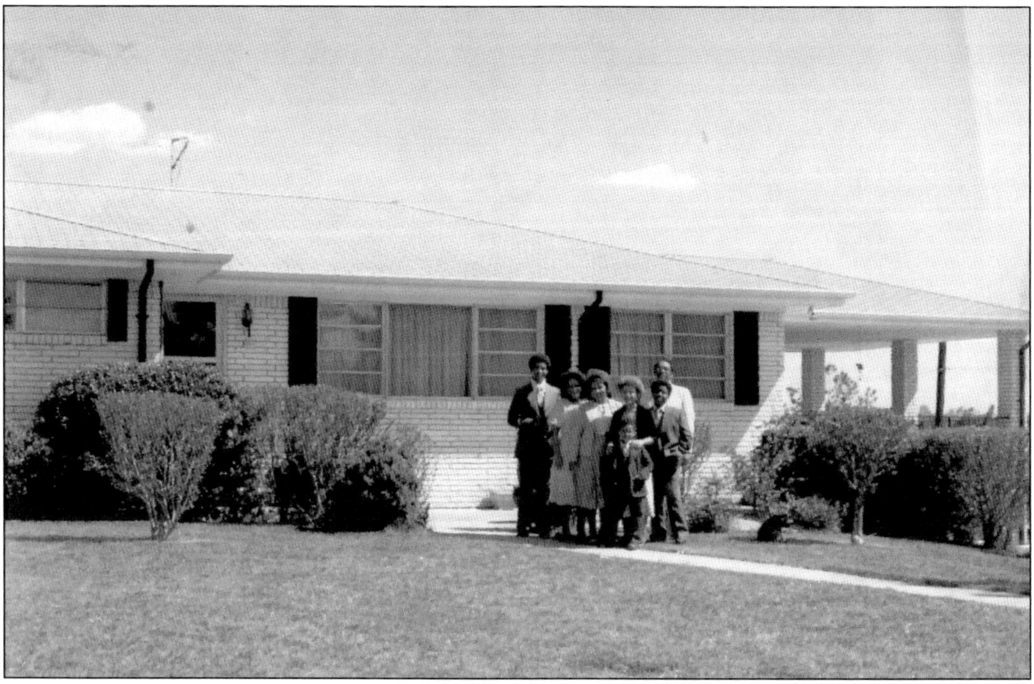

This photograph of the Livsey Family in the 1970s includes, from left to right, Thomas A. Livsey, Sheryl Livsey, Dorethia Livsey, Yolanda Livsey, Kobie Livsey, Kevin Livsey, and Thomas Livsey. (Courtesy of Thomas Livsey.)

Two

Places of Worship

. . . upon this rock I will build my church.
——Jesus Christ

The church is the pillar of the African-American community. Many churches were founded shortly after slavery was abolished. Few churches have roots that began during slavery; however, some plantation owners donated small tracts of land for their slaves to have places to worship. The African-American churches today still have the same worship, love, and faith that was present during the early years. There are over 20 historic African-American churches in the Gwinnett community today.

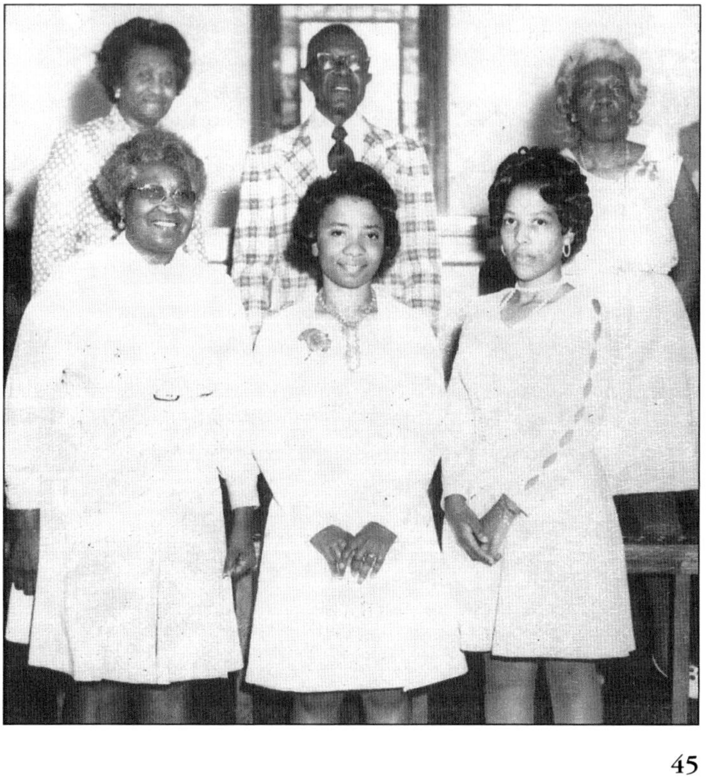

Members of the Mt. Calvary Methodist Church are pictured here from left to right (front row) Julia Dunham, Freddie Norman, and Annie Harris; (back row) Laura Hawkins, Charlie Dunham, and Minnie Brown. This photo was taken in 1975. (Courtesy of Julia Dunham.)

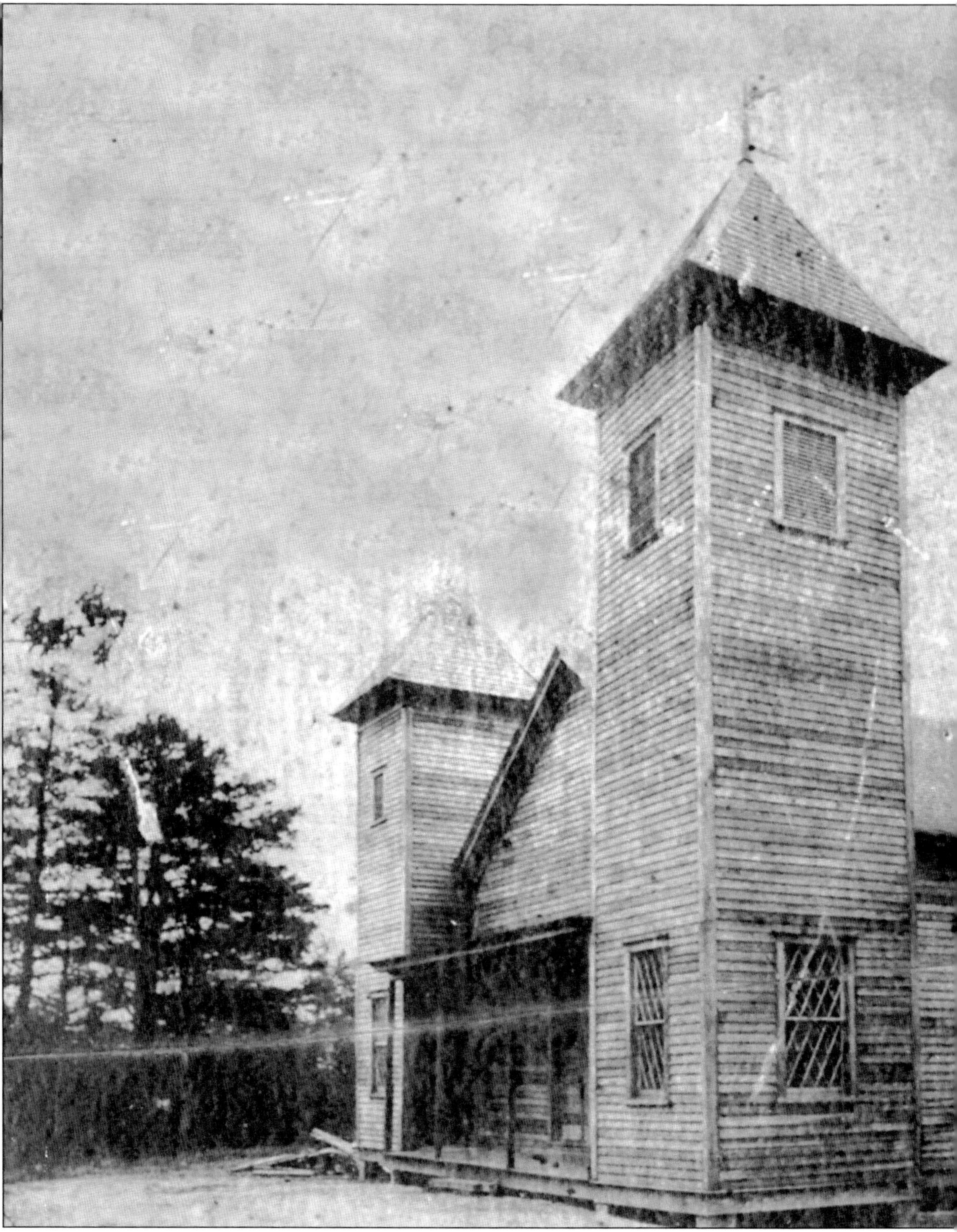

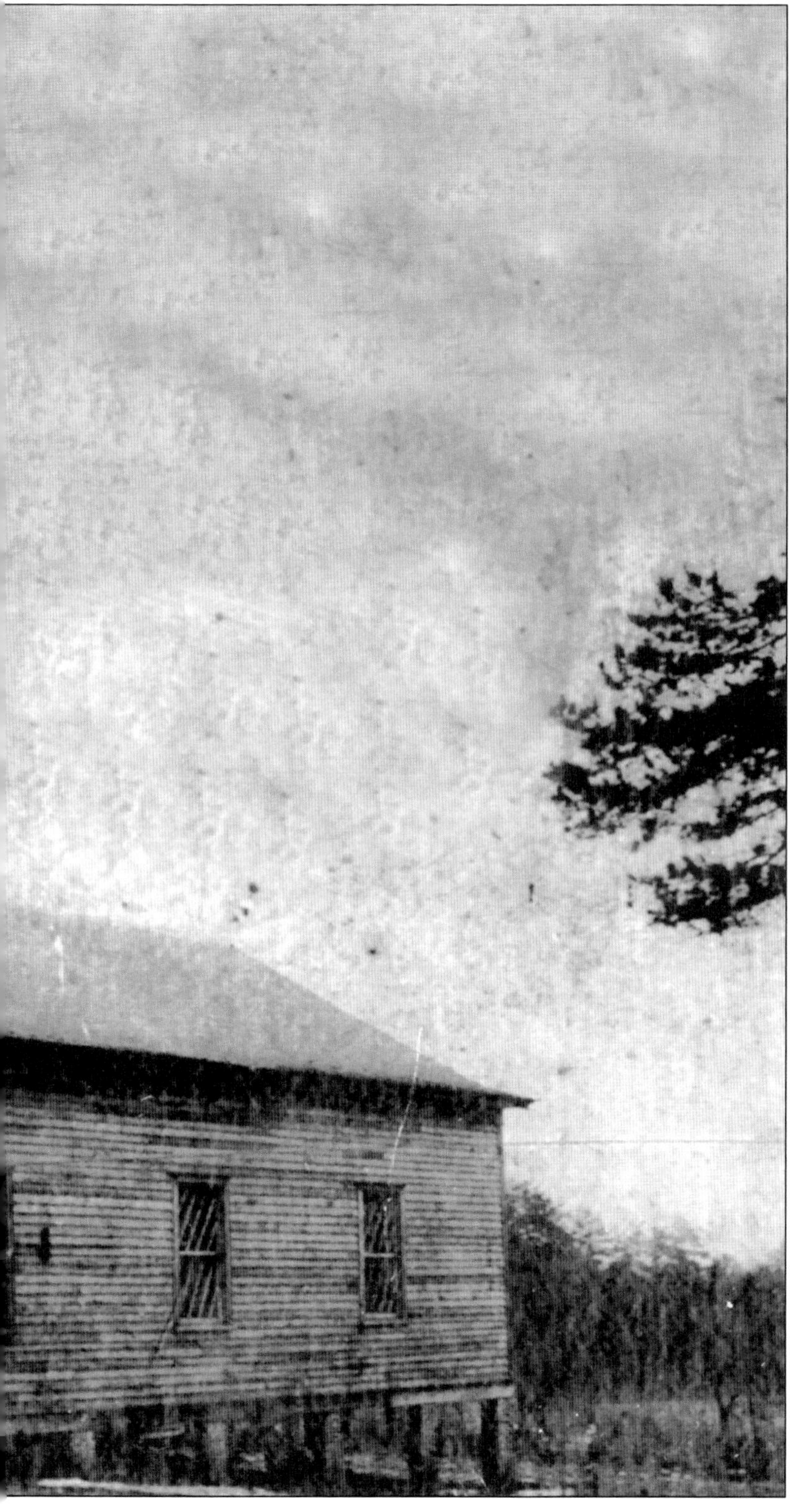

Mt. Calvary Methodist Church is pictured in the late 1800s. Started shortly after the abolition of slavery, this church was destroyed by a tornado in the 1930s. (Courtesy of Dorothy Maxey.)

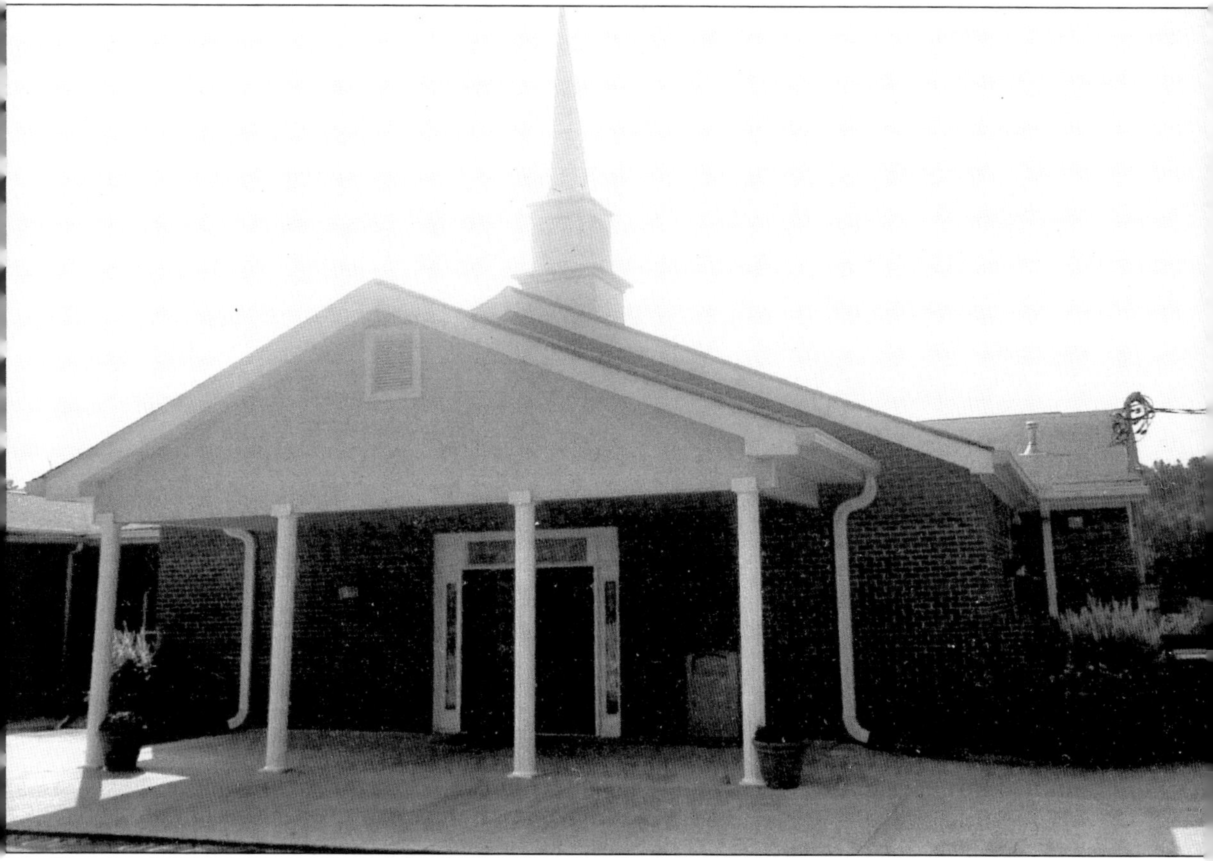

Salem Missionary Baptist Church is the oldest known historically black church in the county. The original tract of land was given to slaves in the community to build a place of worship. (Courtesy of the author.)

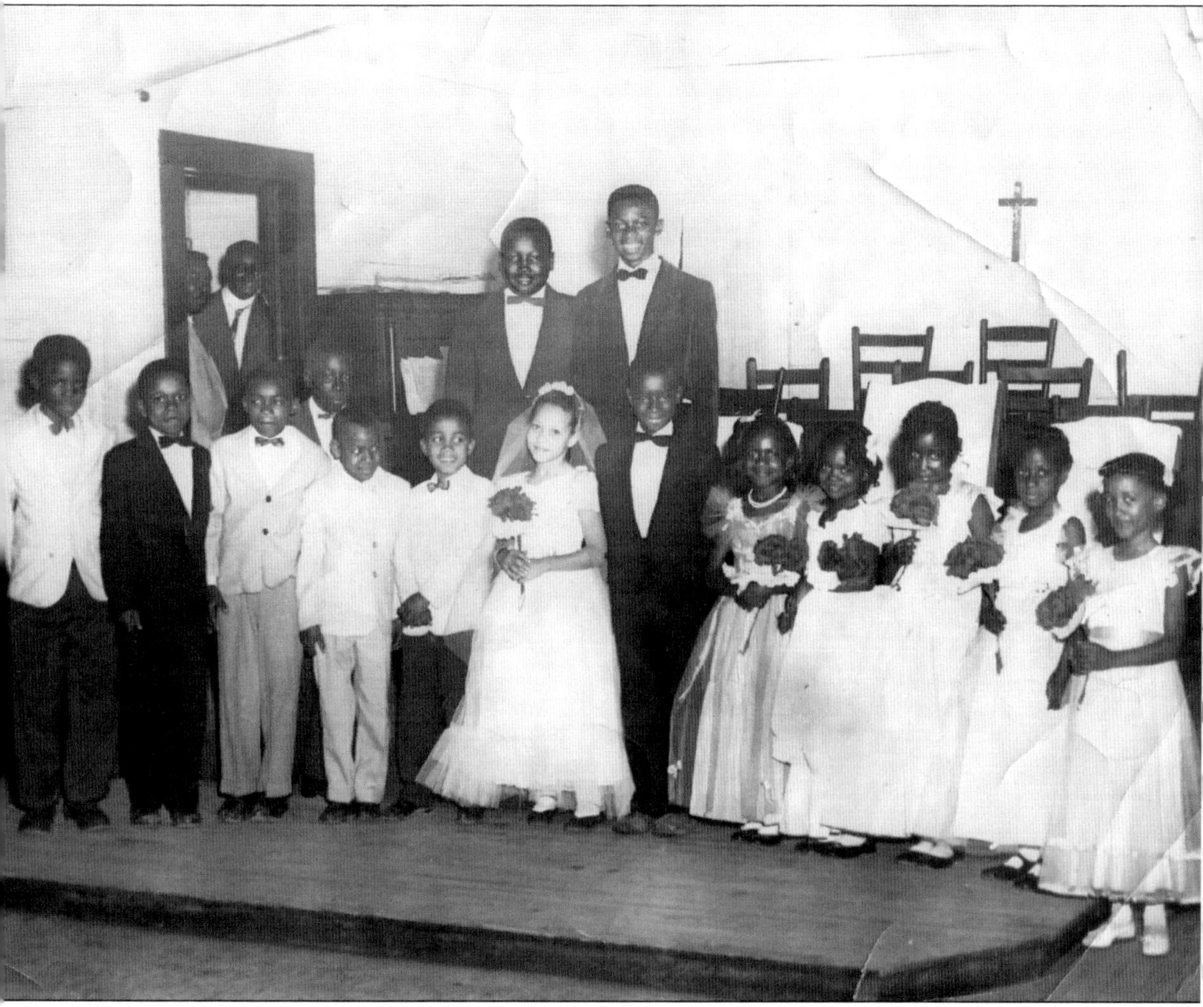

Members of Pleasant Hill Baptist Church pose in the 1940s during a "Tom Thumb" wedding. From left to right are (front row) T.W. Vines, Josh Echols Jr., ? Tucker, Terry Maxey, Johnny Maxey, ? Maxey, Diane Echols, Gloria Paxton, ? Brown, Carolyn Carter, and ? Tucker; (back row) Roy Brown Jr. and Marvin Echols; (in doorway) Josh Echols and Calvin Maddox. (Courtesy of Timothy Summerour.)

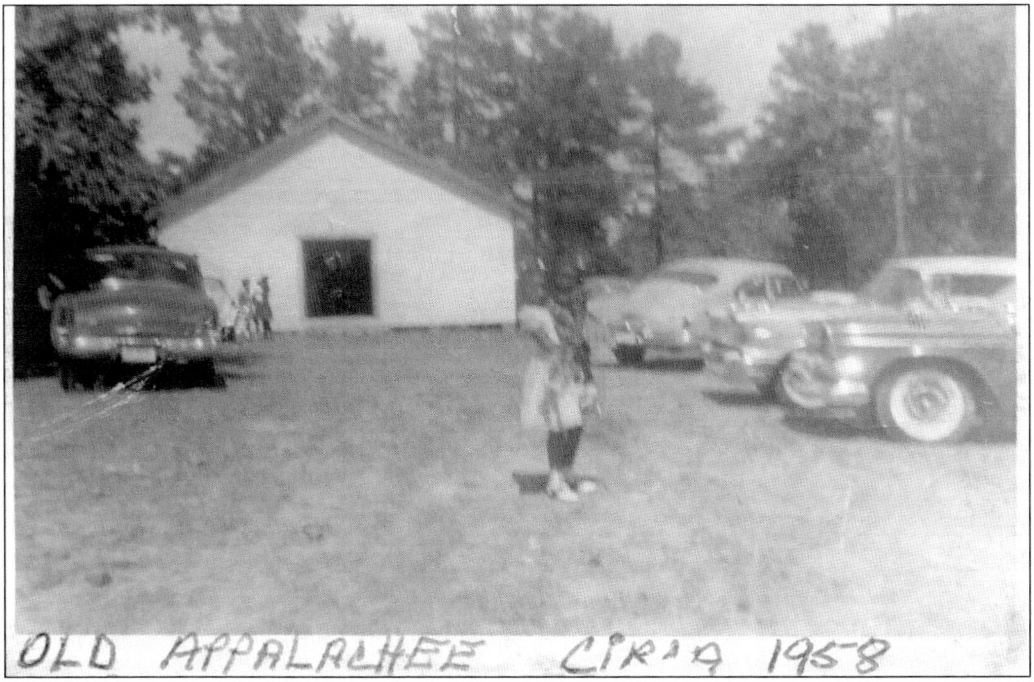

Joyce Moore holds a baby in front of Appalachee Baptist Church *c.* 1950. (Courtesy of Eron and Susan Moore.)

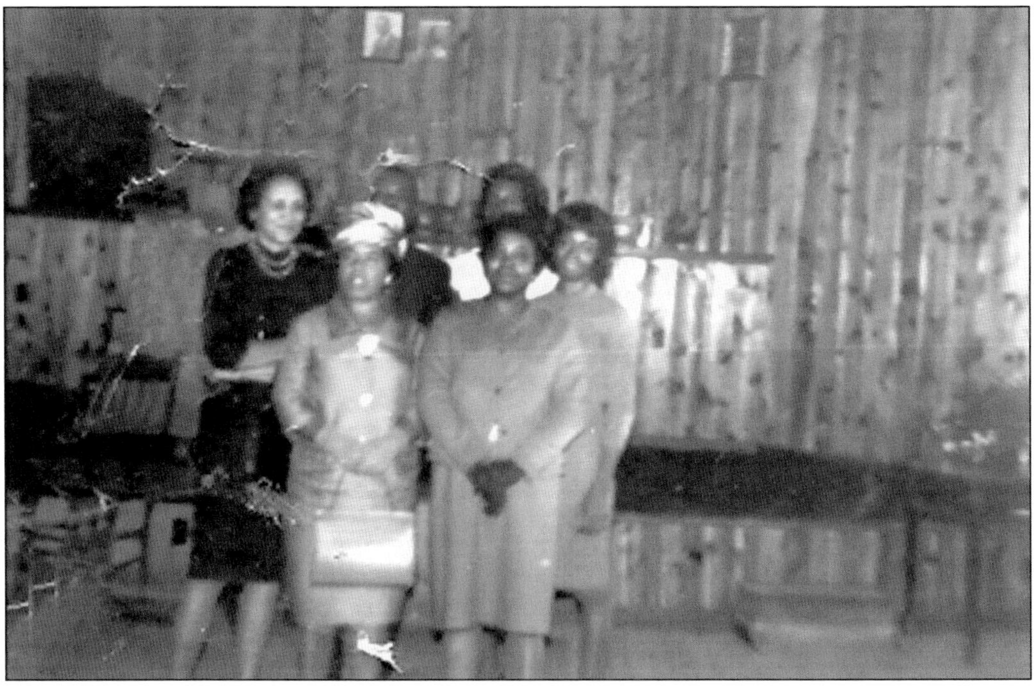

An October 1965 photo at Pleasant Hill Baptist Church depicts, from right to left, Mary Ann Echols, M. Vines, Carolyn Wynn, Linda J. Patillo, and Frannie L. Paxton. (Courtesy of Clara Collins.)

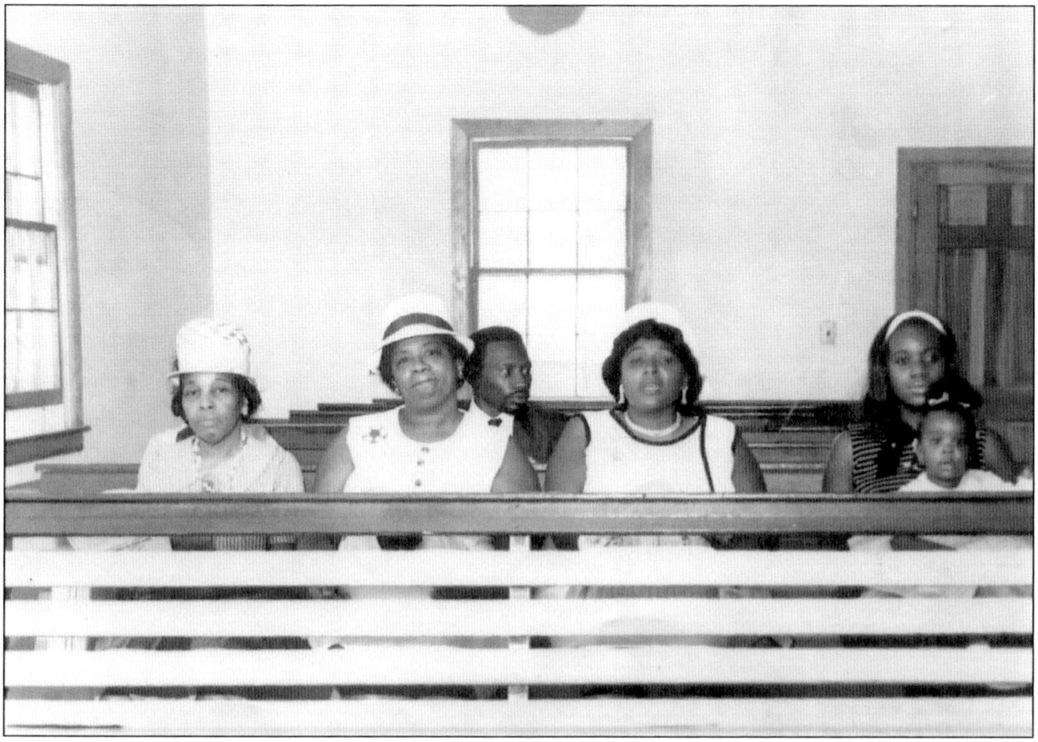

Members at the Pleasant Hill Baptist Church are pictured *c.* 1940. From left to right are Cotericie Maddox, Clara Collins, James Wilburn, Cassie Cain, Dorothy Abney, and Tabathia Abney. (Courtesy of Clara Collins.)

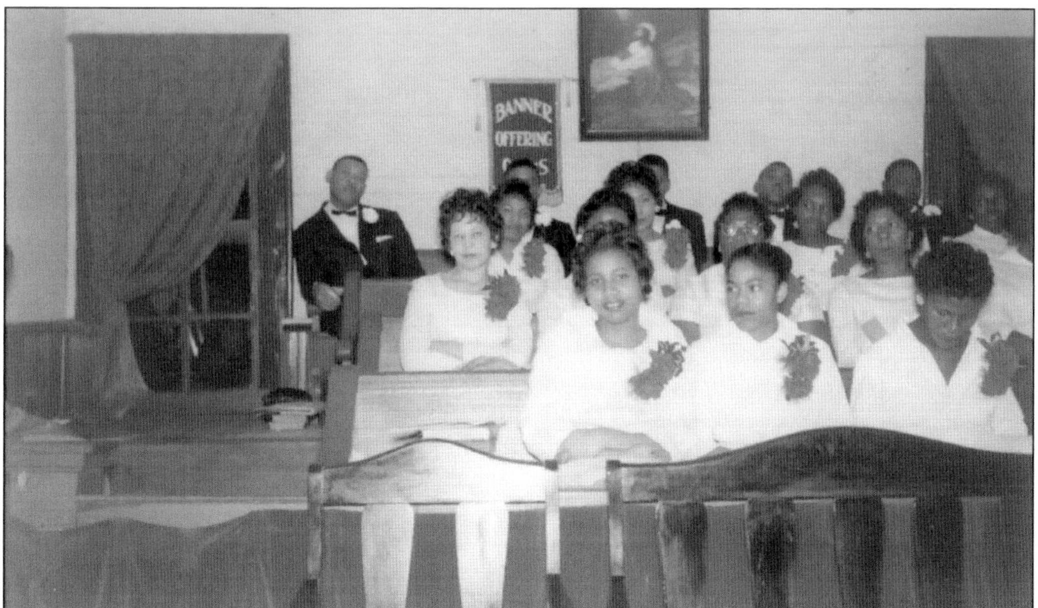

The combined choir is seen at the Hopewell Baptist Church Annual Choir Day in 1958. (Courtesy of Rufus Dunnigan.)

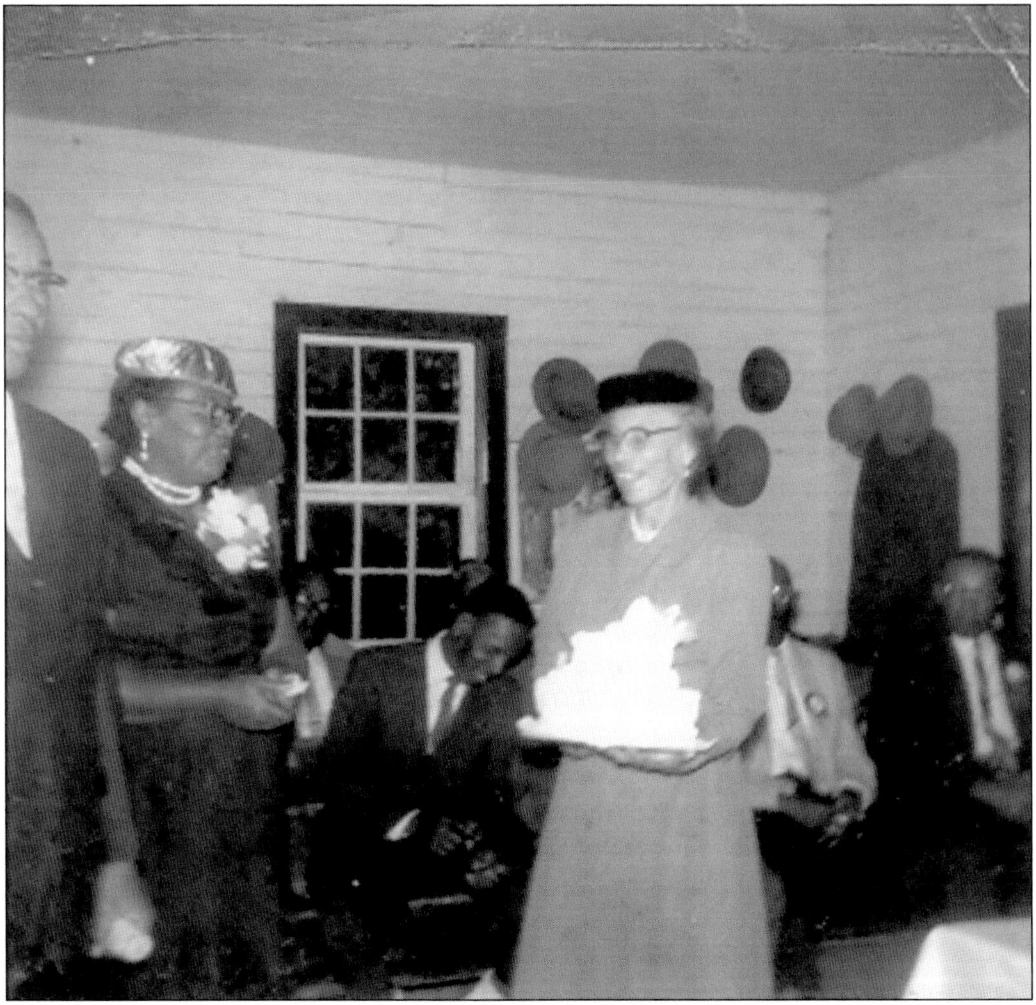

Mother board member Mary Jones presents Reverend Evans with an anniversary cake at the Appalachee Baptist Church. Notice the hats on the wall at the church *c.* 1950. (Courtesy of Eron and Susan Moore.)

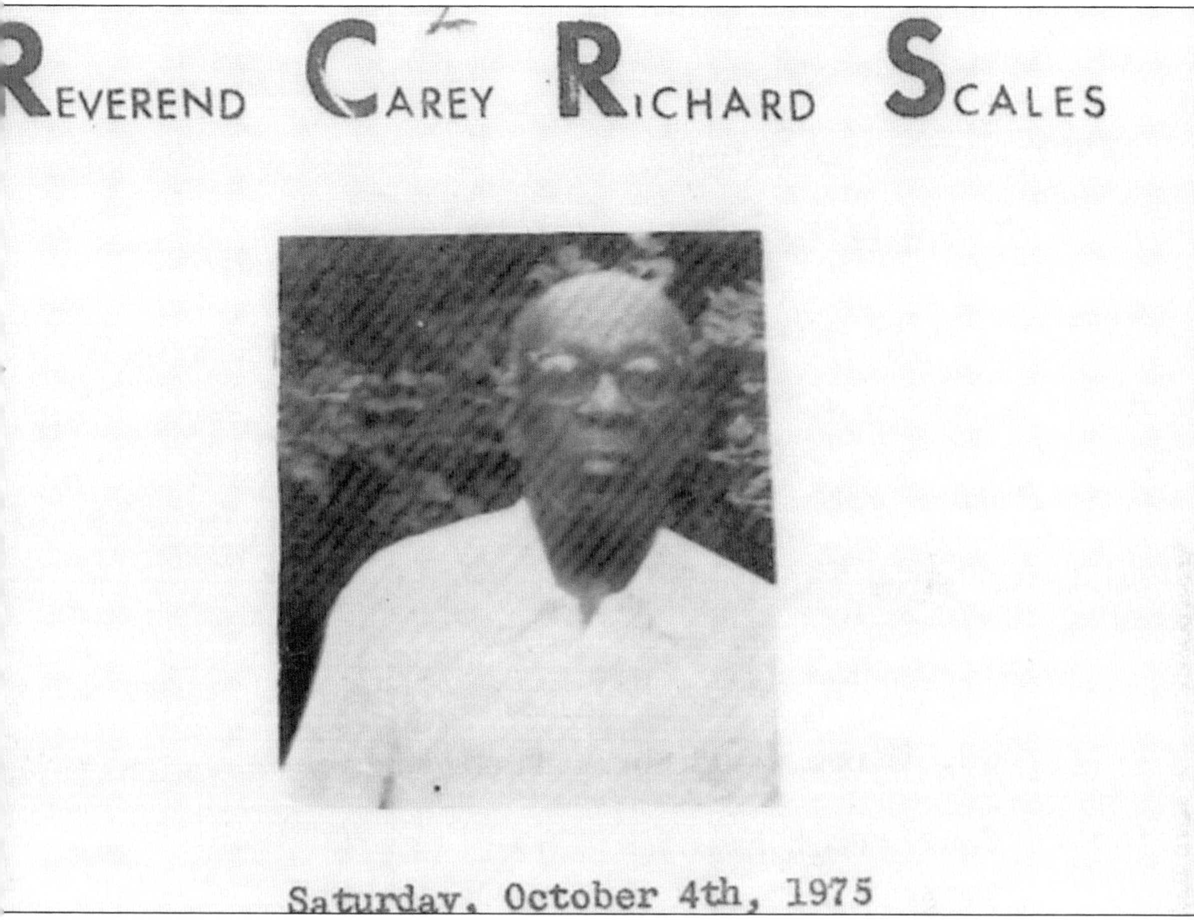

Rev. Richard Scales was photographed on Saturday, October 4, 1975. He served as pastor of Macedonia Baptist Church for many years. (Courtesy of Thomas Livsey.)

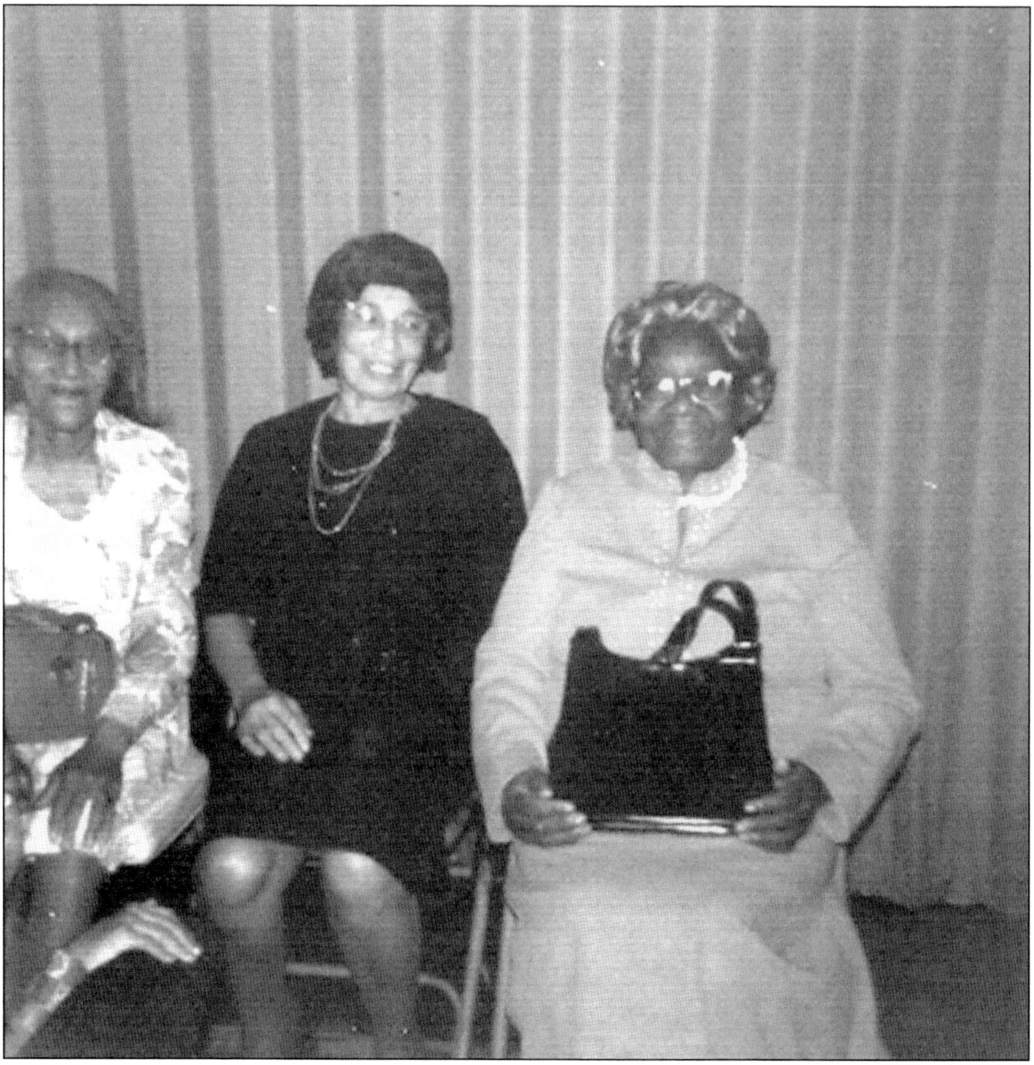

Ms. Luchie Wilburn, Mary Jones, and Edda Mae Hosch participate in a church supper at Appalachee Baptist Church. (Courtesy of Eron and Susan Moore.)

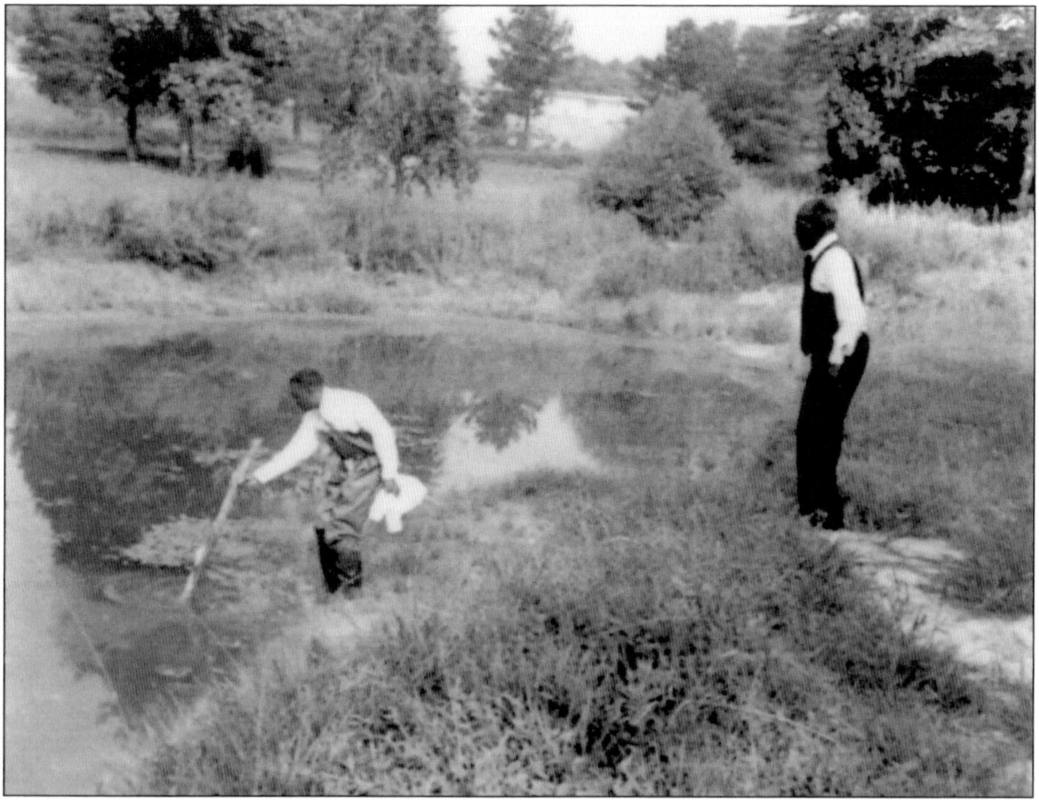

Two men clear Lake Sheryl for the baptizing ceremonies at Macedonia Baptist Church in the southern section of the county. (Courtesy of Thomas Livsey.)

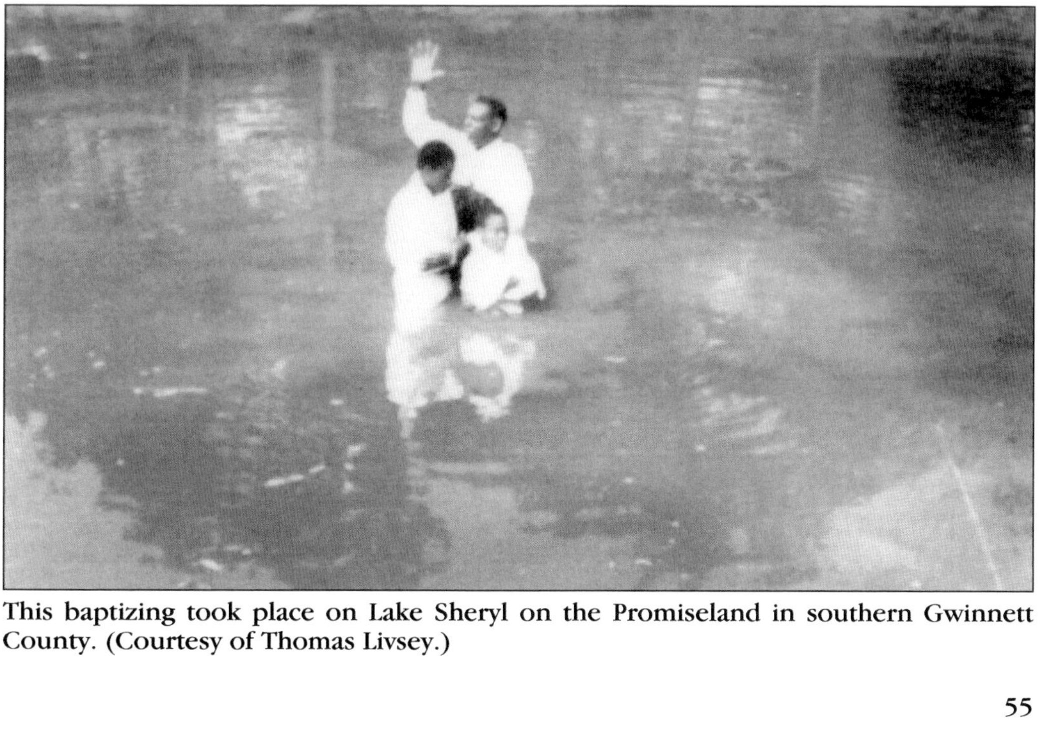

This baptizing took place on Lake Sheryl on the Promiseland in southern Gwinnett County. (Courtesy of Thomas Livsey.)

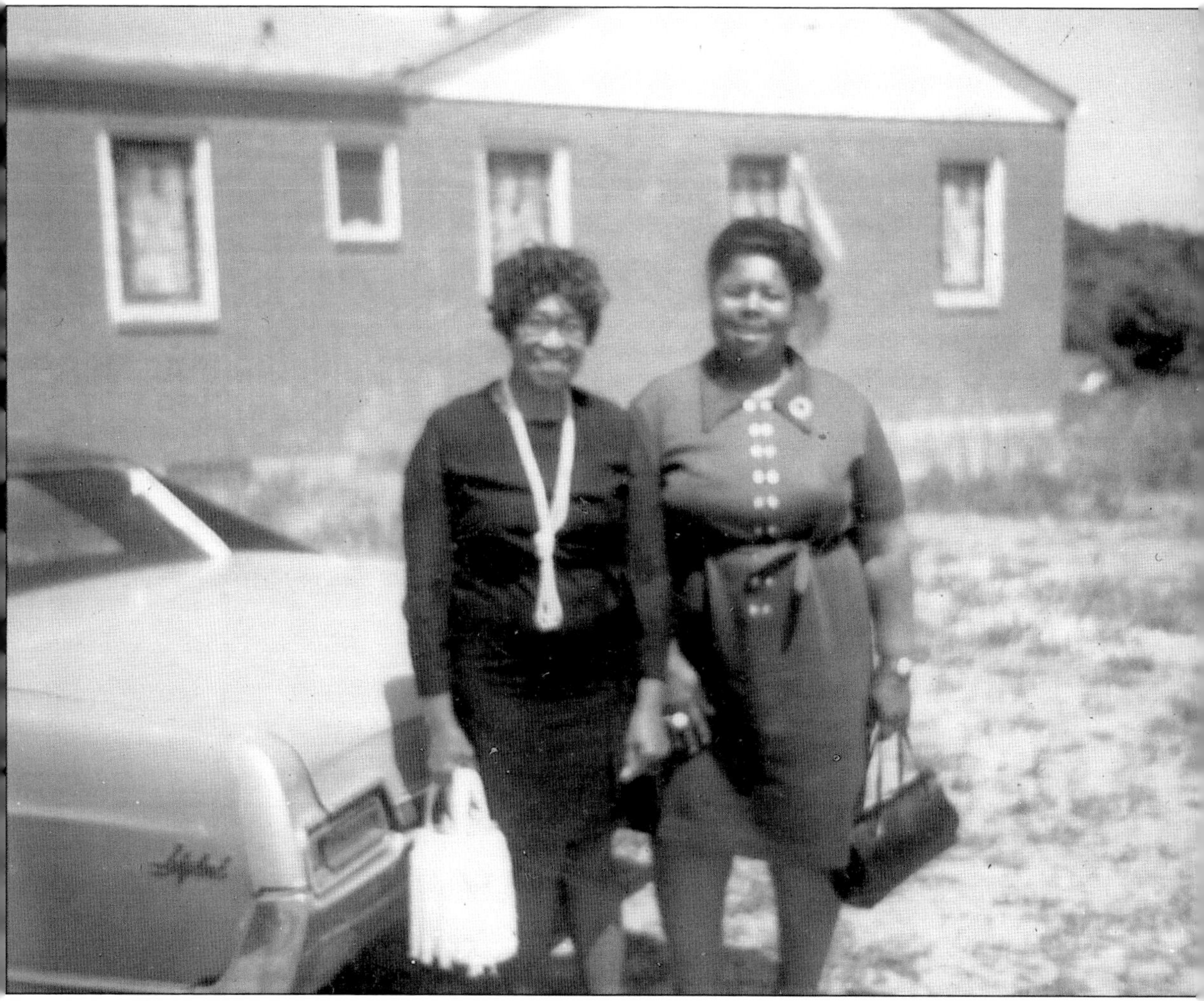

Julia Dunham and Willie Mae Meadows pose for this photo outside the Mt. Calvary Methodist Church in Lawrenceville in 1979. The two women have been lifelong members of the church.

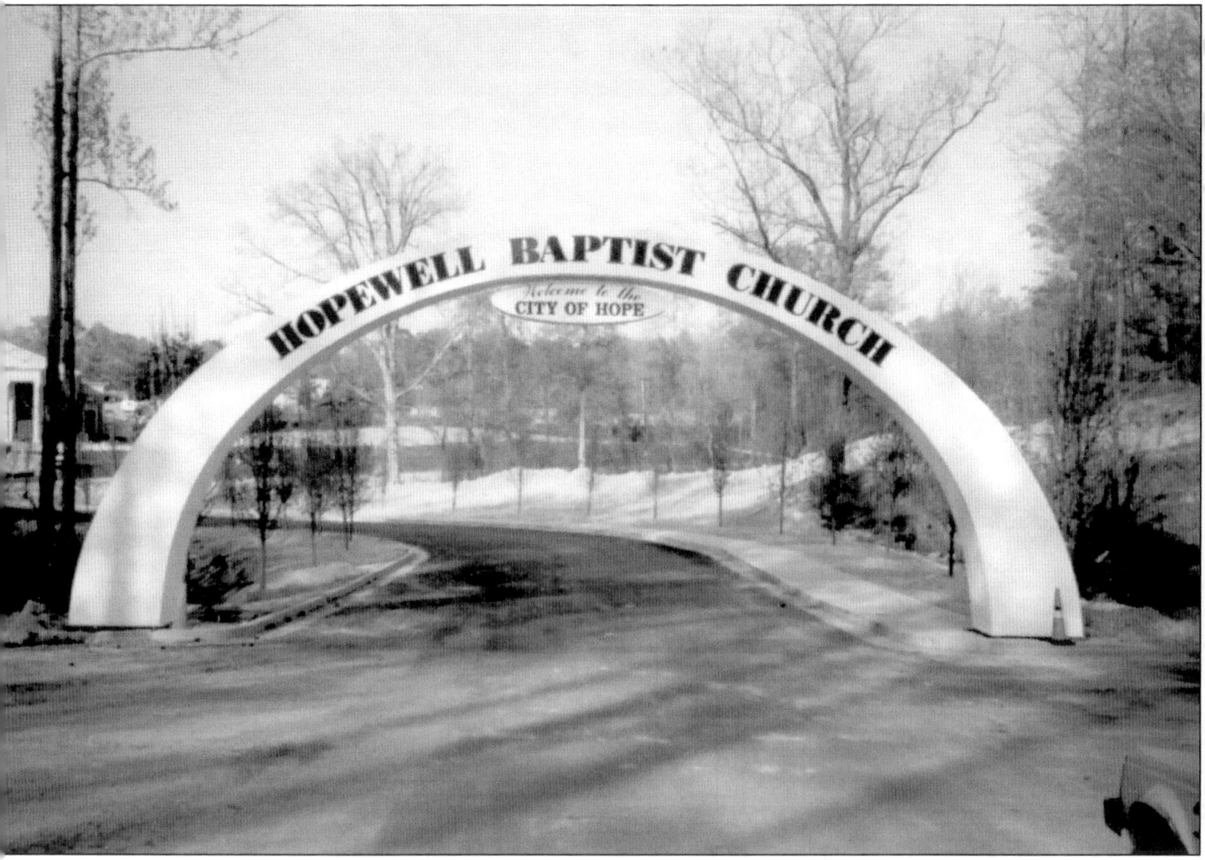

Hopewell Baptist Church is one of the largest historically black churches in the county. The church was established in the late 1800s. (Courtesy of Rufus Dunnigan.)

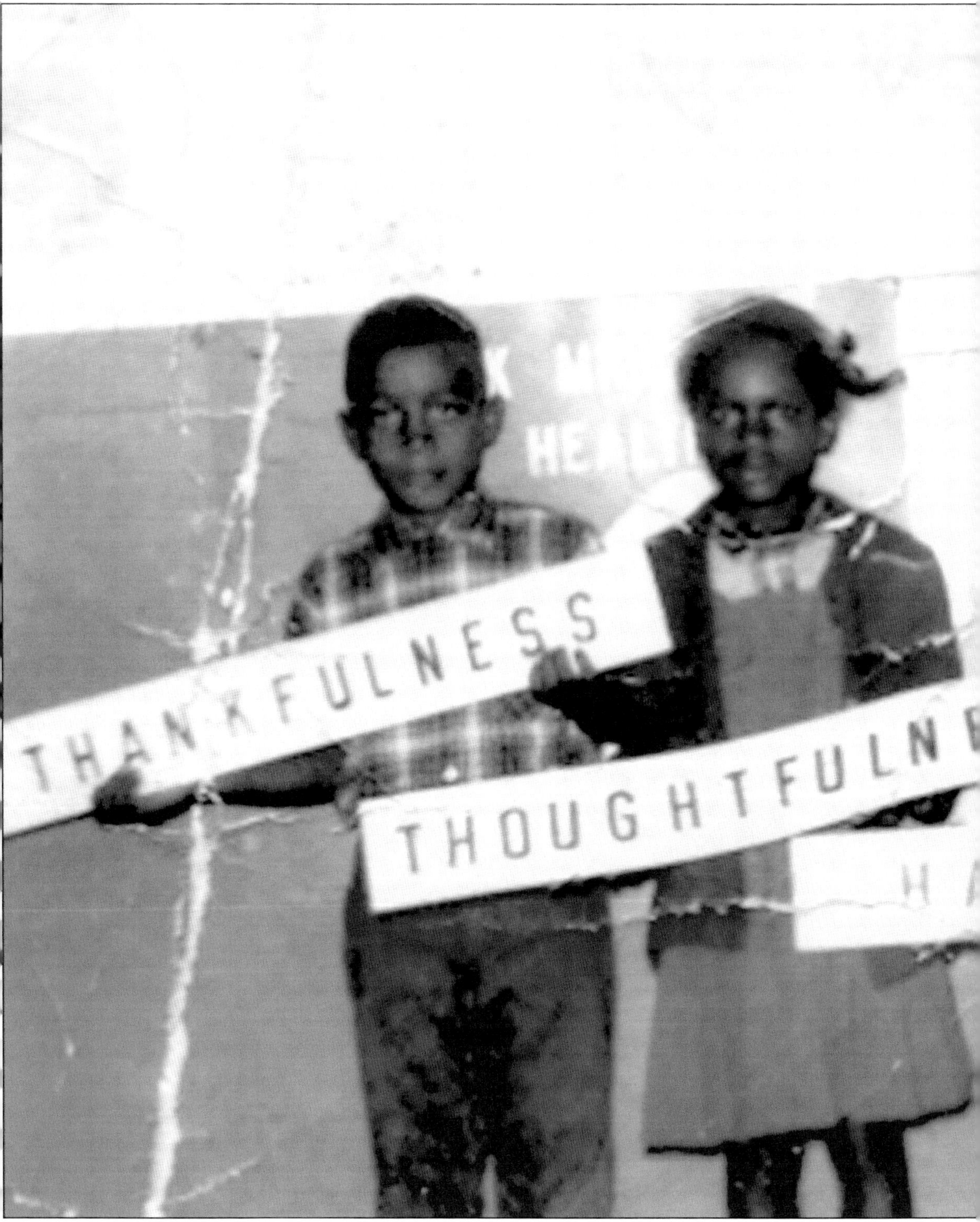

These children participated in a Sunday School play at the Pleasant Hill Baptist Church.

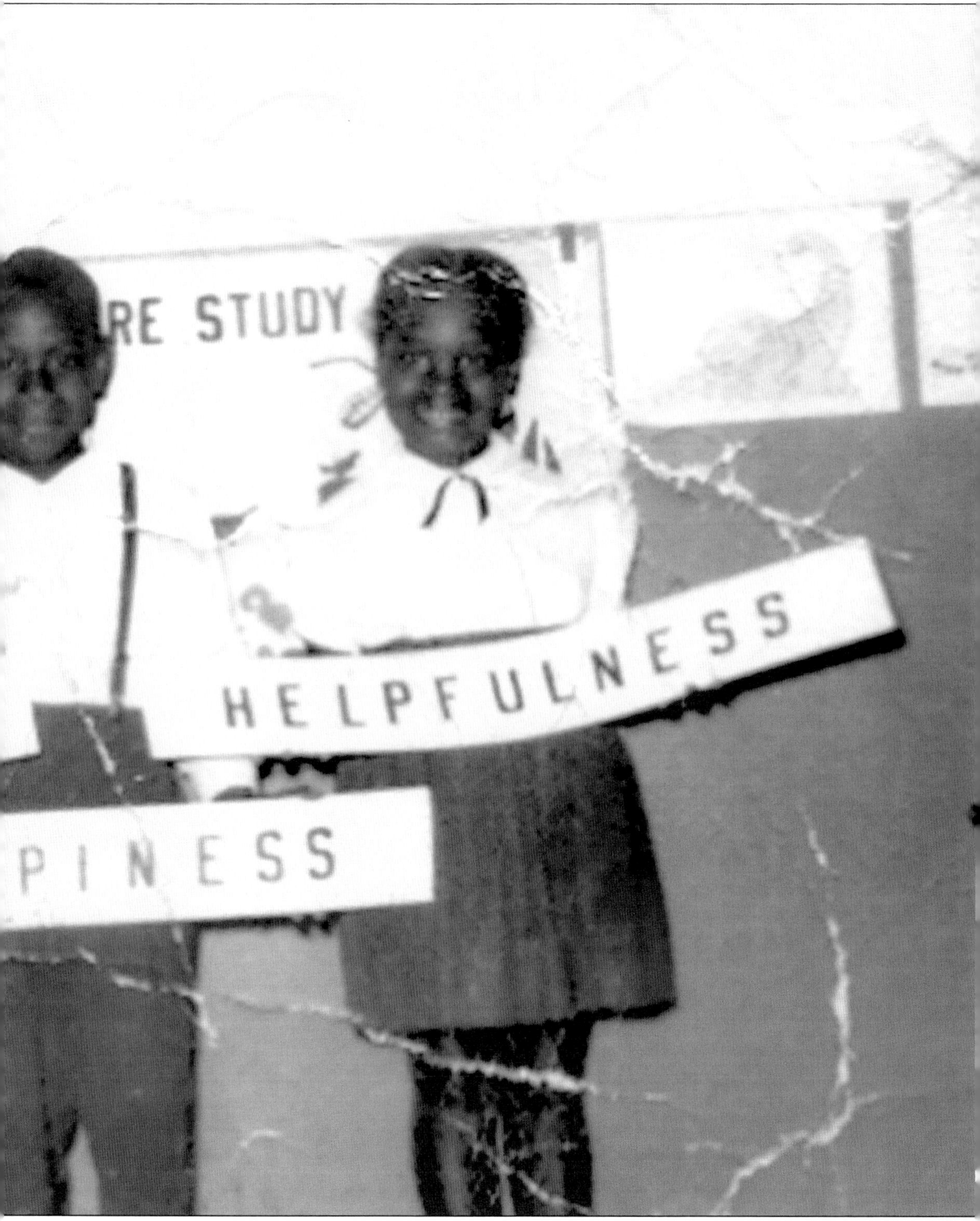

"Happiness" is John Maxey *c.* 1950. (Courtesy of Dorothy Maxey.)

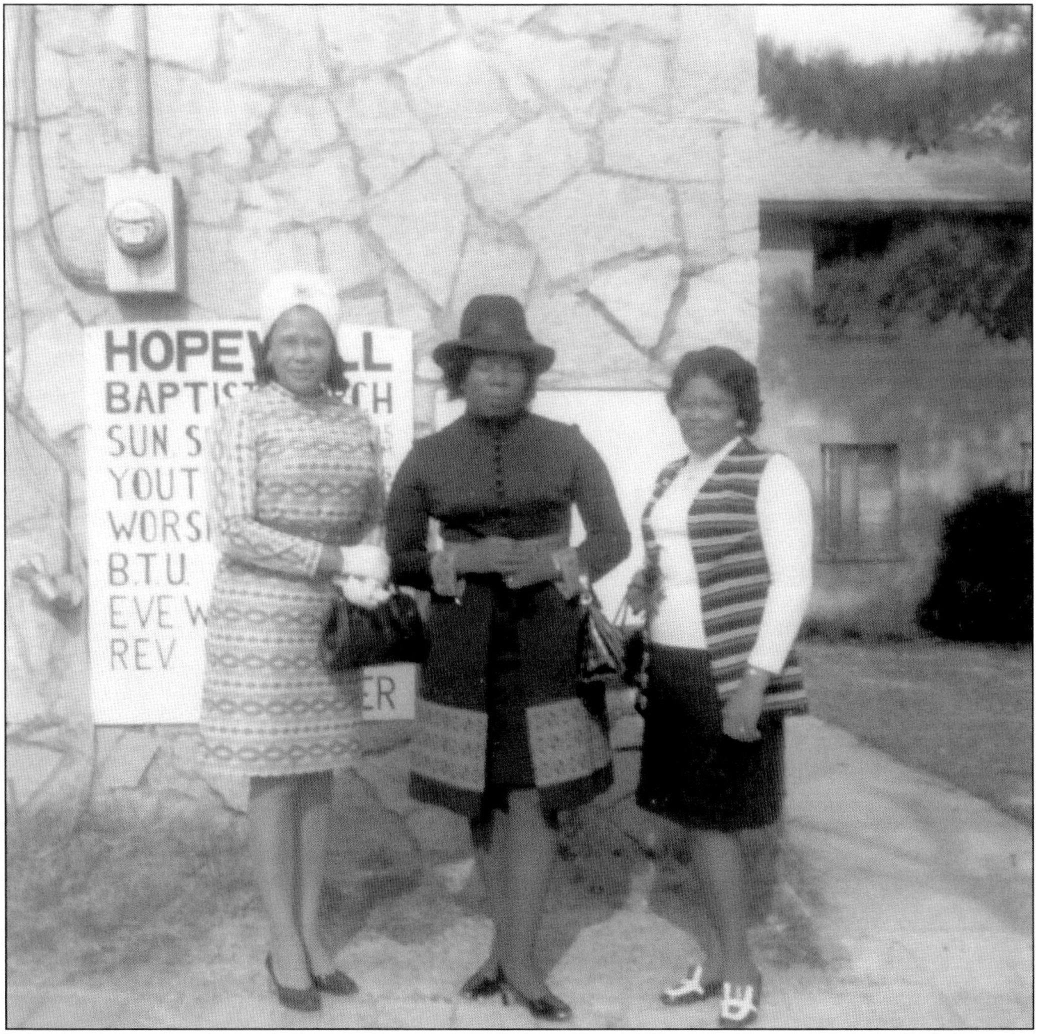

From left to right, Myra Gammage, Francis Sims, and Barbara Dunnigan are pictured in front of Hopewell Baptist Church in the 1970s. (Courtesy of Rufus Dunnigan.)

Three

WEDDINGS

The heart of marriage is memories; and if the two of you happen to have the same ones and savor your reruns, then your marriage is a gift from the gods.
——Bill Cosby

Weddings are gala affairs in the African-American community. Family members come from far and near to celebrate these joyous occasions. In the early years, the bride's dress was usually handmade. It was customary for the newly married couple to "jump the broom" at the end of the ceremony, an old tradition from the days of slavery.

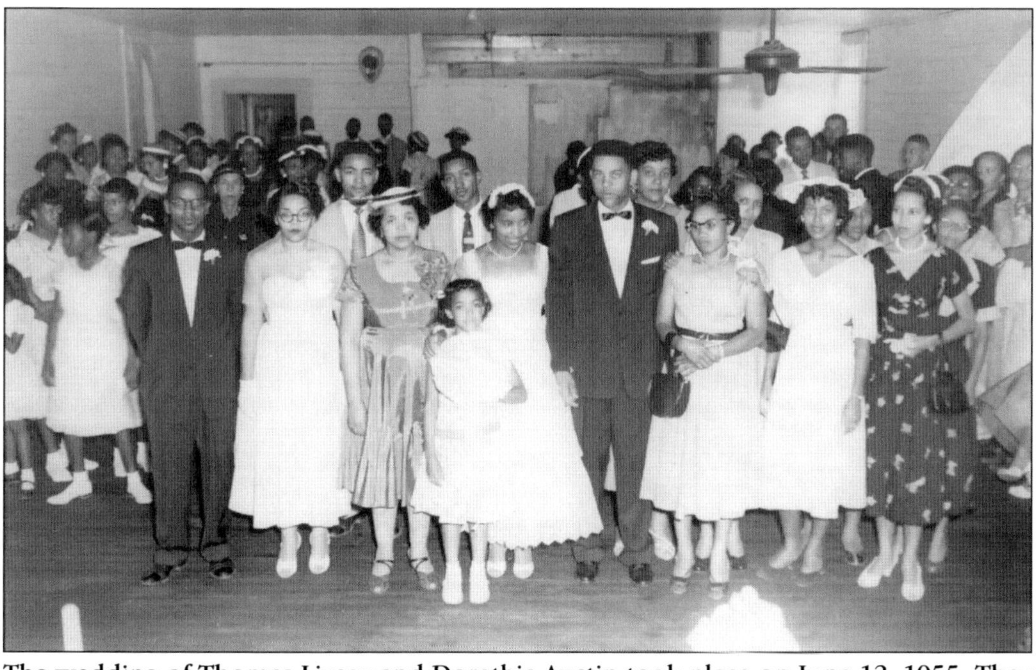

The wedding of Thomas Livsey and Dorethia Austin took place on June 12, 1955. They are lifelong residents of Gwinnett County. Notice the hardwood floors of the church. (Courtesy of Thomas Livsey.)

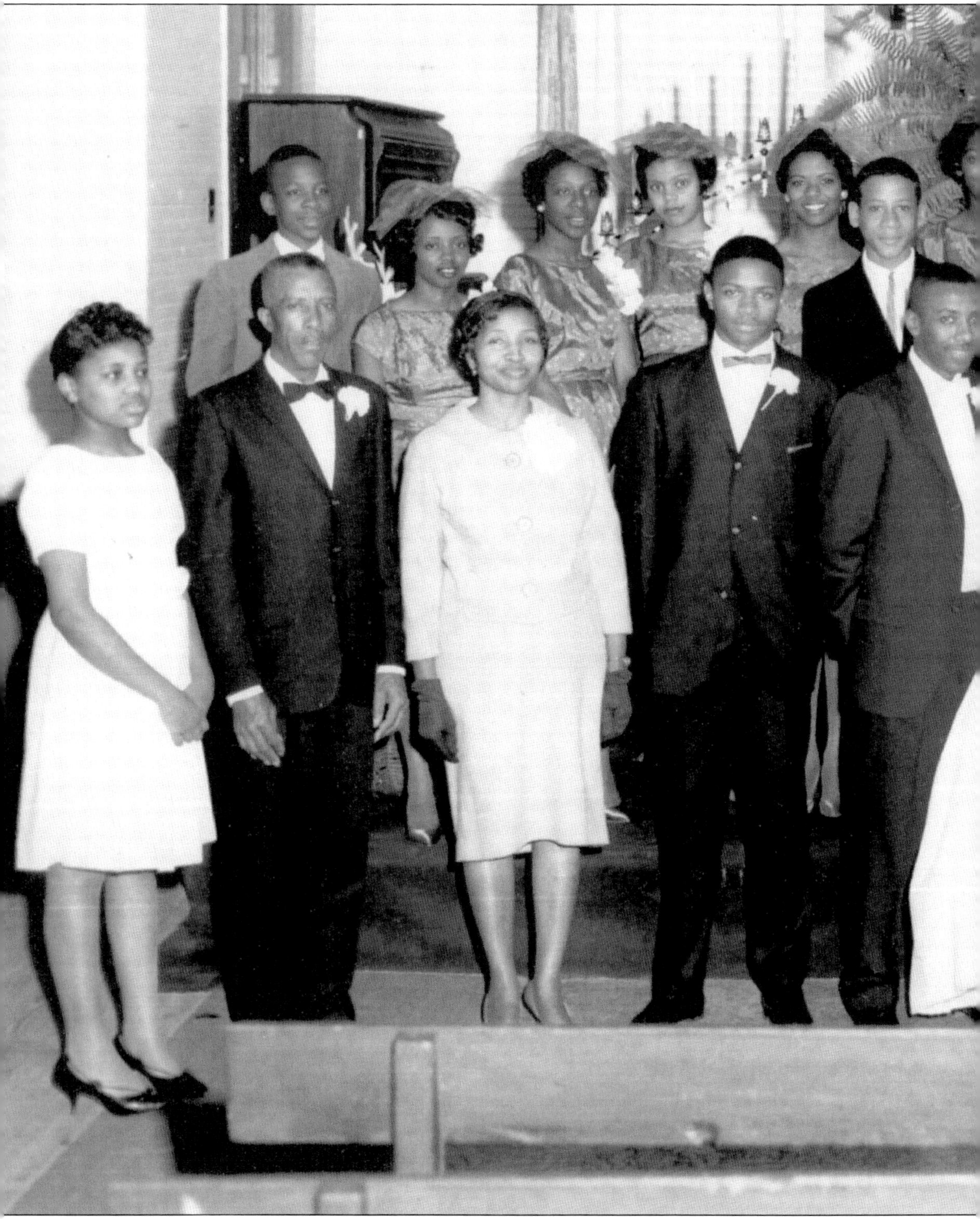

The wedding party of Eron and Susan Moore are seen on December 25, 1962.

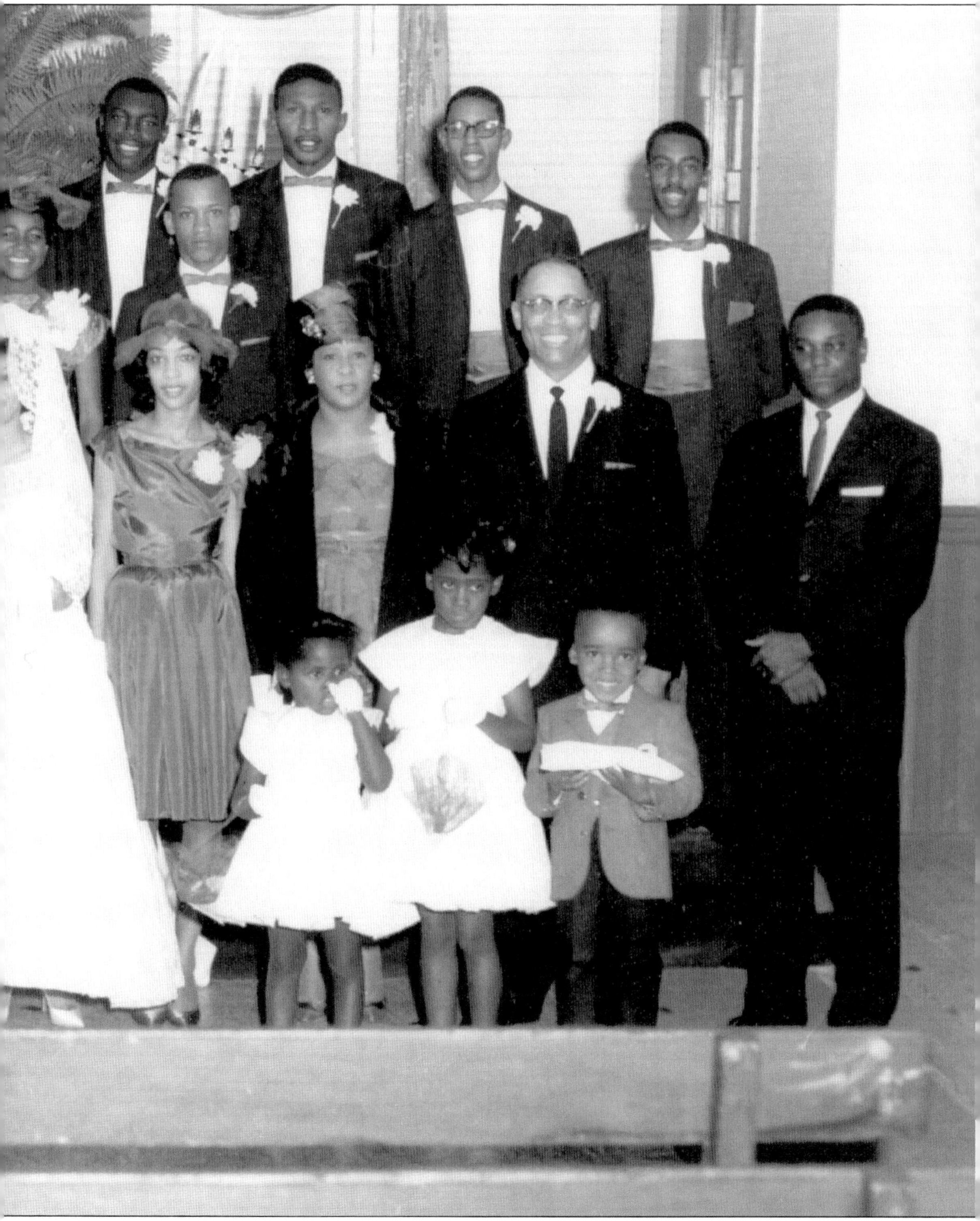

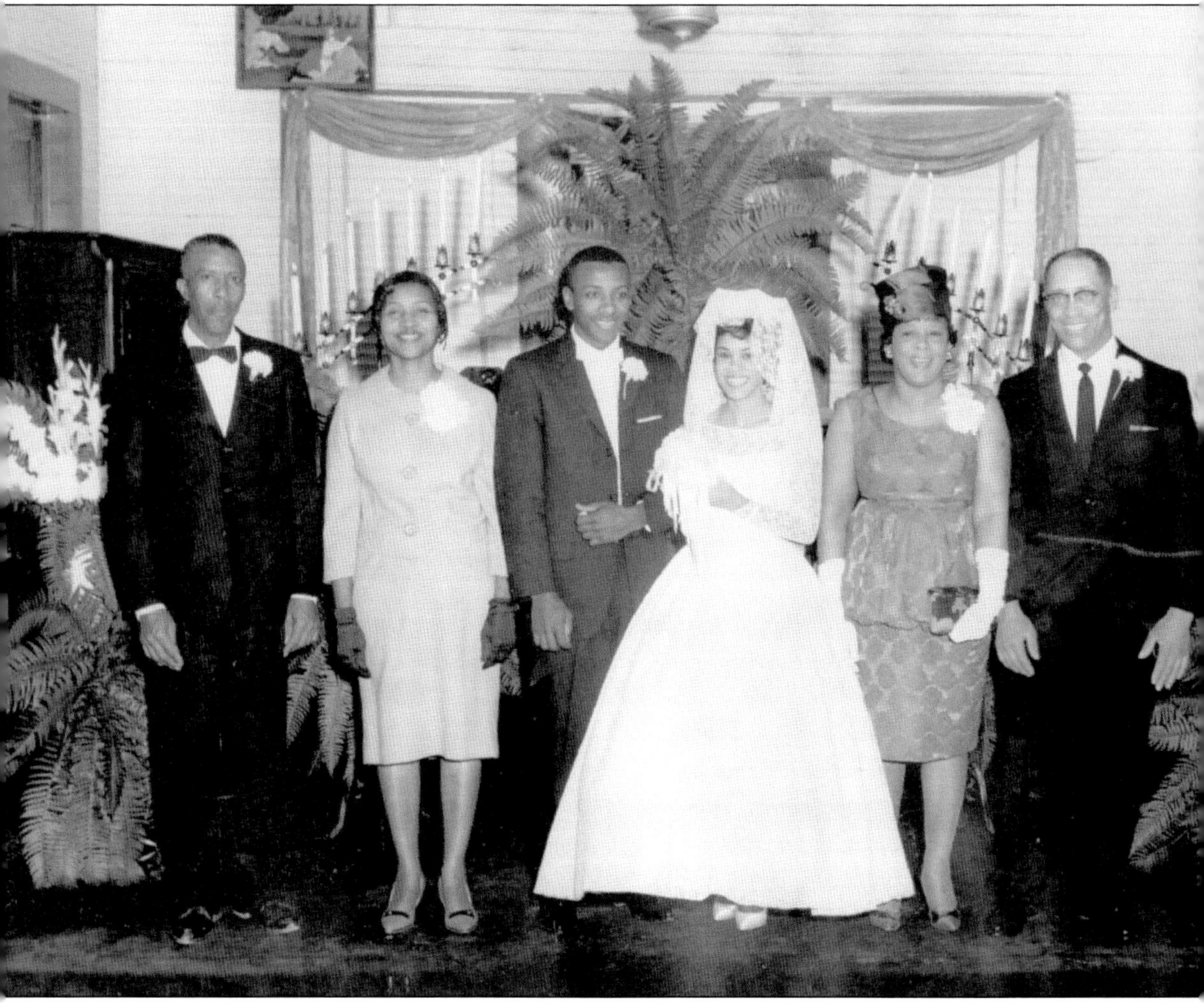

The parents of the bride and groom joined this wedding photo on December 25, 1962. Pictured from left to right are Eron Moore, Lila Bell Moore, Eron Moore Jr., Robbie Susan Teasley Moore, Robbie Teasley, and McKinley Teasley. Eron and Susan Moore are longtime residents of the county. (Courtesy of Eron and Susan Moore.)

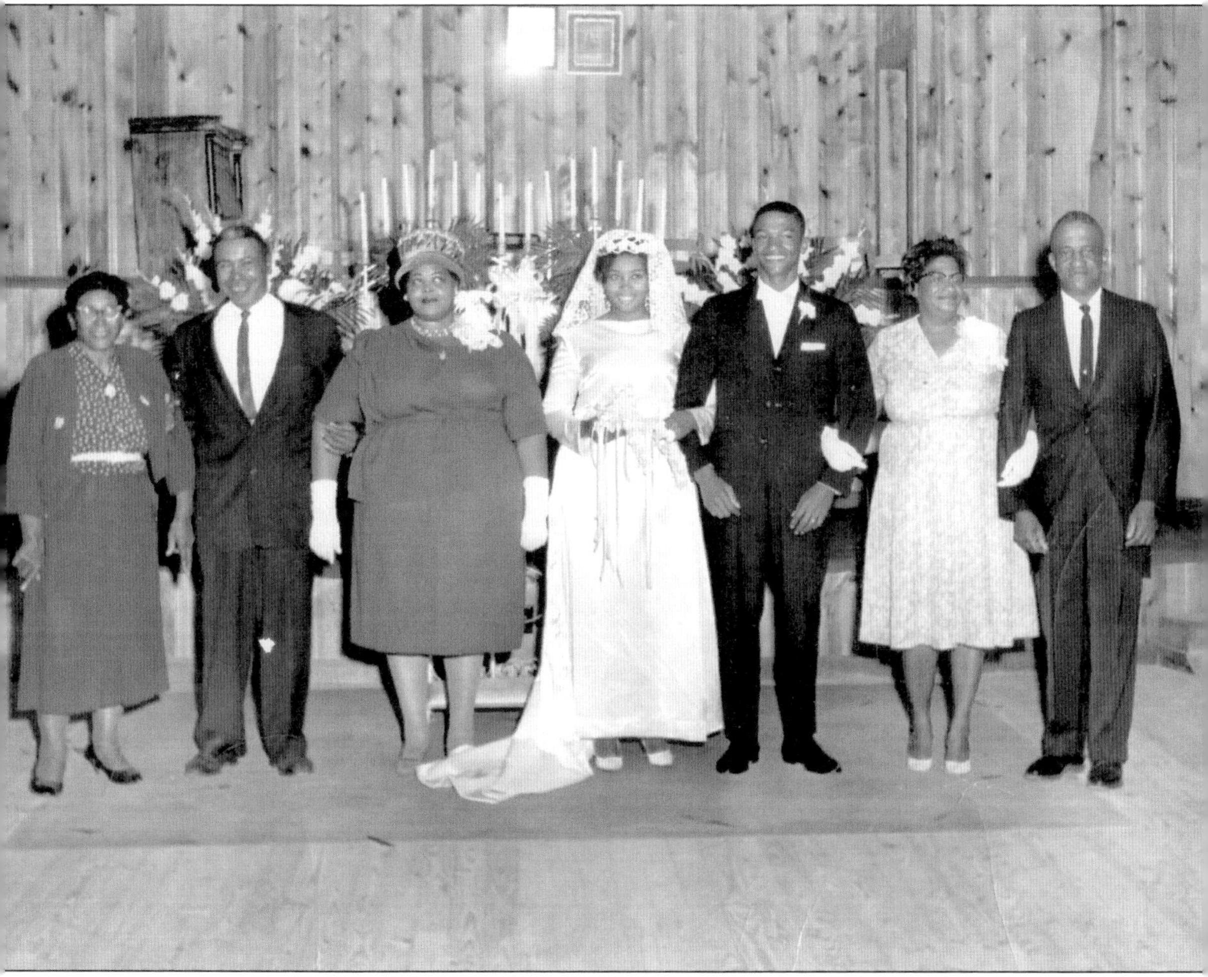

Another wedding photo depicts parents with the bride and groom on October 18, 1964. From left to right are Martha Taylor Gordon, Willie B. Taylor, Susie Mae Hosch Taylor, Iri Williams, Bobby Williams, Jewel Williams, and Walter Williams. The hardwood floors and wood benches were common in the church during those years. (Courtesy of Iri Williams.)

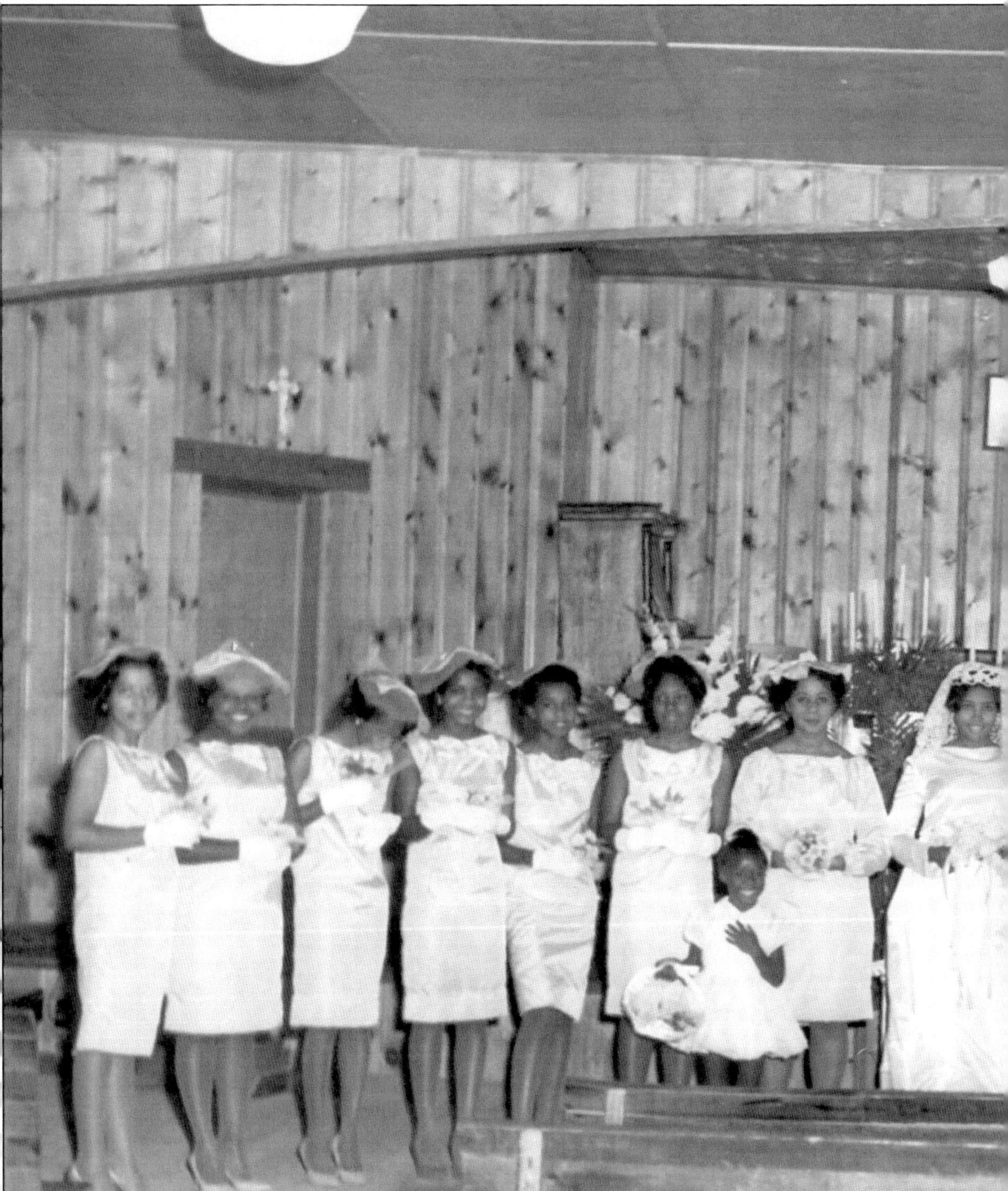

Bobby and Iri Williams wed on October 18, 1964. Seen from left to right are Annie Harris, Hazel Harris, Christine Summerour, Barbara Ann Patillo, Linda Jean Patillo, Linda Brown, Vivian Taylor, Evett Patillo, Rev. J. Jones, Marvin Griffin, Jonathan Keith

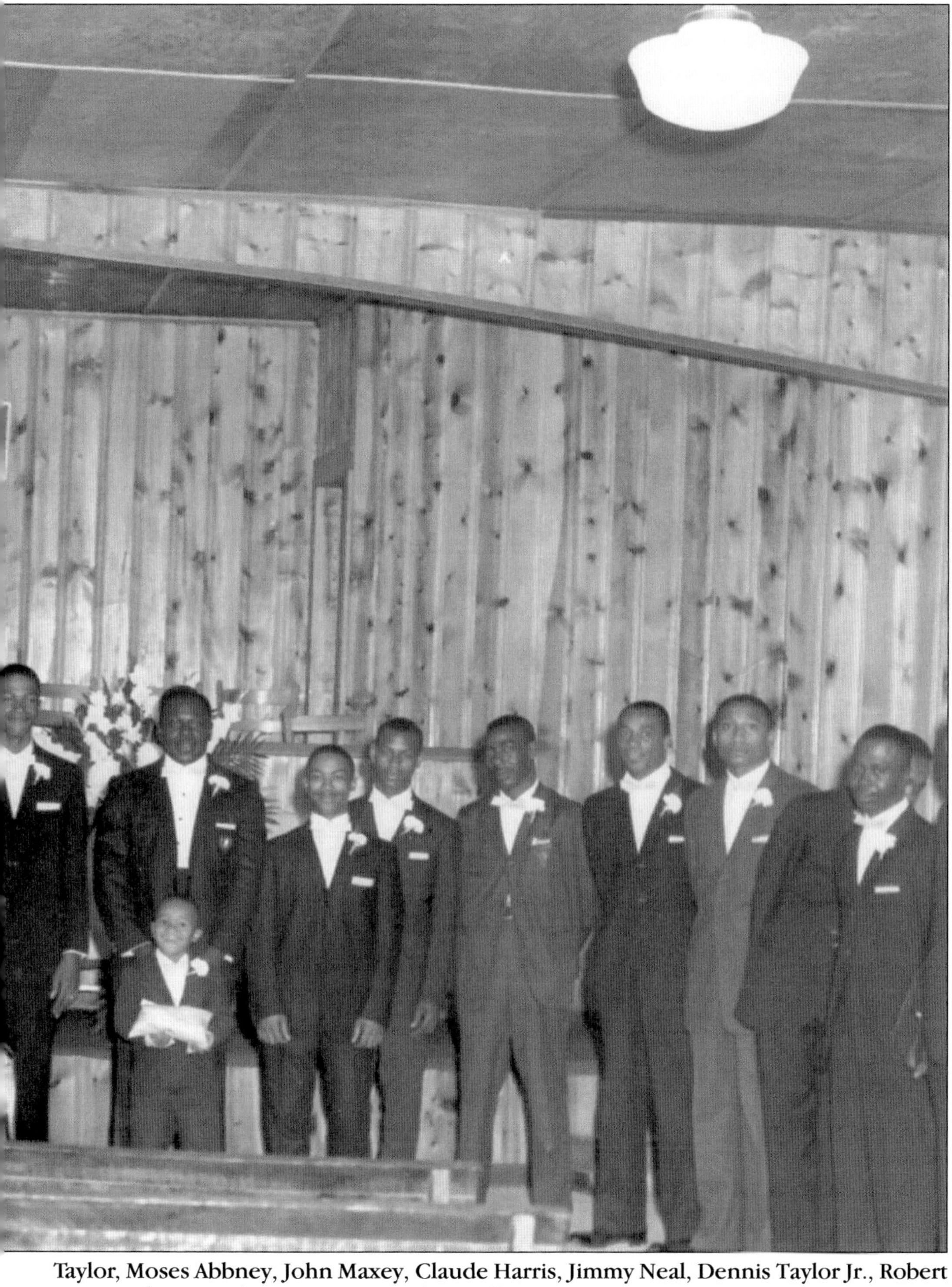

Taylor, Moses Abbney, John Maxey, Claude Harris, Jimmy Neal, Dennis Taylor Jr., Robert King, and O. Hutchins. (Courtesy of Iri Williams.)

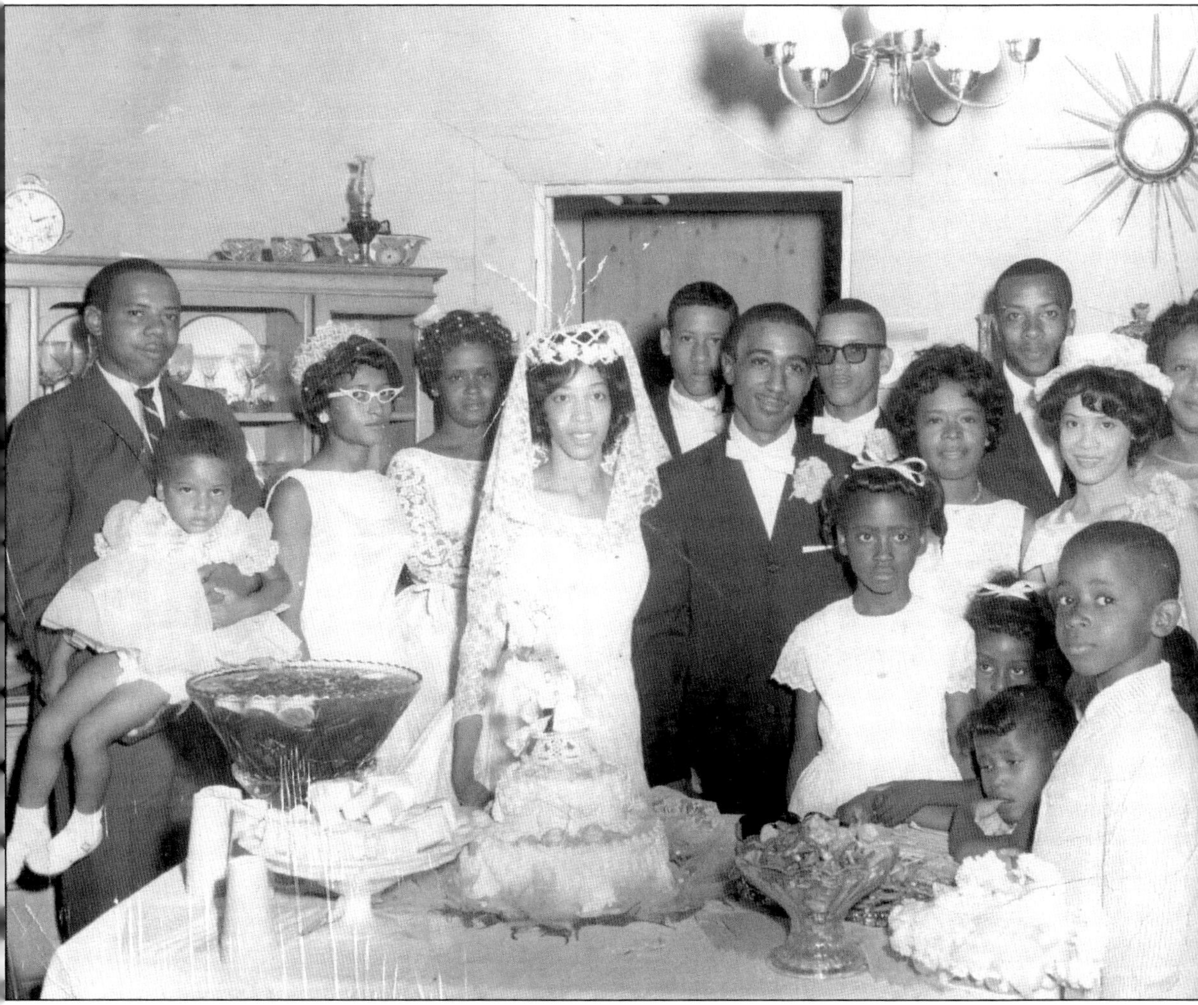

Walter Timley married Mary Ann Teasley in August of 1963. The couple had two children—Walter III and Patrick. (Courtesy of Eron and Susan Moore.)

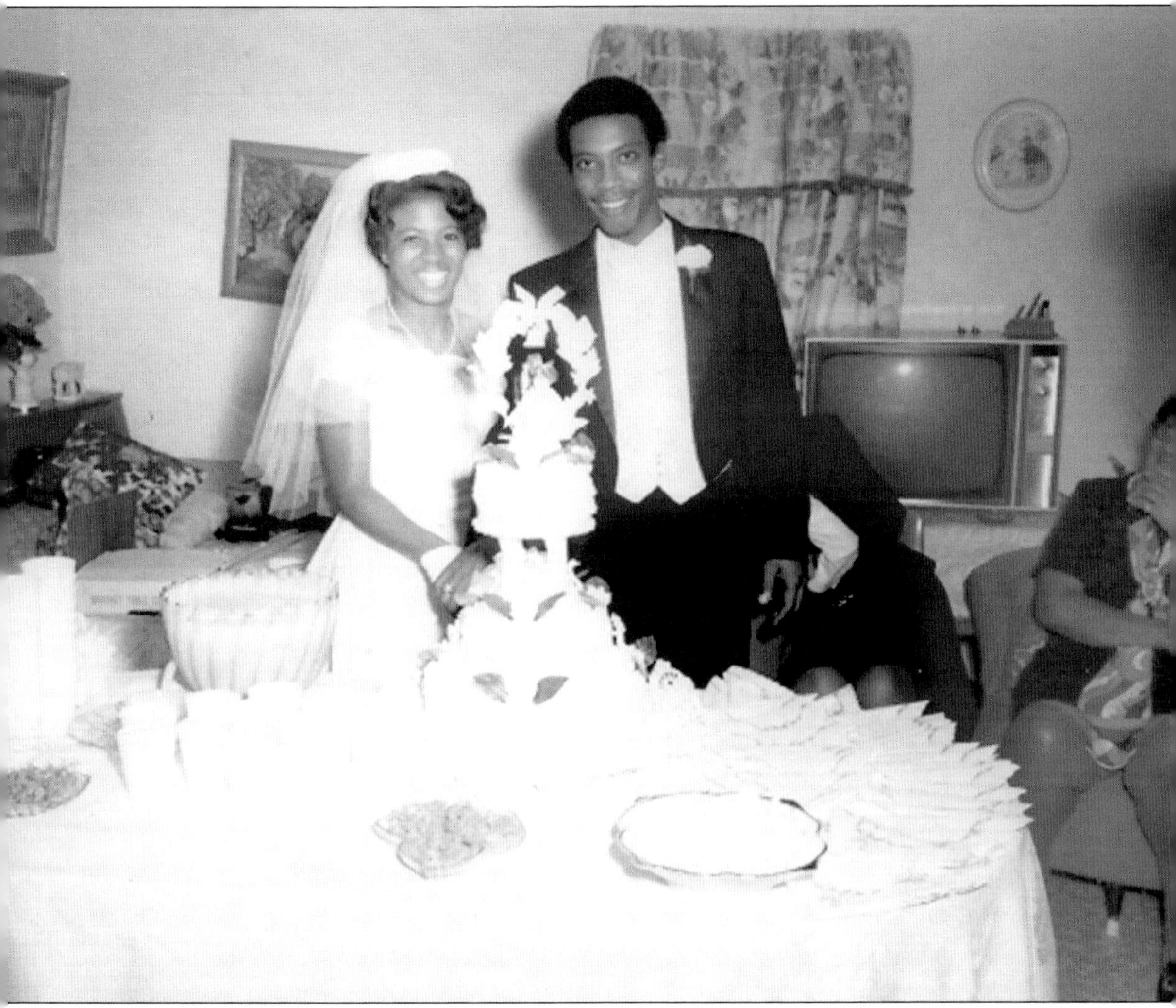

James Brown and Carrene Maxey are a couple full of happiness on their wedding day, November 20, 1970. They still reside in Gwinnett County and are the parents of two children—Andre and Melissa. (Courtesy of Dorothy Maxey.)

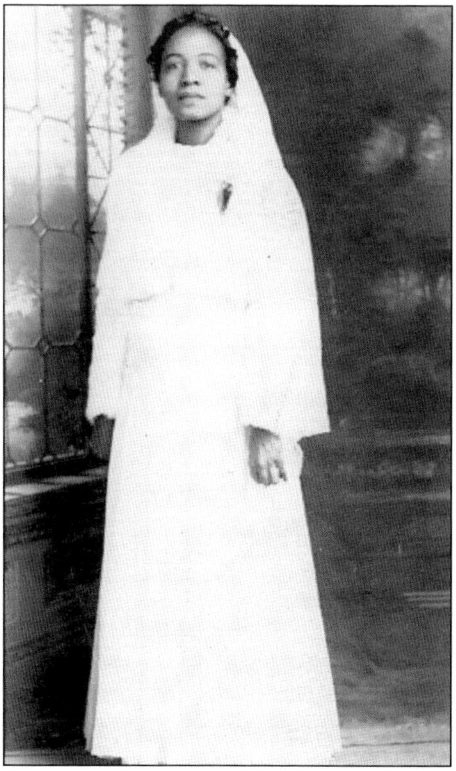

Lena Maxey is pictured on her wedding day in 1942. The bride-to-be stands with poise and beauty on her special day. (Courtesy of Dorothy Maxey.)

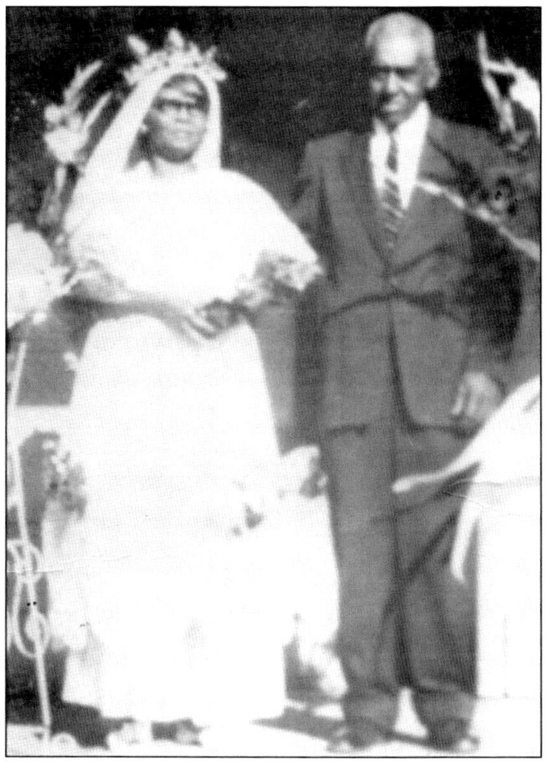

Robert and Morena Livsey pose for a photograph on their wedding anniversary. The couple shared over 50 years together. (Courtesy of Thomas Livsey.)

Four

School and Pageantry

The first thing to do is to get into every school, private and public . . .
——Booker T. Washington

Education was strongly advocated after slavery in the African-American community. There were fewer schools for people of color, and the schools were often in need of repair. School supplies such as books and paper were hard to come by. African-American teachers were paid far less than white teachers in the county. Pageantry was a means to honor the beauty and intelligence in the community and the church. Many pageants were held at local churches and schools annually. This was a major event for young men and women in various communities.

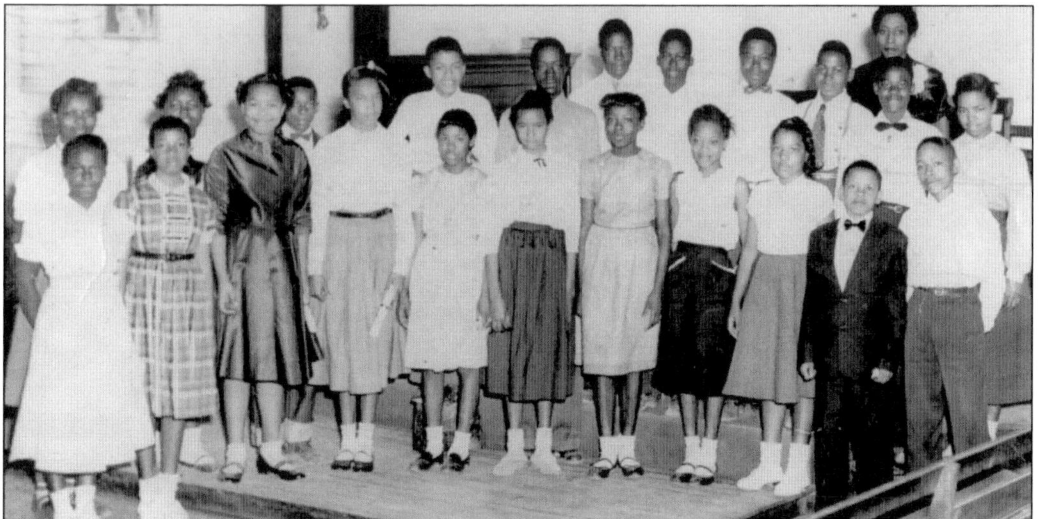

Pictured at Pleasant Hill Baptist Church school in 1956 are, from left to right, (front row) Hazel King, Sarah Cooper, Justine Bell, Benny Anderson, Ethel Mae King, Thelma R. Daniel, Essie Lou Hayes, Mary Echols, Annie Harris, "Meatball" Franklin, and Glenn Smith. (back row) Pearlie Mae Maxey, Mary McIntyre, Claude Harris, Andrew Williams, Ross Brothers, Parker McFadden, Robert King, Robert Hayes, Herbert Wilburn, Mildred Cooper, and Viola Smith (teacher). (Courtesy of Thelma R. Yarbough.)

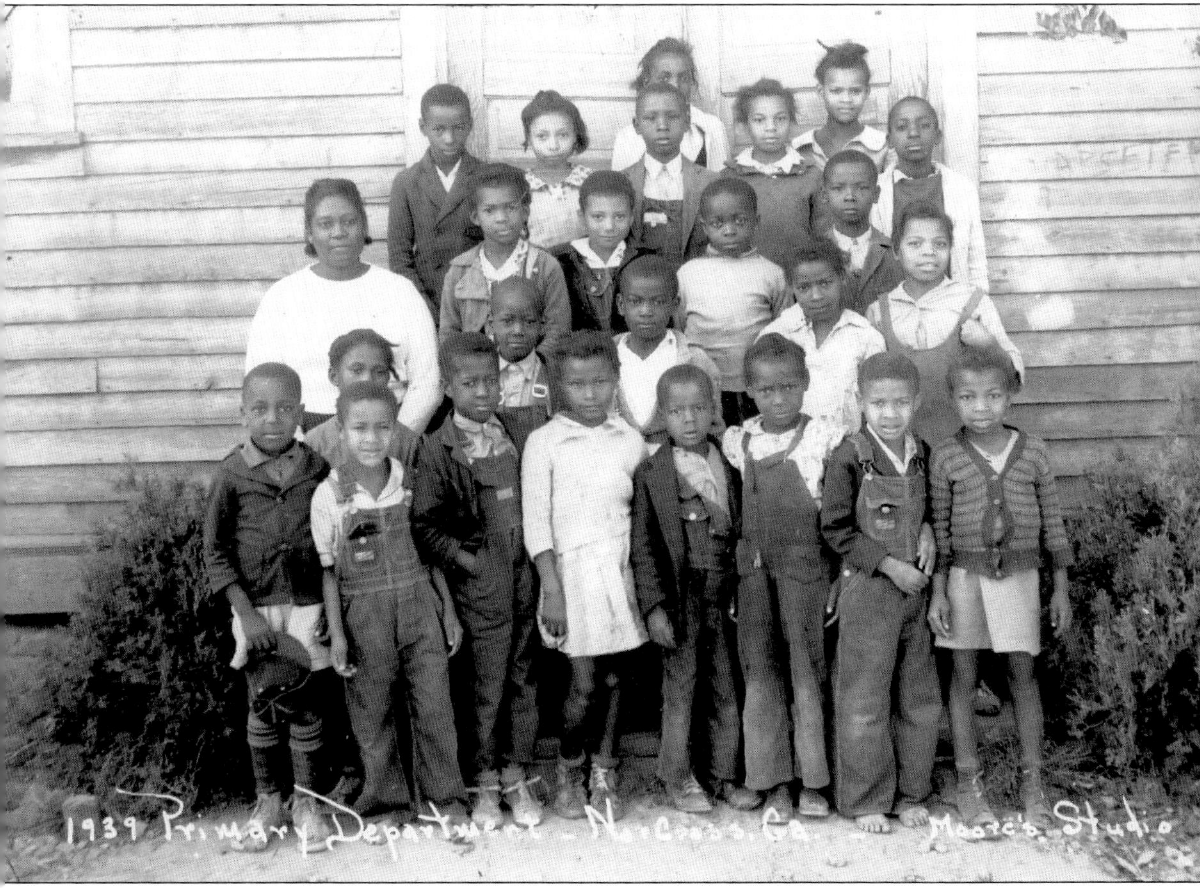

Students at the colored elementary school in Norcross are seen here in 1939. From left to right are (front row) John Crawford McKinney, Hattie Mae Brown, Albert Burson, Charles Newton, Elizabeth Simpson, Margaret Trimble, Horace Simpson, Benjamin Cothran, Katie Mae Brown, George Bailey, Winnie Sue Bailey, Leon Simpson, and Everlyn McKinney; (middle row) Ms. Jo Ann Parks (teacher), Virginia Bailey, Mancest Jones, Oscar Smith Jr., and Nathaniel Brown; (back row) Rufus Dunnigan, Melody Jones, Francis Davis, Willie Brown, Jessie Mae Trimble, Dorothy Simpson, and Charles Crosby. (Courtesy of Rufus Dunnigan.)

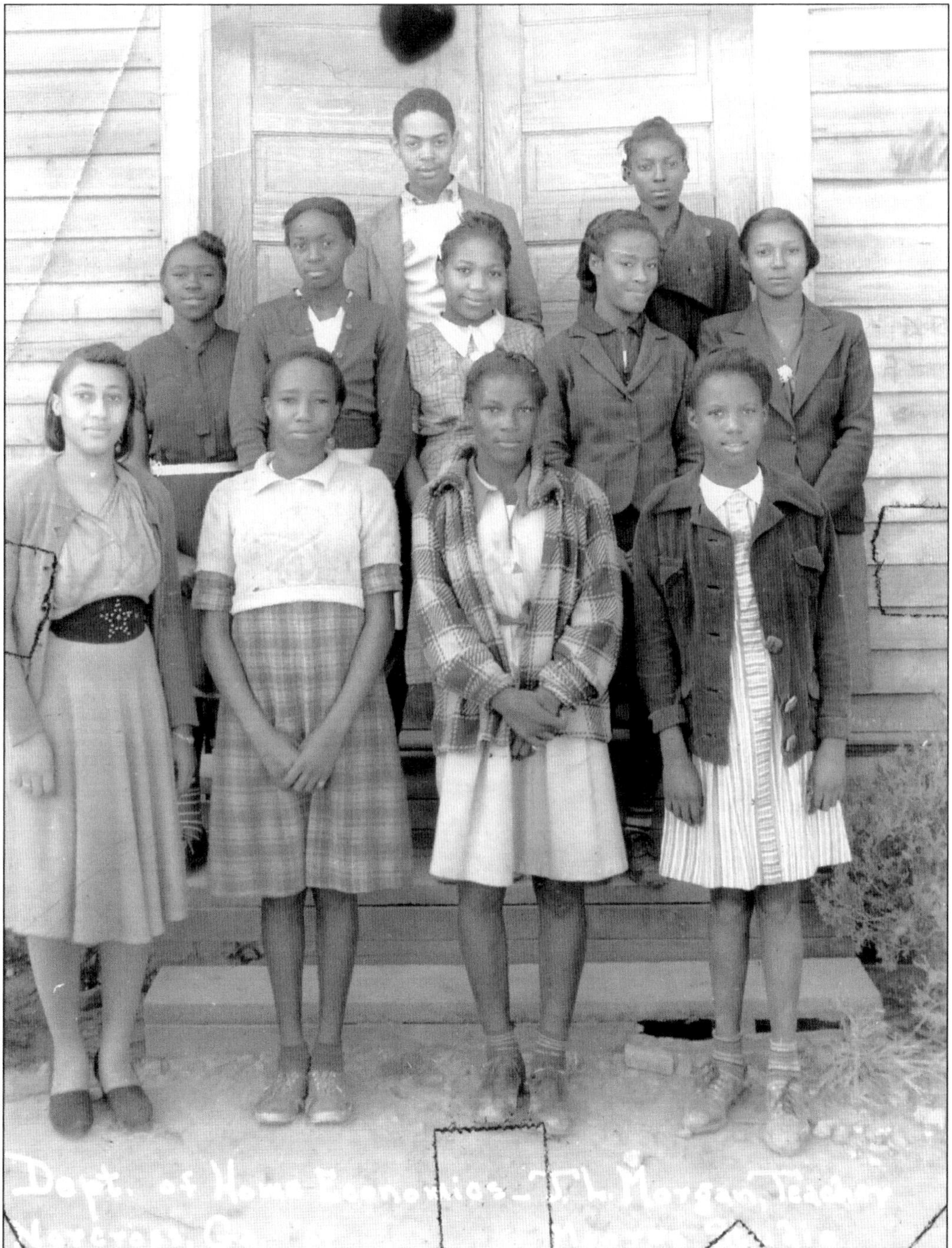

Students at the colored middle school in Norcross are pictured in 1939. Seen from left to right are (front row) Ms. Morgan (teacher), Dorothy Woodford, Janet Newton, and Cora Dunnigan; (middle row) Annie Ruth Gilbert, Elizabeth Smith, Betty Thompson, Margaret Simpson, and Martis Benton; (back row) unidentified. (Courtesy of Rufus Dunnigan.)

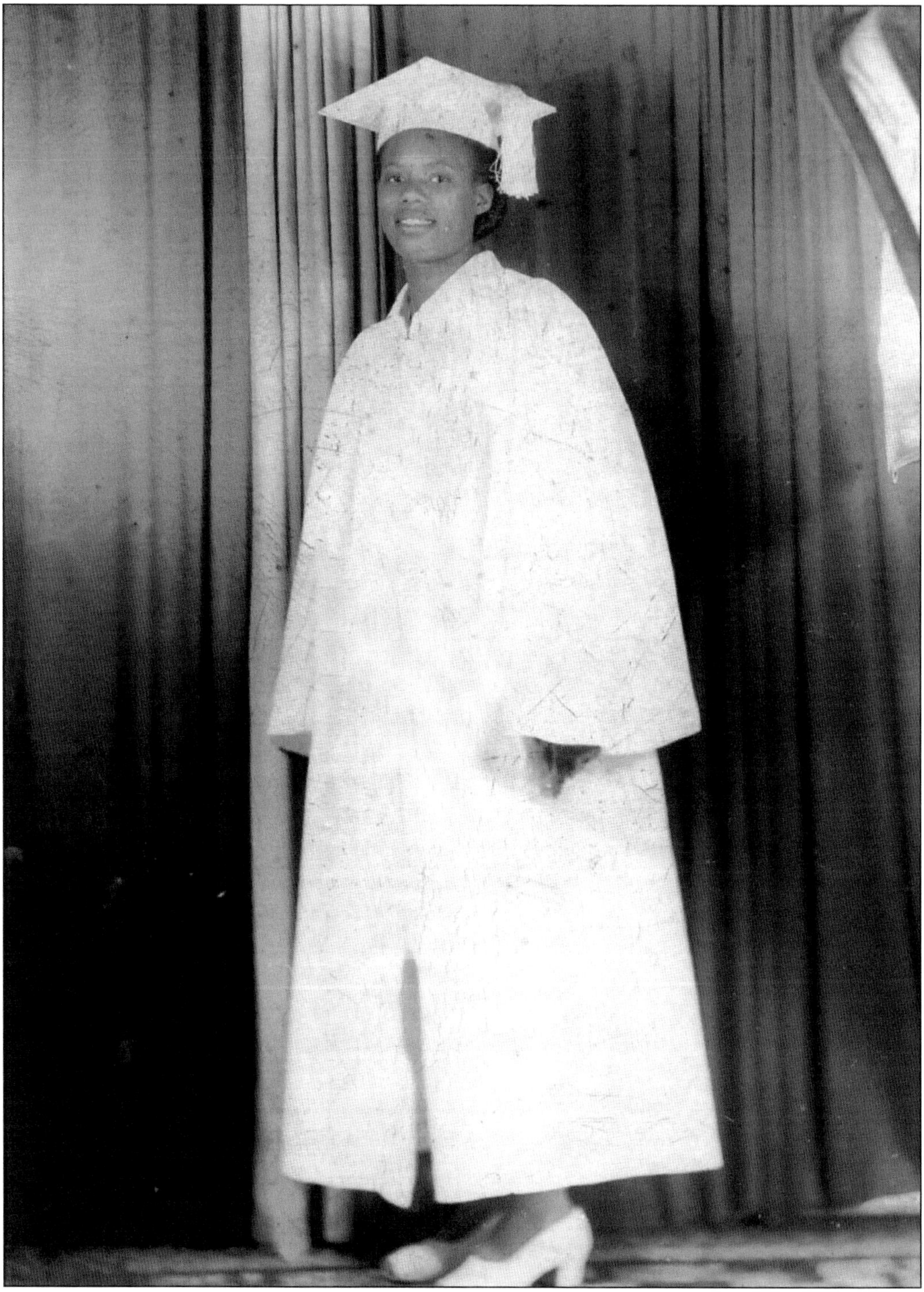

Cora Dunnigan graduated from Atlanta Beauty School in 1946. Ms. Dunnigan was a beautician in Norcross for over five years and later became a licensed nurse. (Courtesy of Rufus Dunnigan.)

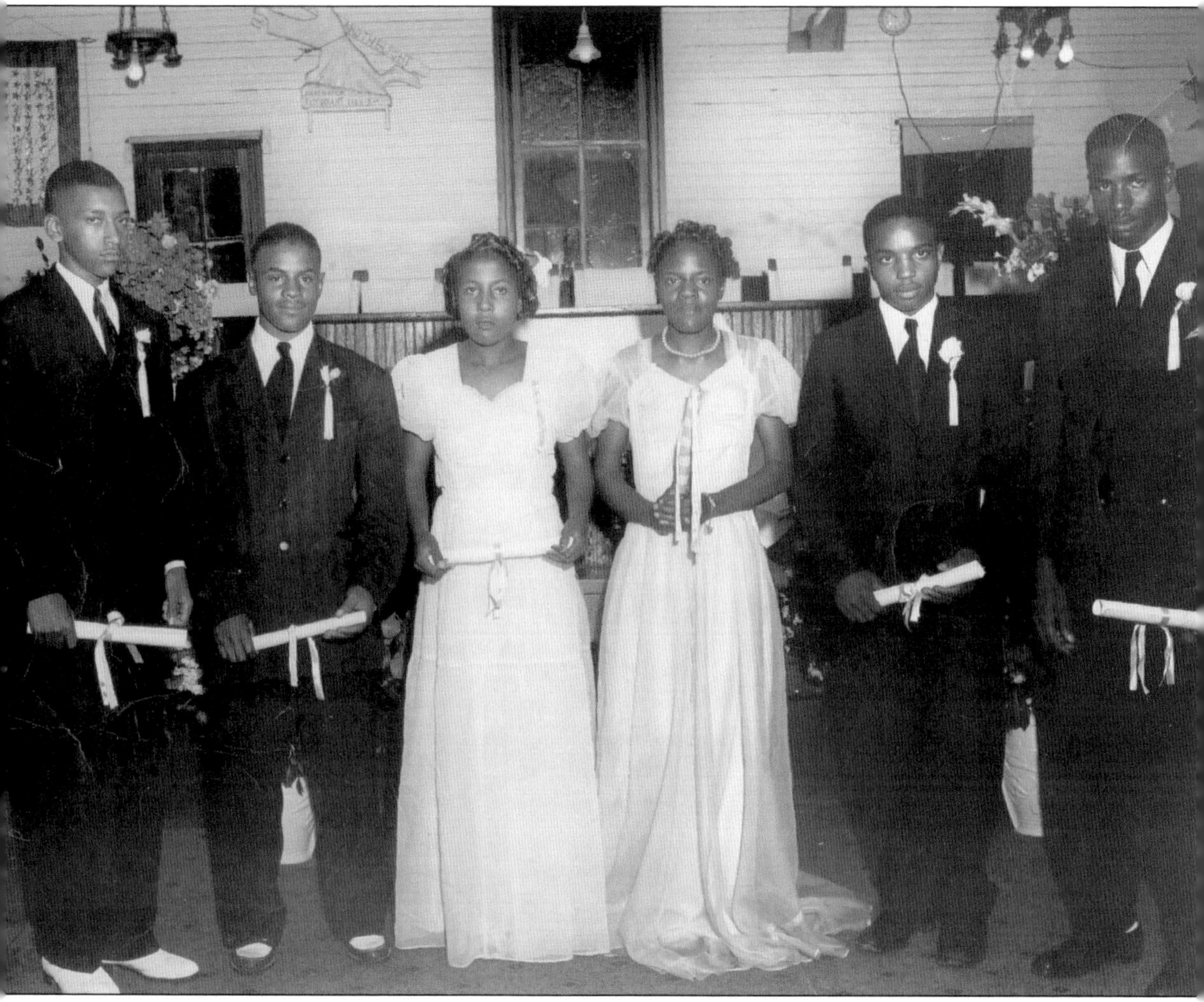

This is the graduating class of 1949 at Chamblee High School in DeKalb County. Black students in the Norcross area who wanted to finish high school had to go to DeKalb County because Gwinnett County did not have a high school that black students could attend. Seen from left to right are Wallace Jones, Thomas Lester, Olivia Lyons (from Gwinnett), unidentified, Sam Summerour, and Rufus Dunnigan (from Gwinnett). (Courtesy of Rufus Dunnigan.)

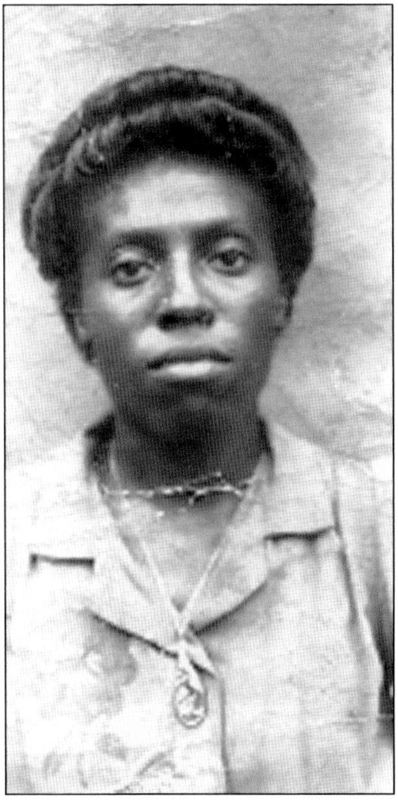

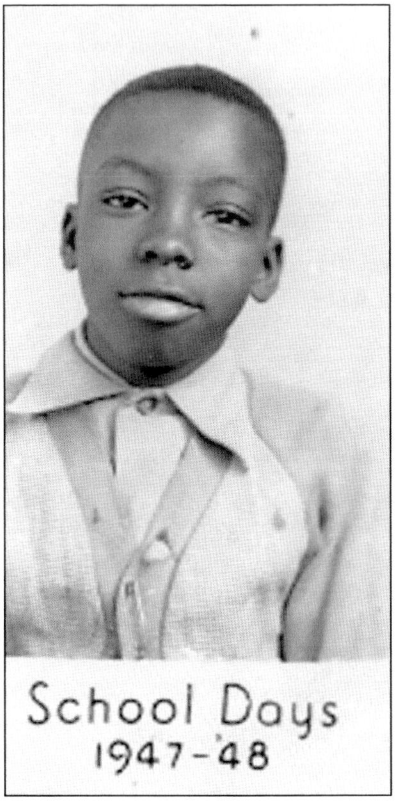

(*above left*) This is Jesseline Yarbough's school photo from the early 1950s. (Courtesy of Eron and Susan Moore.)
(*above right*) Henry Lott Jr. is pictured in a school days photo. He was 11 years old when this photo was taken at the Hooper Renwick School. (Courtesy of Dorothy Maxey.)

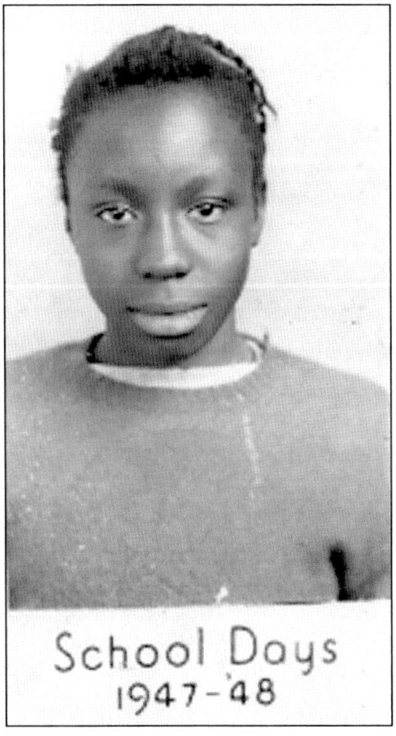

This is Margaret Lott's school photo. She was 12 years old when this photo was taken at the Hooper Renwick School. (Courtesy of Dorothy Maxey.)

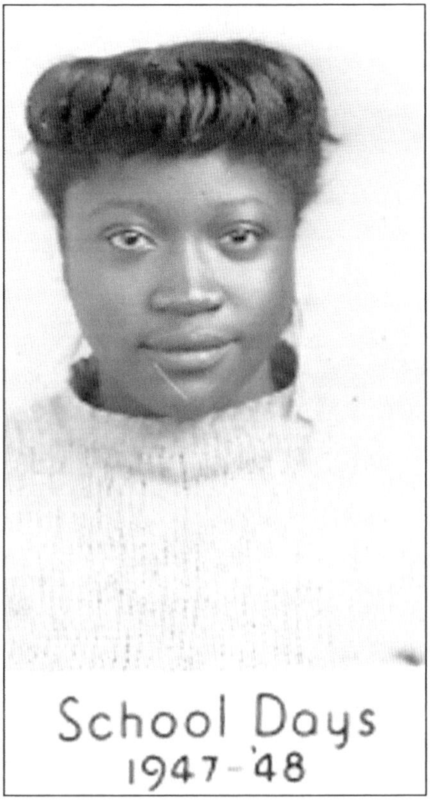

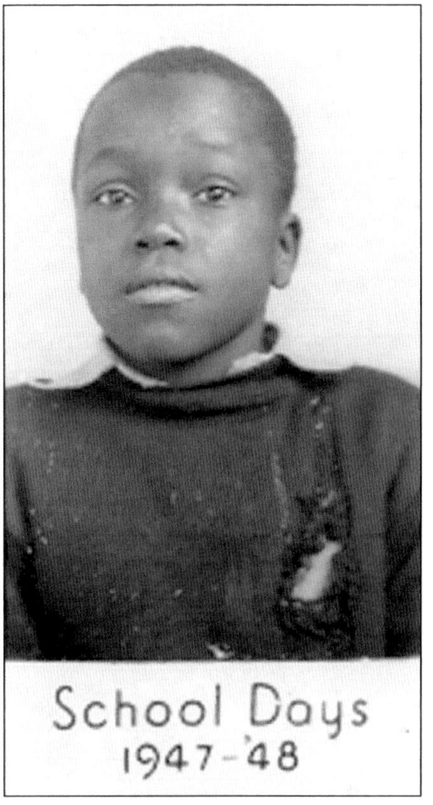

(*above left*) Annie Francis Brown was 12 years old in this Hooper Renwick school days photo. (Courtesy of Dorothy Maxey.)
(*above right*) Thomas Maxey is seen at age 8 in his Hooper Renwick school days photo. He currently resides in Gwinnett County. (Courtesy of Dorothy Maxey.)

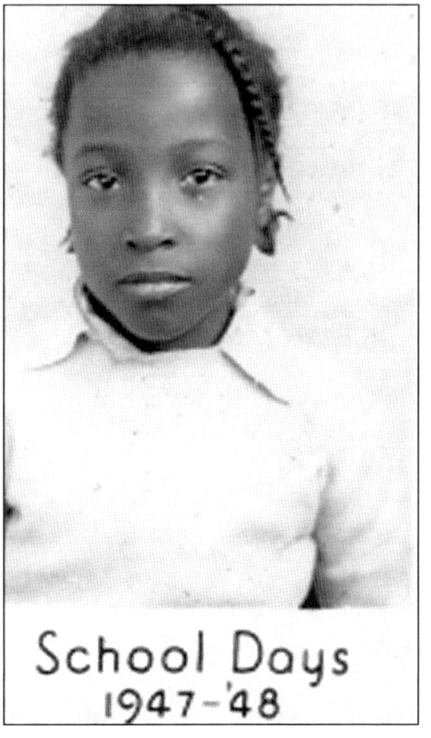

Charlie Mae Maxey is pictured at age 7. The sister of Thomas Maxey (above), she also attended Hooper Renwick School. (Courtesy of Dorothy Maxey.)

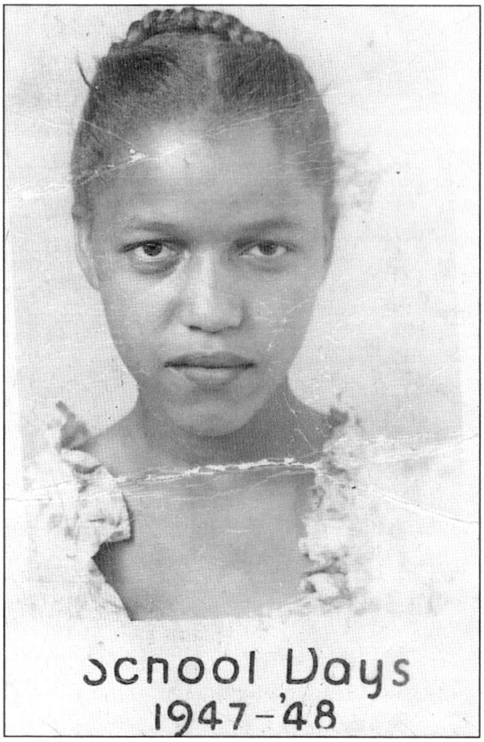

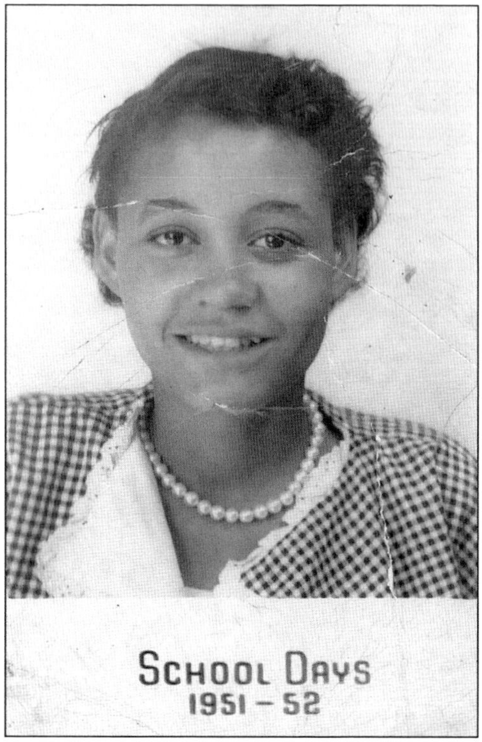

(*above left*) Julia "Patsy" Williams was 13 years old when this photo was taken. She lived in the family home on Clayton Street in Lawrenceville. (Courtesy of Julia Williams.)
(*above right*) Hattie Williams, Julia's sister, participated in basketball, softball, and track during her time at Hooper Renwick School. (Courtesy of Hattie Peters.)

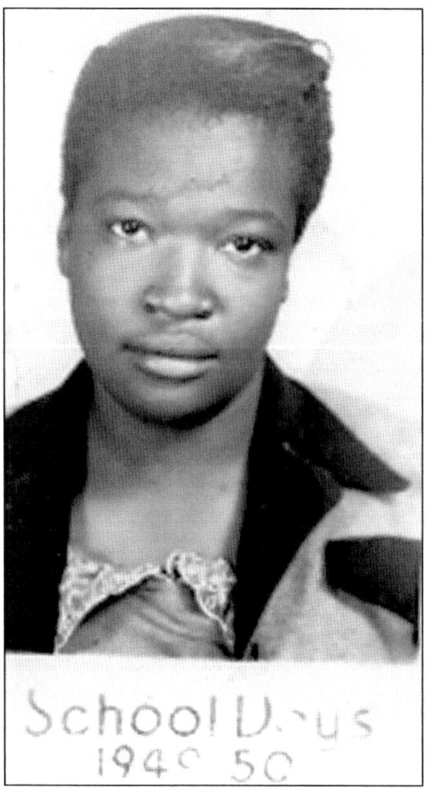

Laura Brown also attended Hooper Renwick; she later became a beautician in Gwinnett County. (Courtesy of Dorothy Maxey.)

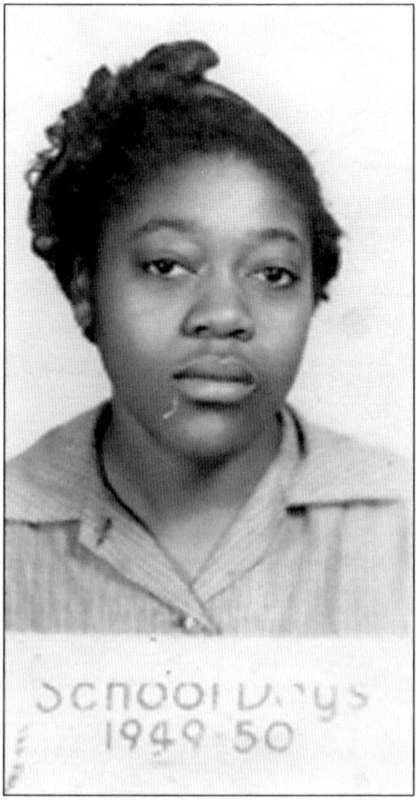

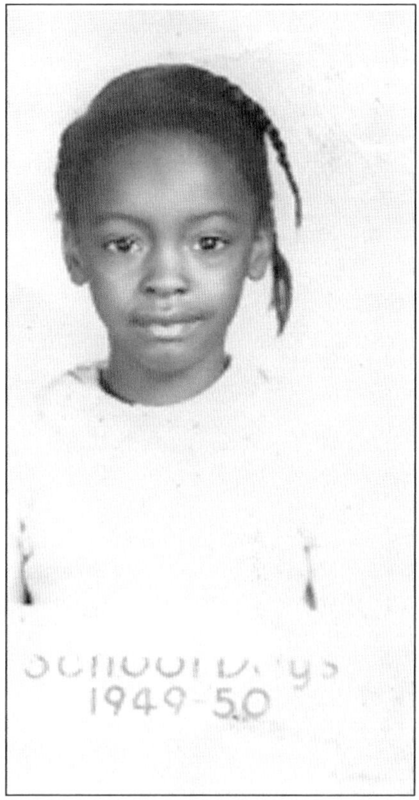

(*above left*) Julia Griffin, seen here in her Hooper Renwick photo, still resides in Gwinnett County. (Courtesy of Eron and Susan Moore.) (*above right*) Christine Summerour was six years old when this school photo was taken. She still lives in Gwinnett County. (Courtesy of Dorothy Maxey.)

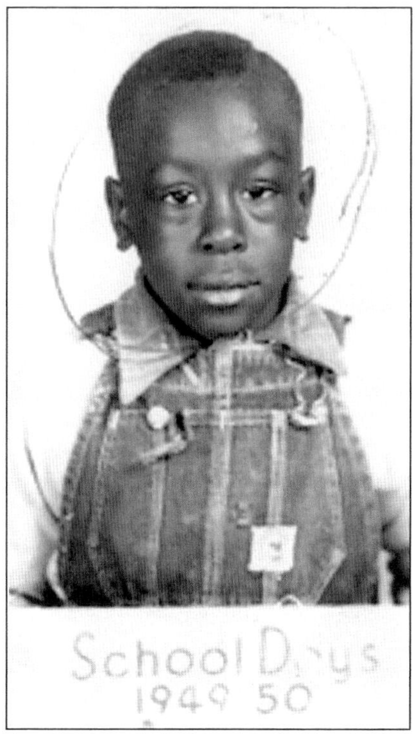

Terry Maxey is pictured at age six in his Hooper Renwick photo. (Courtesy of Dorothy Maxey.)

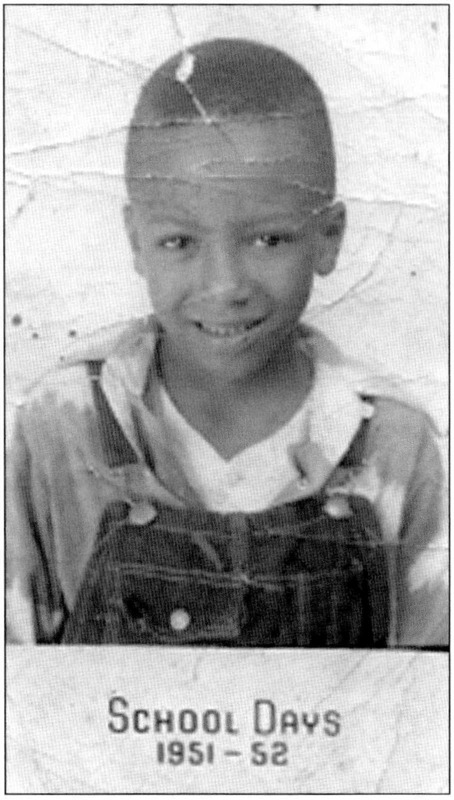

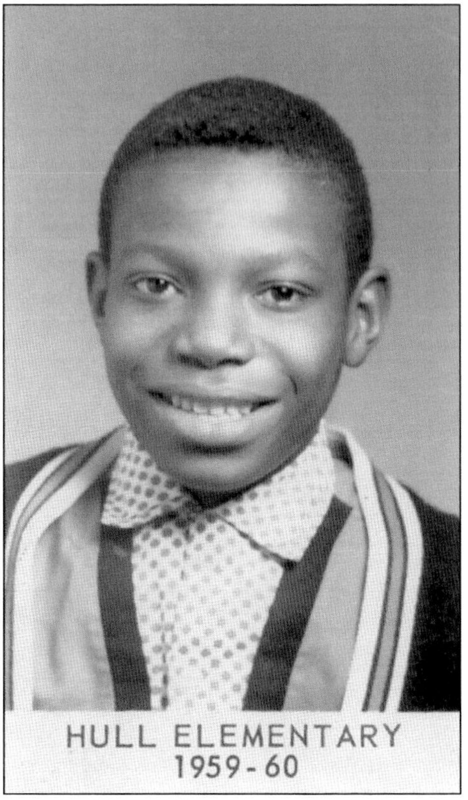

(*above left*) Michael Smith, who is now a preacher in Gwinnett County, was eight years old in this school days photo. (Courtesy of Eron and Susan Moore.)
(*above right*) This is Harold Dunnigan's school days photo from Hull Elementary. (Courtesy of Eron and Susan Moore)

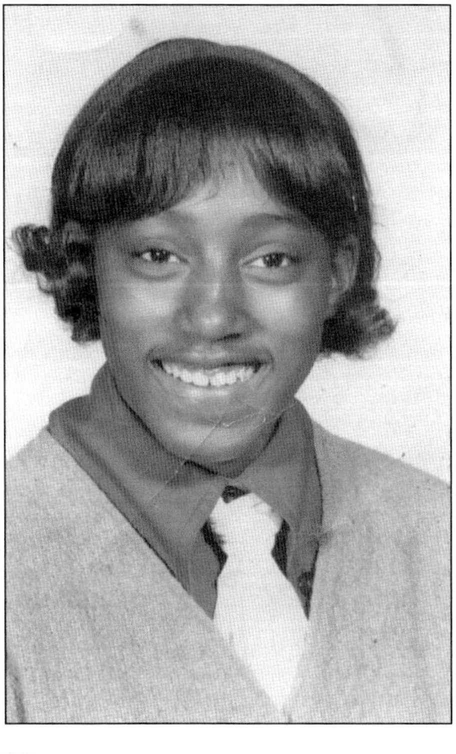

Vivian Summerour poses for her Hooper Renwick school photo. (Courtesy of Ruth Summerour.)

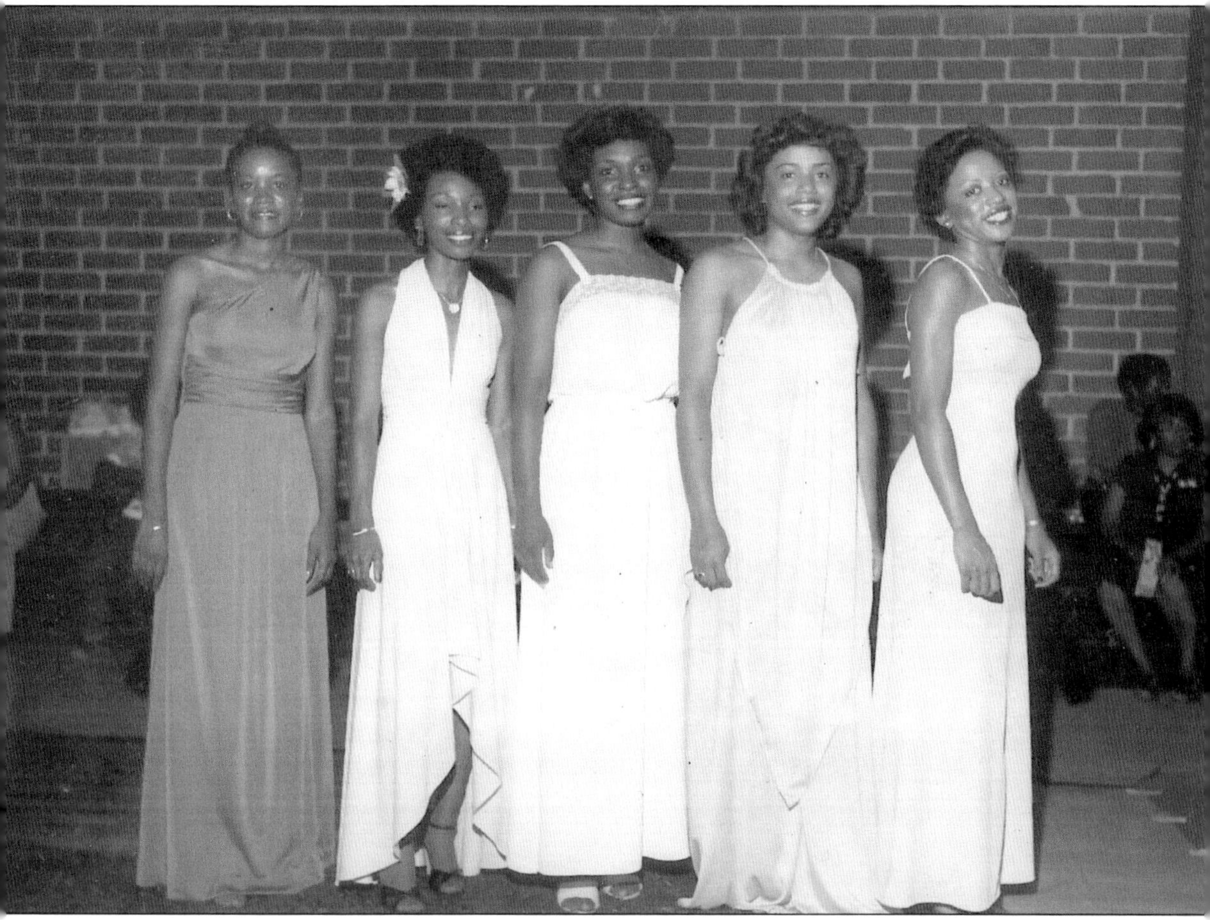

Contestants in the 1980 Miss Black Gwinnett pageant included (from left to right) Brenice Bailey, Prince Grimes, Vanessa Brown, Tracey Riden, and Elizabeth Bailey. (Courtesy of Eron and Susan Moore.)

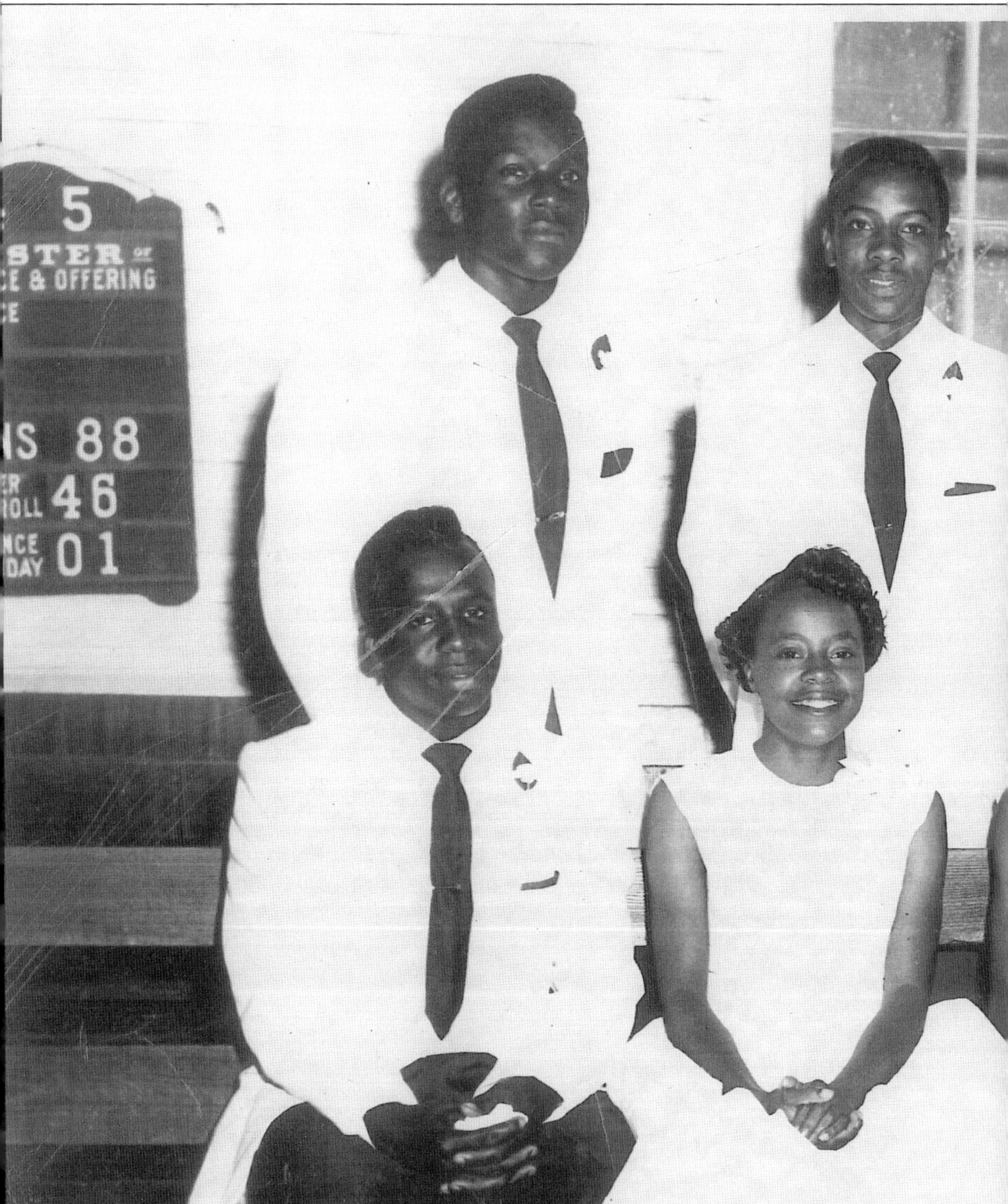

Pictured here is the 1956 graduating class at Hooper Renwick School. From left to right are (front row) Earnest Yarbough Jr., Cora Putman, Ruby Wilburn, Mary Echols, and L.D.

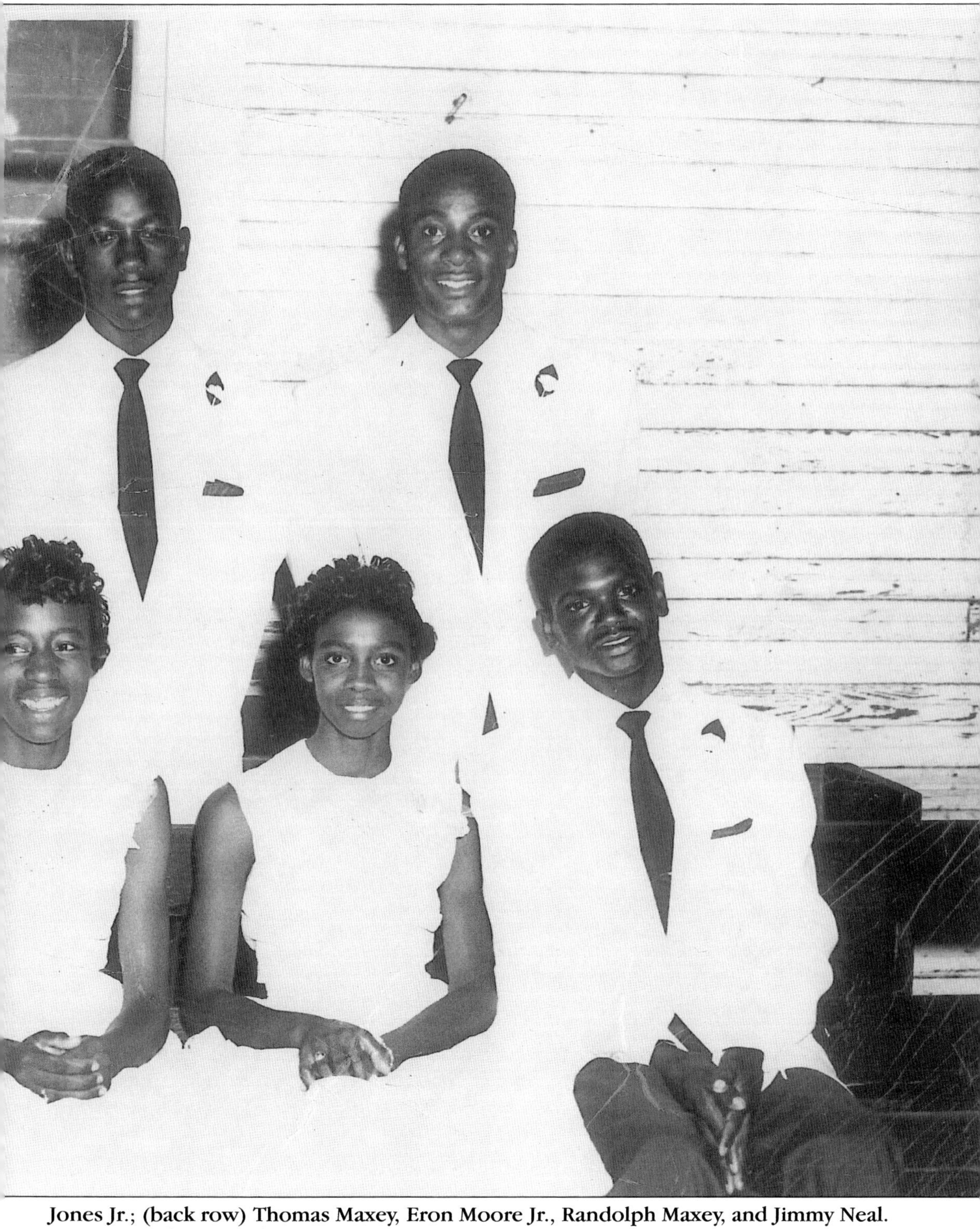

Jones Jr.; (back row) Thomas Maxey, Eron Moore Jr., Randolph Maxey, and Jimmy Neal. (Courtesy of Eron and Susan Moore.)

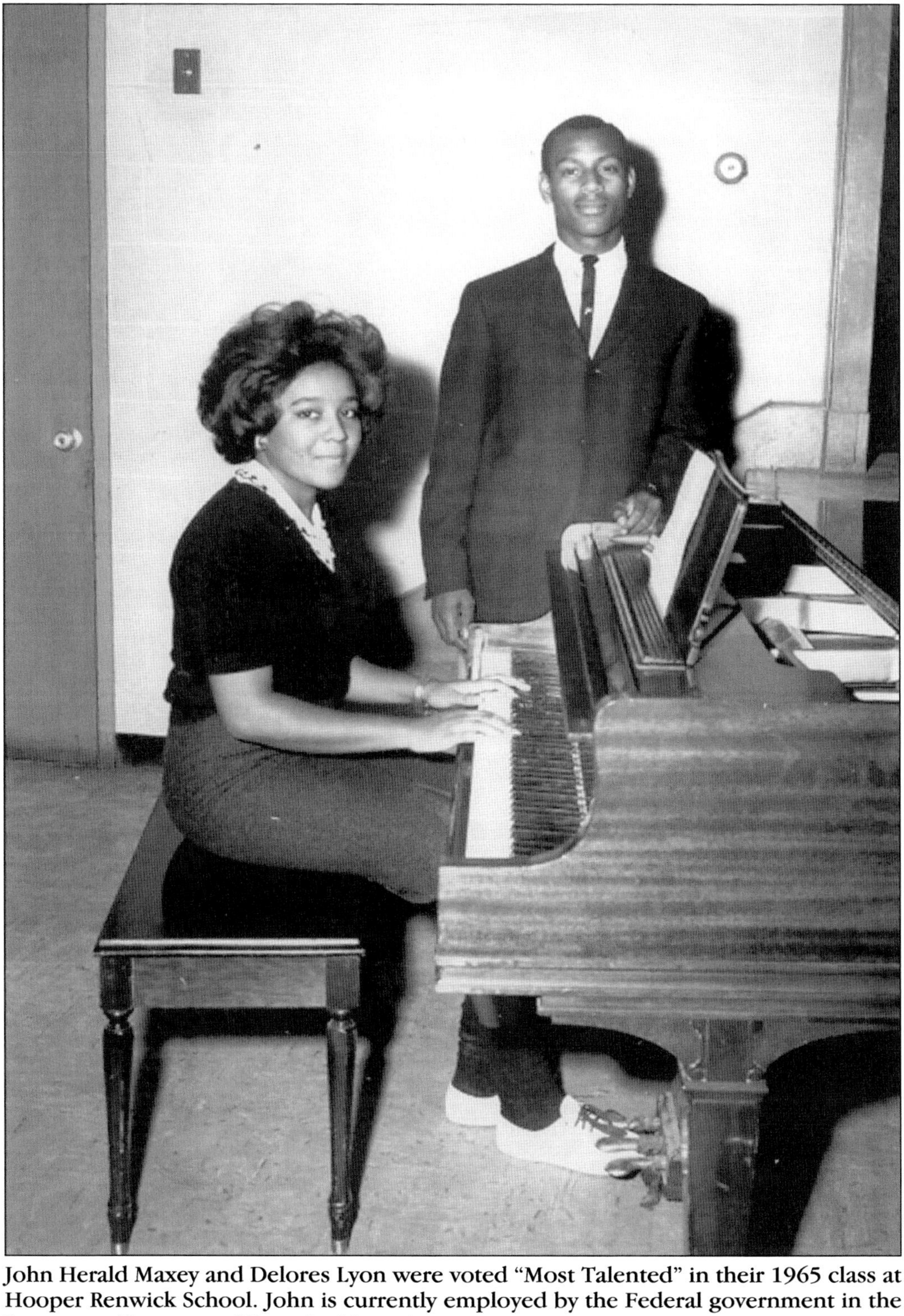

John Herald Maxey and Delores Lyon were voted "Most Talented" in their 1965 class at Hooper Renwick School. John is currently employed by the Federal government in the Pentagon. (Courtesy of Dorothy Maxey.)

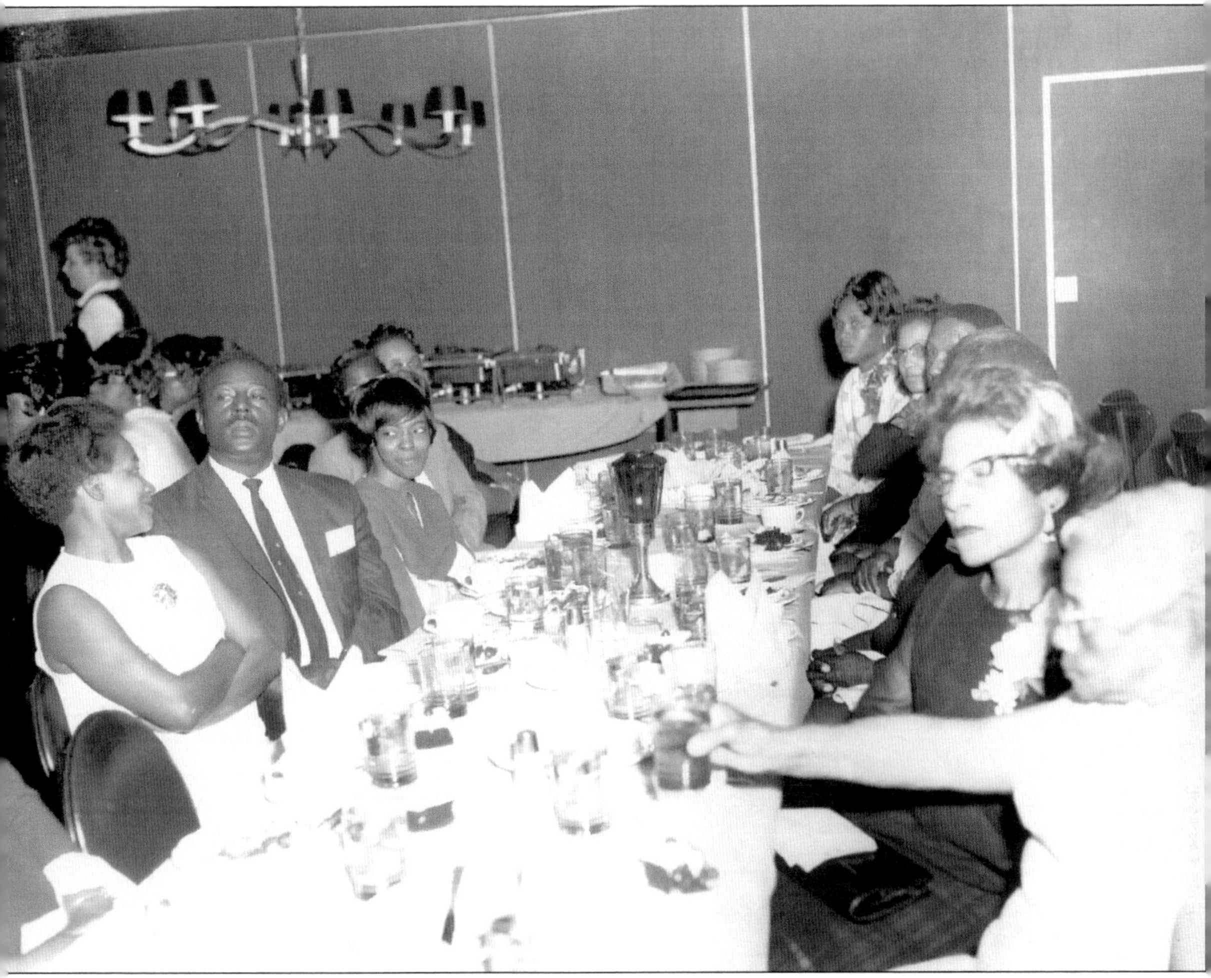

The Hooper Renwick School Integration Banquet included Ruth Summerour, T.S. Summerour, Christine Royster, Ethel Watson, Geneva Hutchins, Clifford Hutchins, and Lena Reese. The group gathered together to celebrate the desegregation of schools across the nation. (Courtesy of Ruth Summerour.)

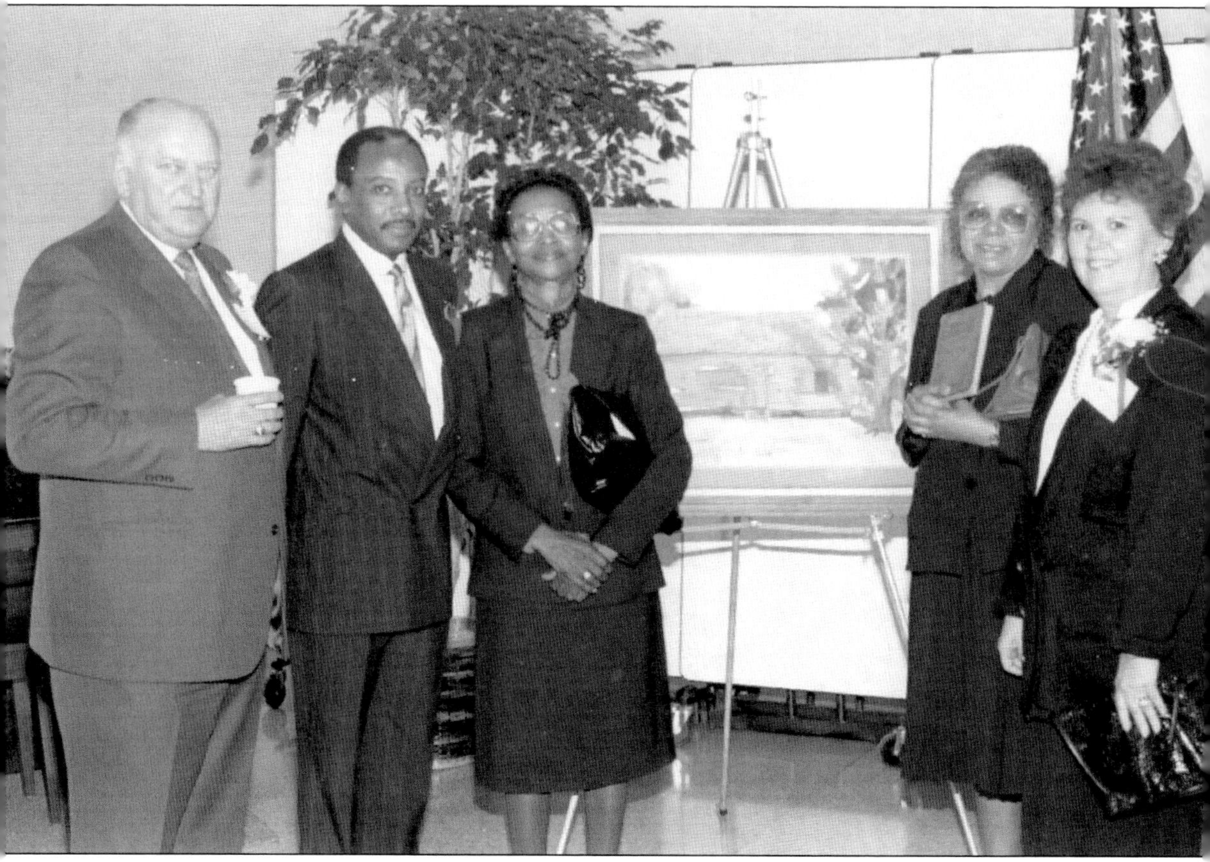

The dedication of the Cedar Hill School took place in the mid-1980s. Seen from left to right are Superintendent of Schools Mr. Cruise, Eron Moore, Leila Moore, Louise Ruth Mahaffey, and Becky Bagget. (Courtesy of Eron and Susan Moore.)

Lenard Hall, Mr. Appalachee 1956, is pictured at the Appalachee Baptist Church. (Courtesy of Eron and Susan Moore.)

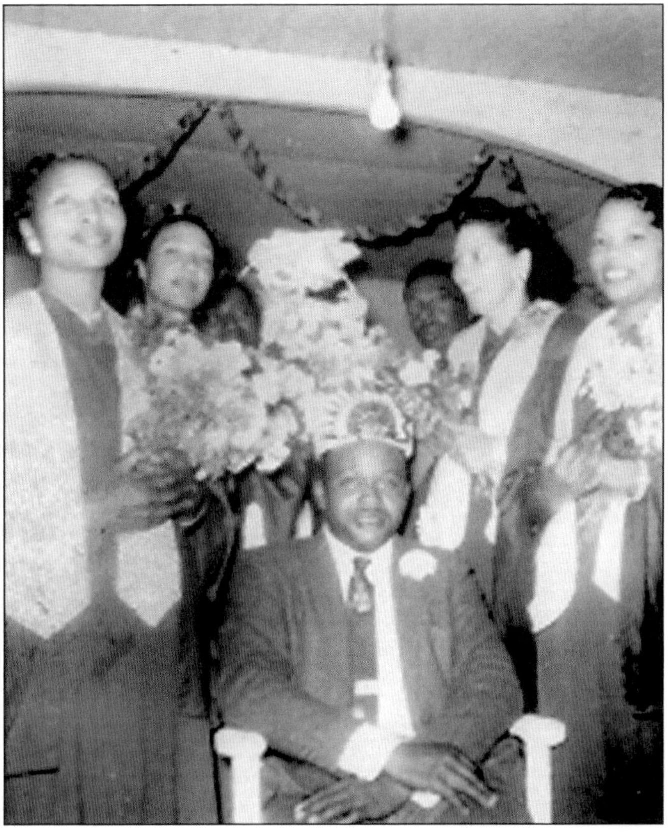

The Miss Black Gwinnett Pageant in 1979 included the following contestants (from left to right): Adrienne Kimbrough, Senior Miss Black Gwinnett; Monique King, Junior Miss Black Gwinnett; Tammi Lynn Riden, Little Miss Black Gwinnett; Tia Apege Maxey, Tiny Miss Black Gwinnett; and unidentified. (Courtesy of Eron and Susan Moore.)

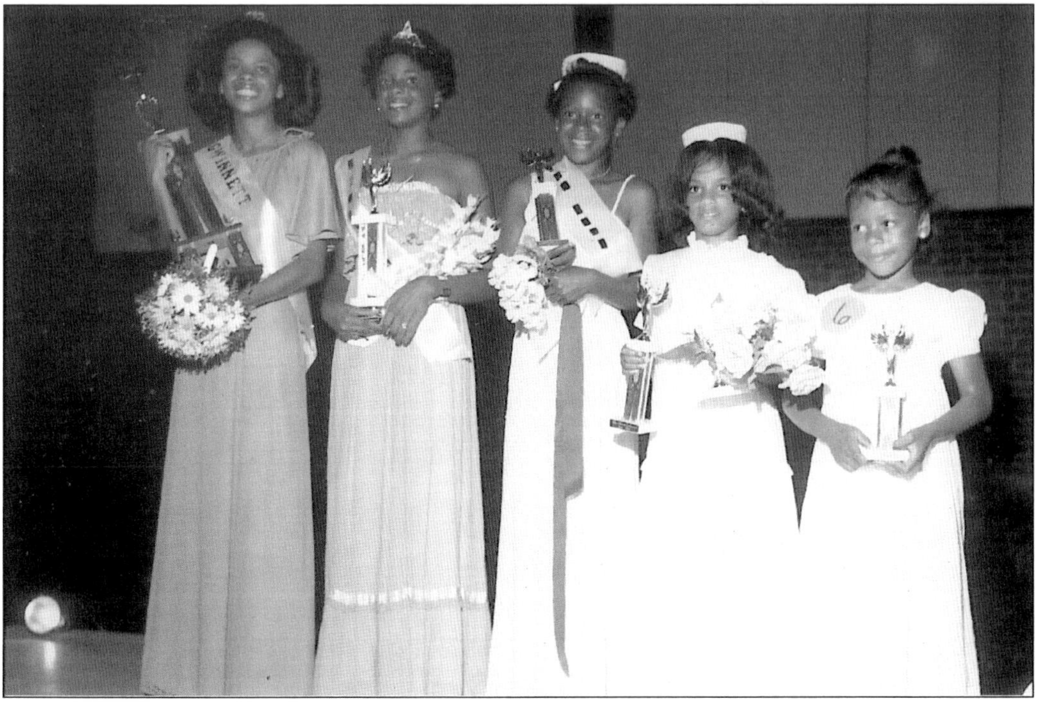

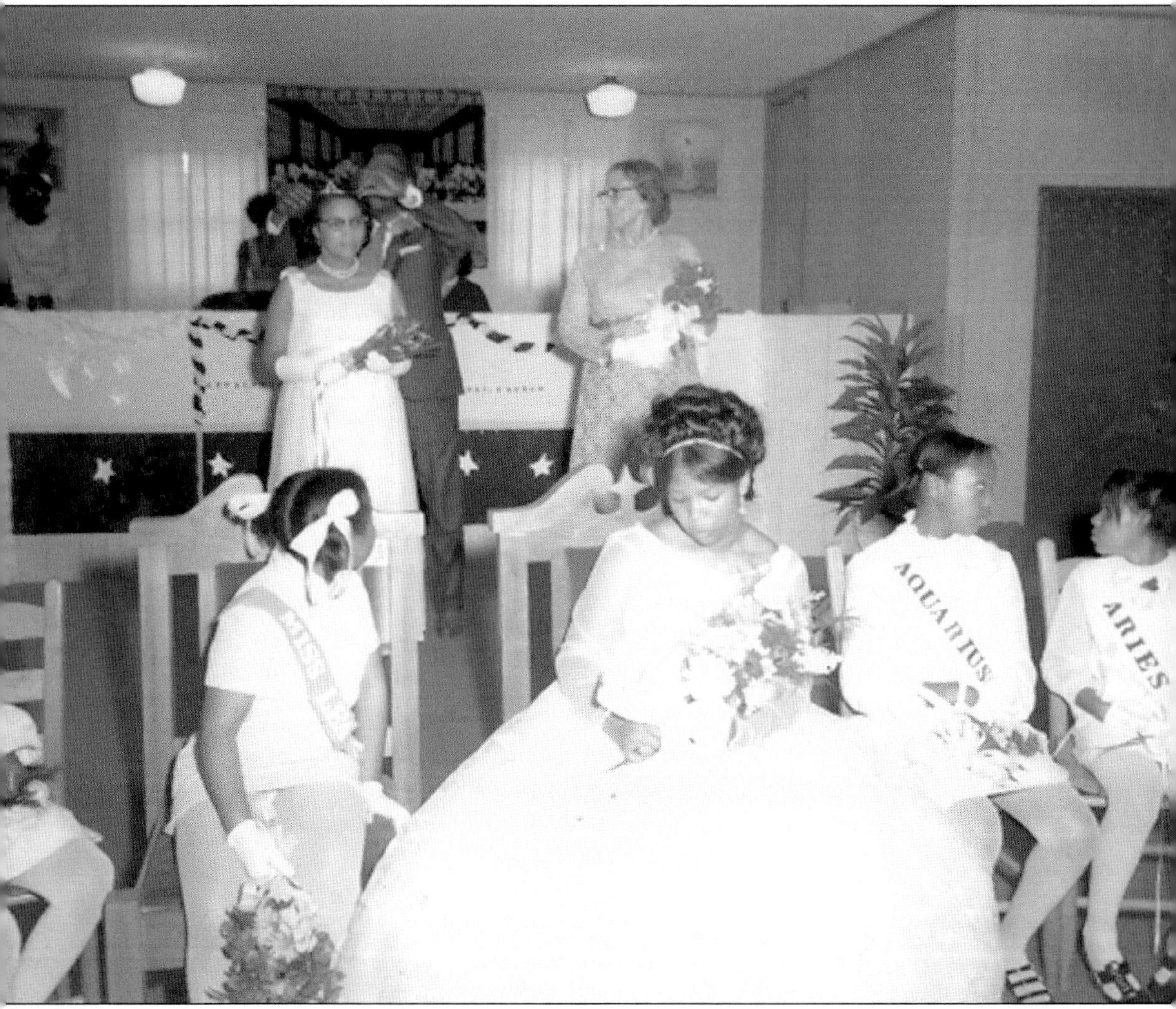

Reverend Thomas crowns Geneva Hutchins as Miss Appalachee. Mrs. Hutchins is currently a nurse in Gwinnett County. (Courtesy of Eron and Susan Moore.)

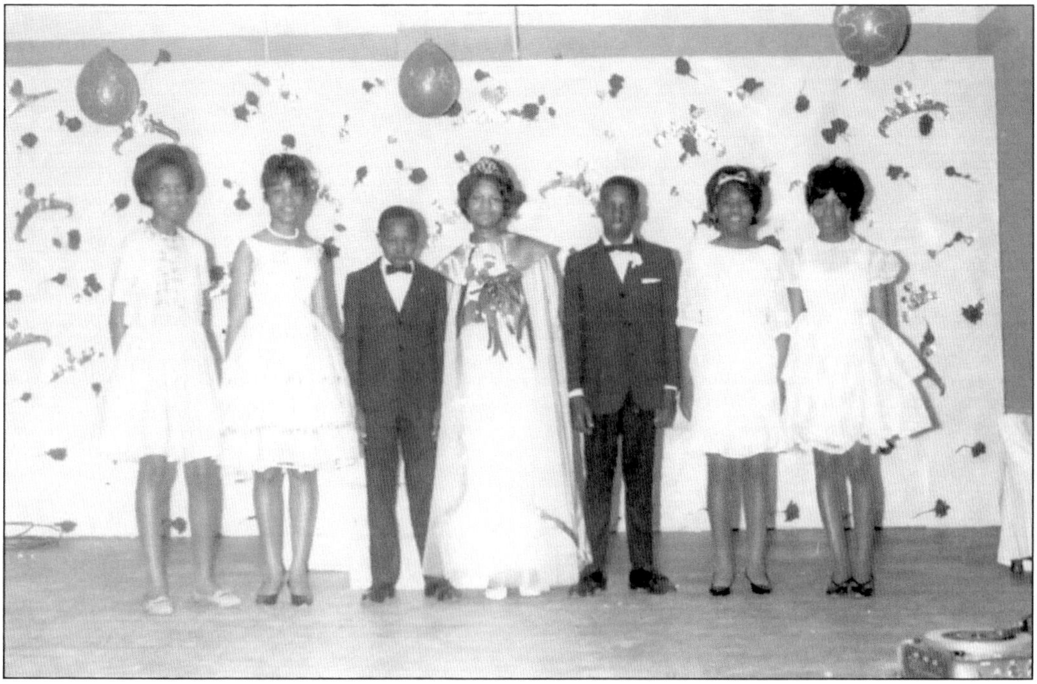

This pageant took place in March 1965 at Hooper Renwick School. (Courtesy of Dorothy Maxey.)

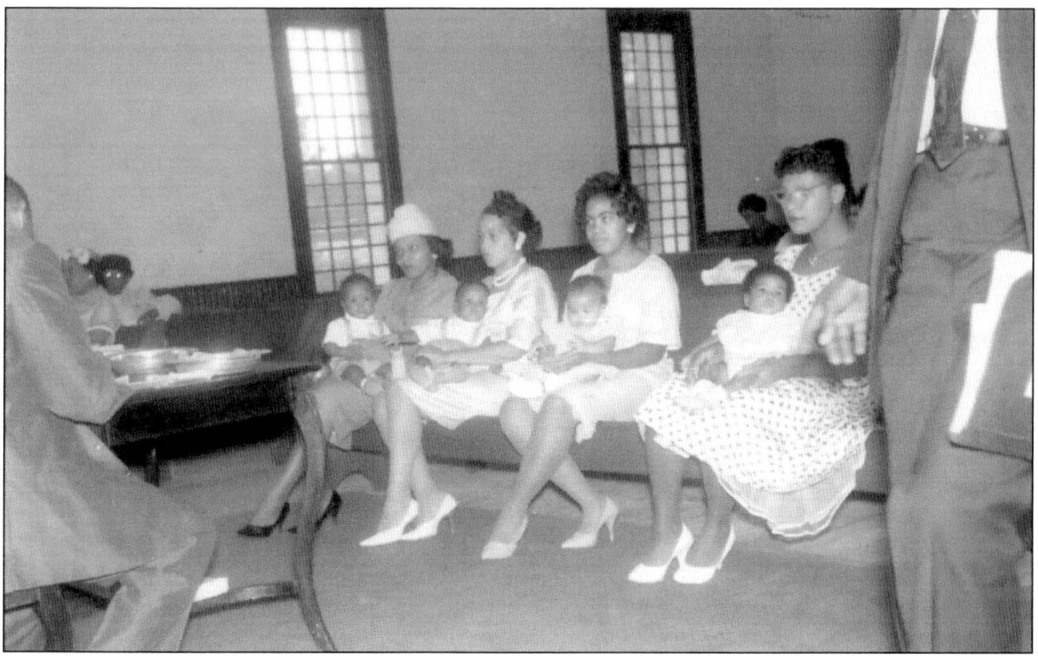

A baby pageant was held at Hopewell Baptist Church in May 1961. Pictured from left to right are Barbara Dunnigan (mother), Annie Bess Bailey (mother), Dewey Walker (mother), Danny Walker (baby), and twin boys Ronald and Donald Dunnigan. (Courtesy of Rufus Dunnigan.)

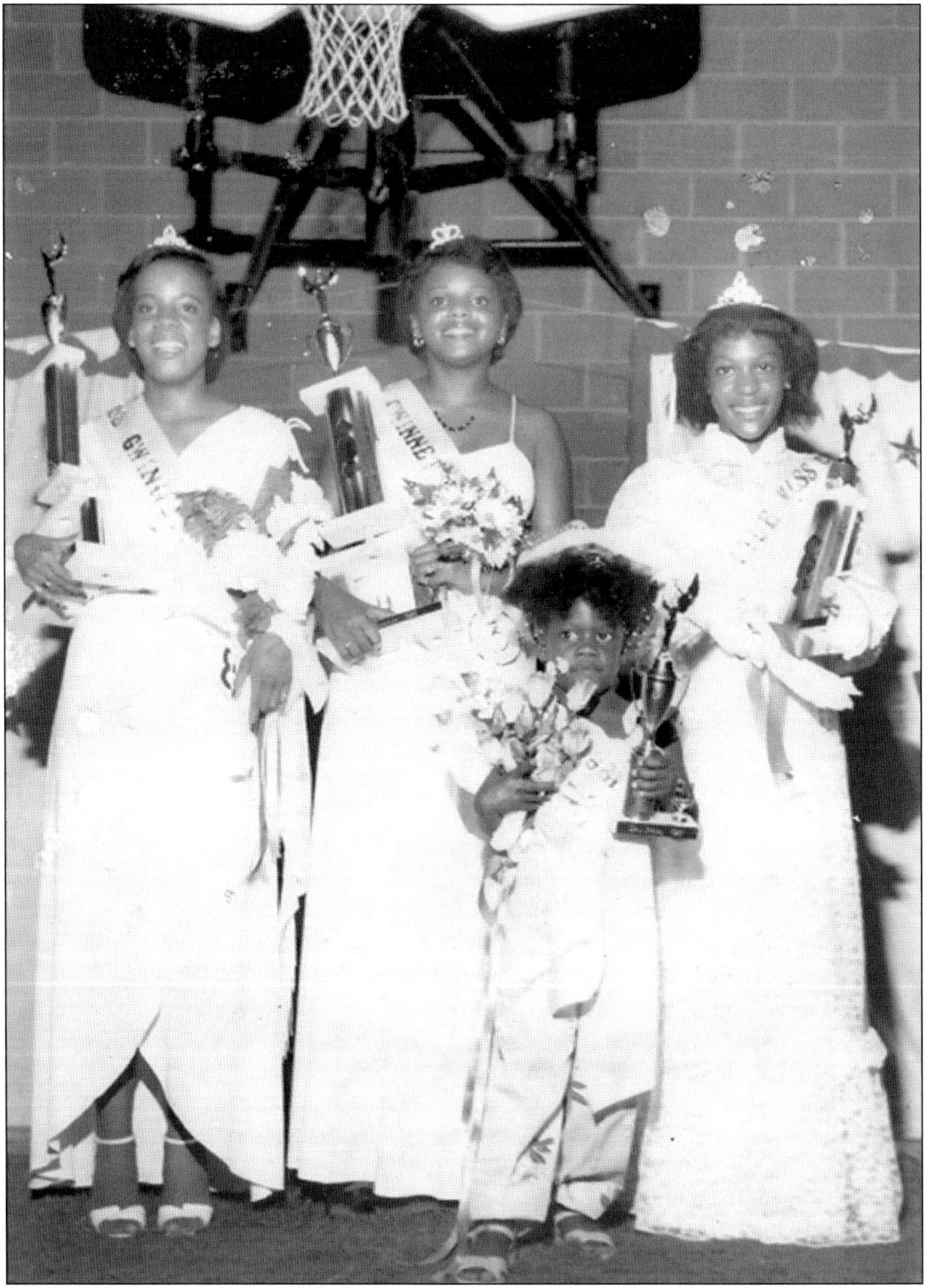

Another Miss Black Gwinnett pageant in the 1980s included, from left to right, Sr. Miss Monique King, Jr. Miss Cindy Wilburn, Little Miss Hood and Little Miss Brandy Dailey. (Courtesy of Eron and Susan Moore.)

Five

MILITARY VALOR

Either move or be moved!
——Colin Powell

The African-American men of Gwinnett have served in the armed services for generations. Many took the opportunity to see America and the world; others felt it was a chance to make a better living for their families. These men of color served in wars and conflicts alongside other races. African Americans were among the enlisted ranks as well as the officer ranks.

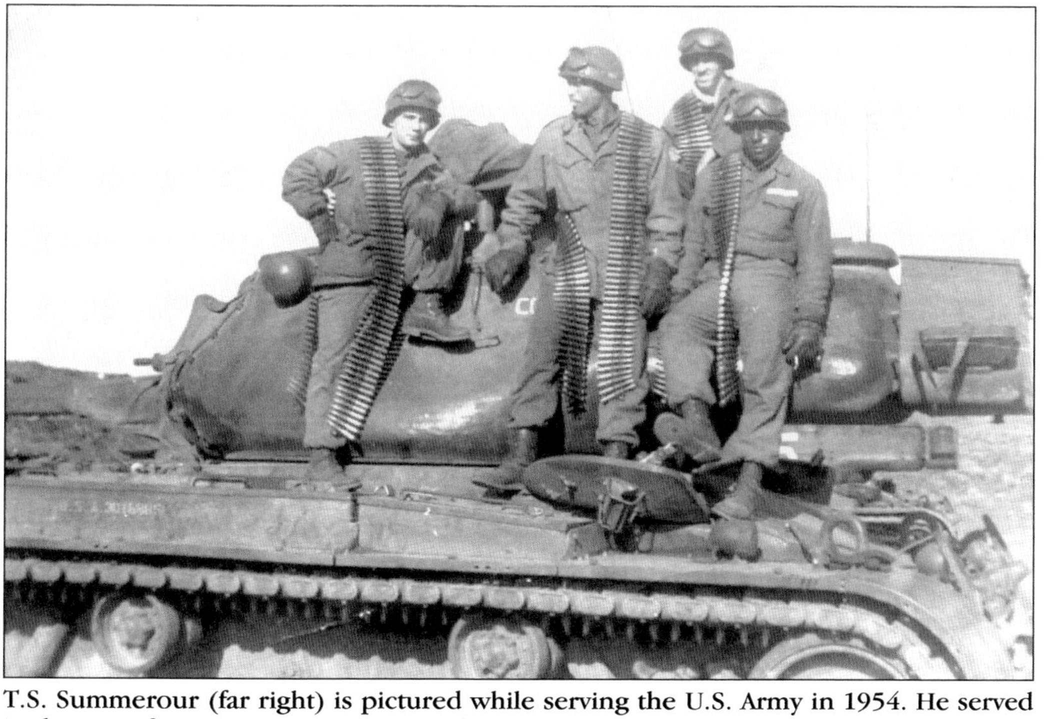

T.S. Summerour (far right) is pictured while serving the U.S. Army in 1954. He served in the army for two years. (Courtesy of Ruth Summerour.)

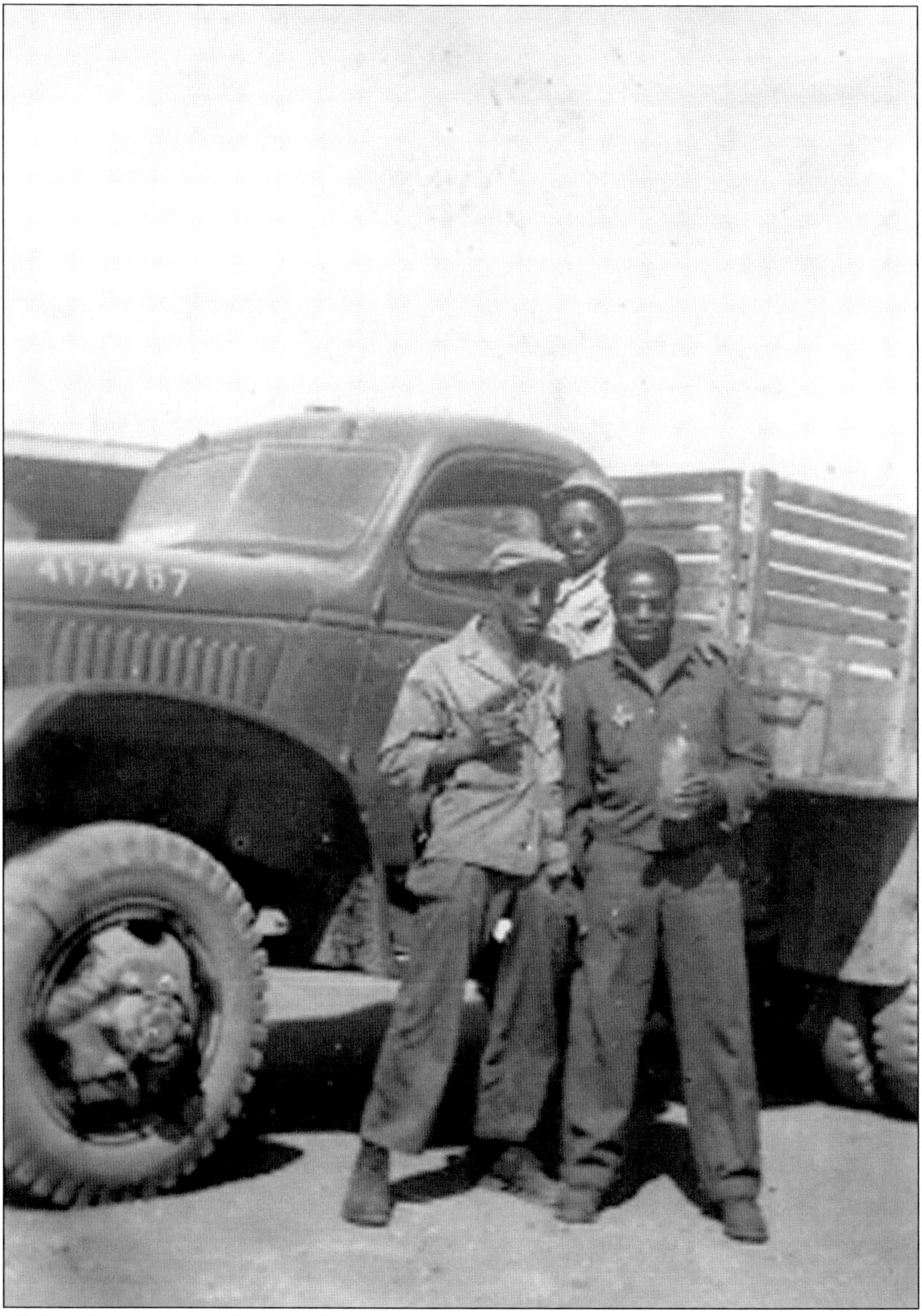

Clifford Maxey Jr. (soldier holding pistol) is seen during World War II. (Courtesy of Dorothy Maxey.)

Robert Gholston is pictured in the U.S. Navy in 1941. He was attending Stillman Institute in Tuscaloosa when he was drafted to serve during World War II. (Courtesy of Dorothy Maxey.)

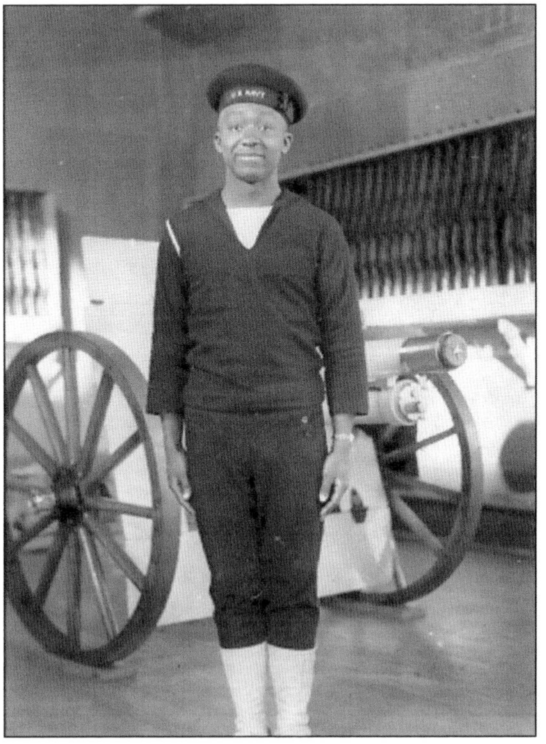

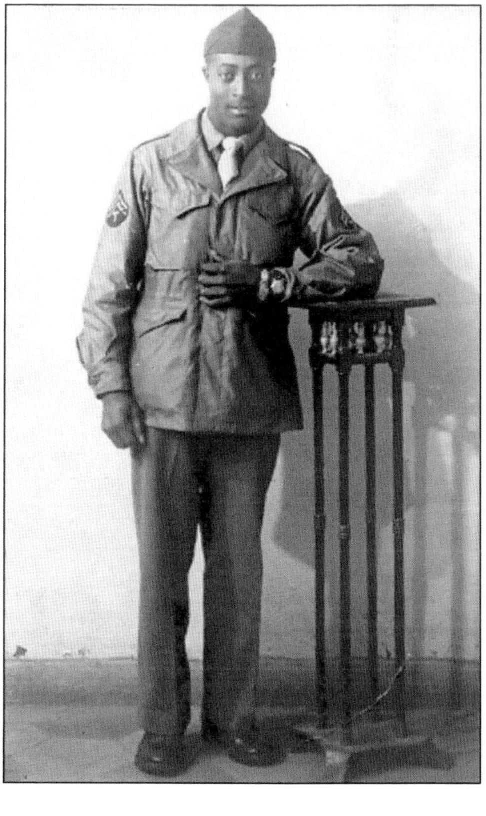

Clifford Maxey Jr. is photographed in Italy in 1942. A veteran of World War II, he was gone from March of 1943 to December of 1945. (Courtesy of Dorothy Maxey.)

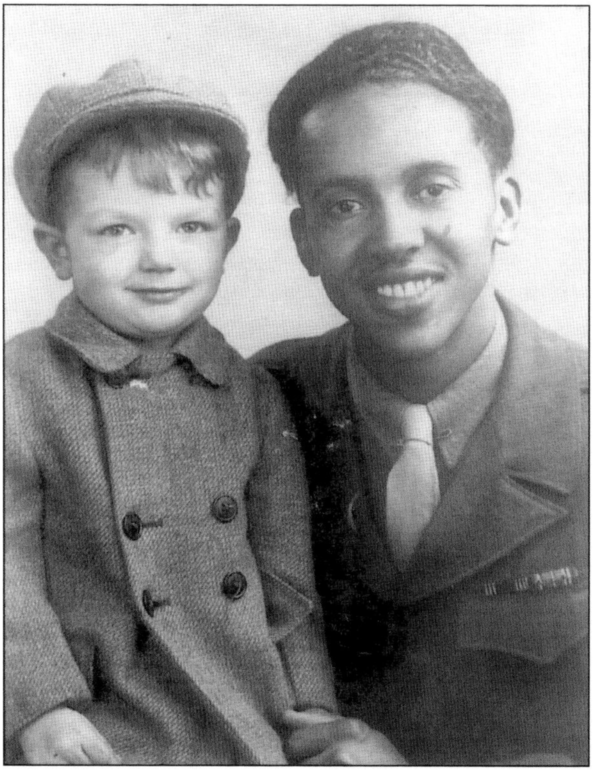

CPL Felix Livsey of the Georgia Technical Co. E 1349th Engineer Ground Support Regiment is pictured during World War II in Germany with his son. (Courtesy of Thomas Livsey.)

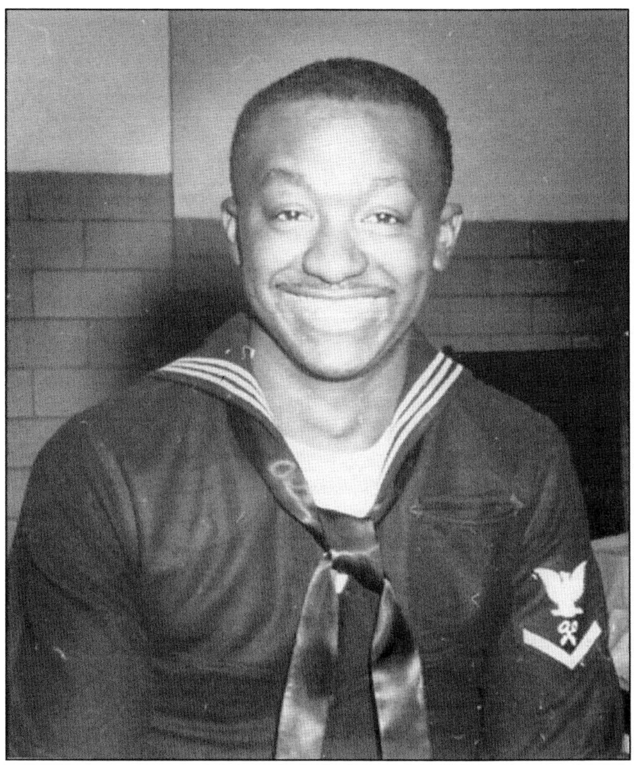

Robert Gholston Jr. served during World War II. (Courtesy of Dorothy Maxey.)

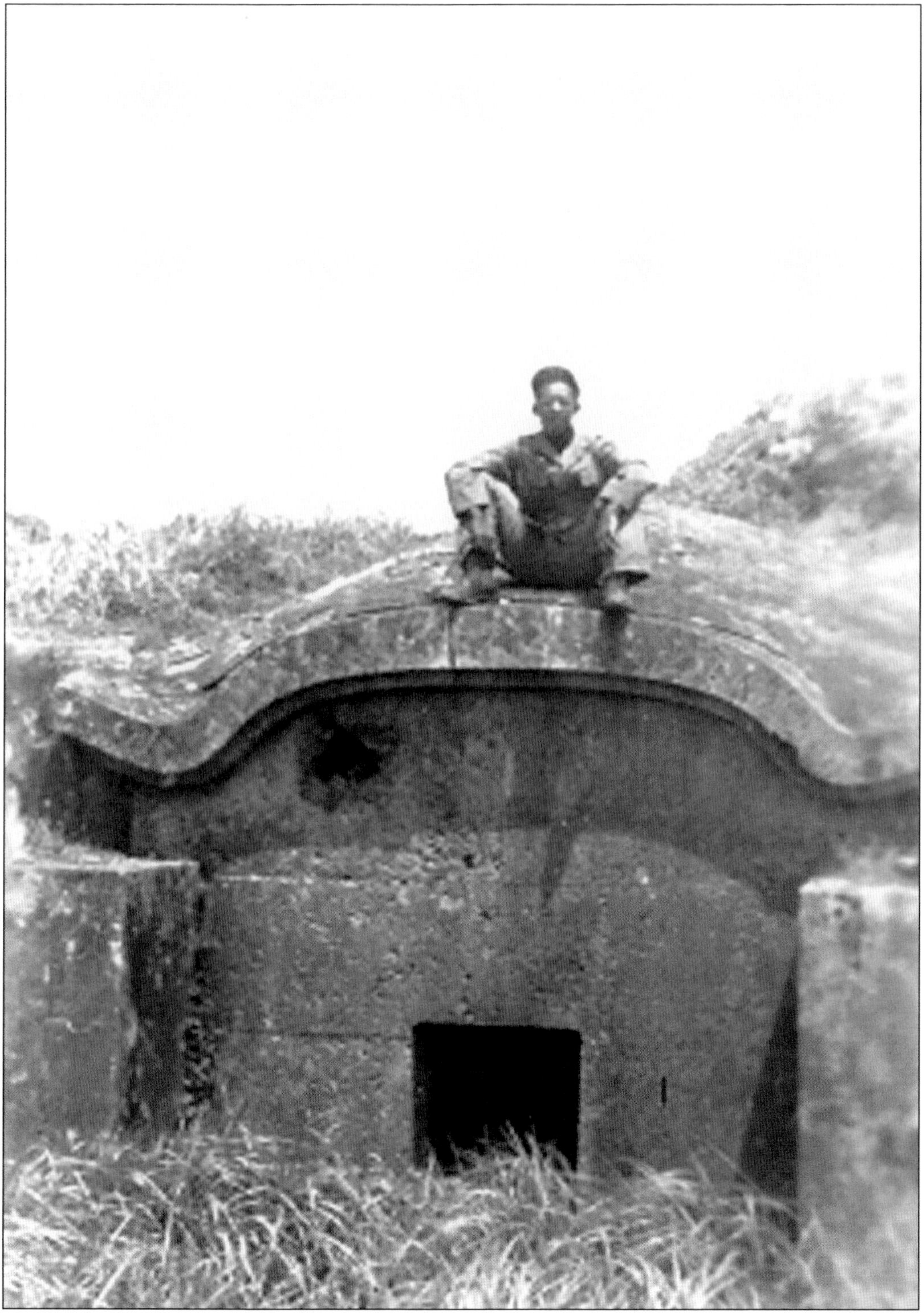

John H. Gholston is seen during the Korean Conflict; he served in the U.S. army. (Courtesy of Dorothy Maxey.)

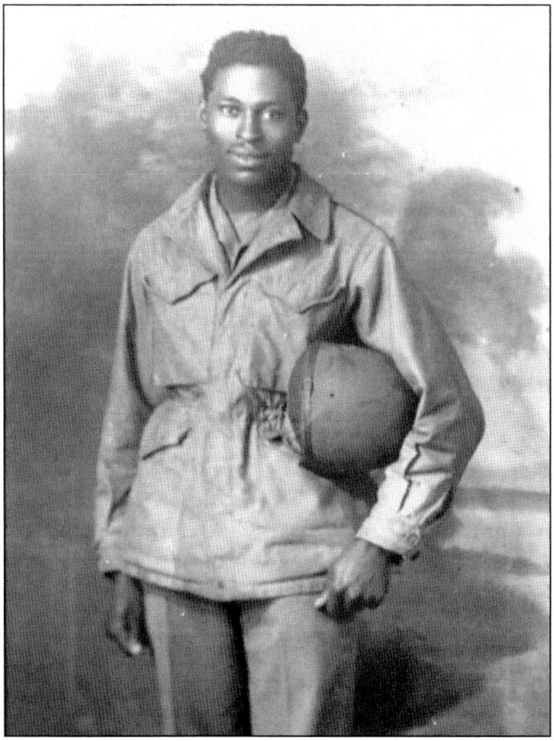

Gwendola J. Everson served during the Korean Conflict. (Courtesy of Gwinnett Historical Society.)

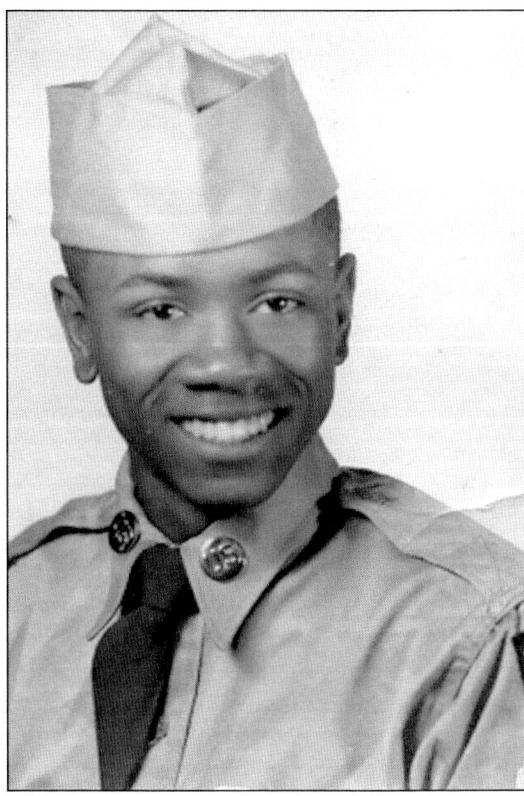

Billy Gholston served as a para trooper in the U.S. Military. (Courtesy of Dorothy Maxey.)

John H. Gholston served during the Korean Conflict. (Courtesy of Dorothy Maxey.)

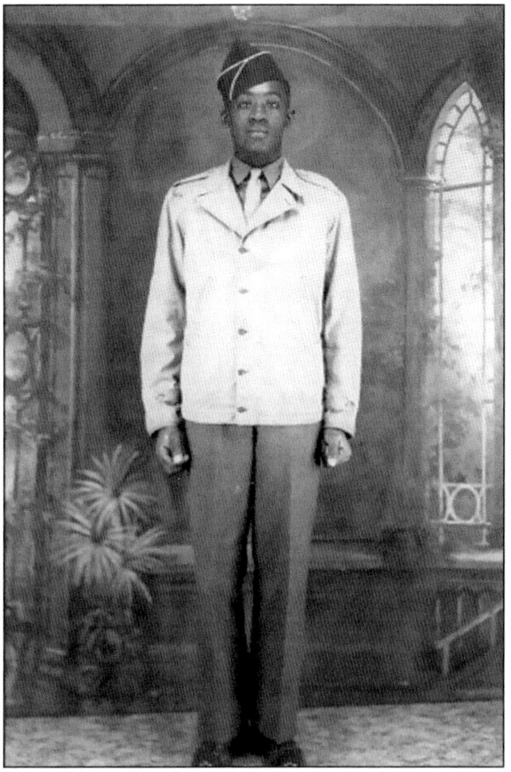

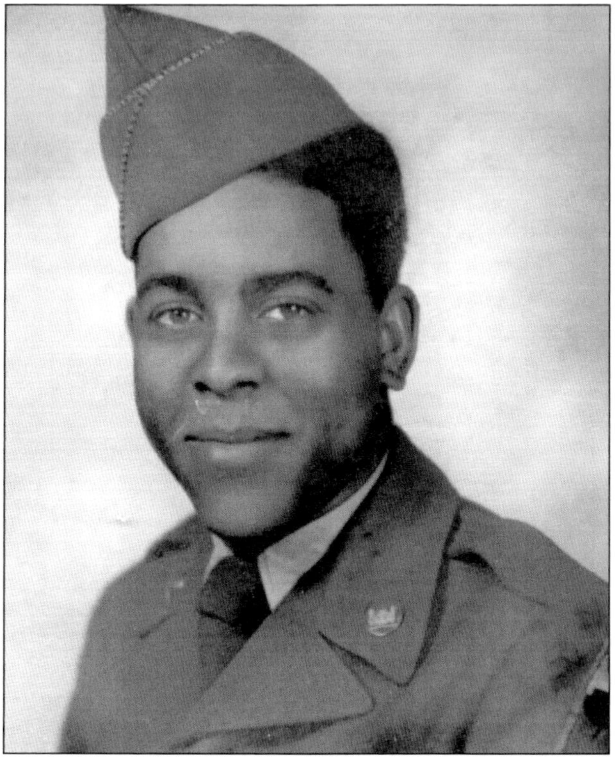

Cpl. Thomas Livsey served in the 40th Infantry Division of the U.S. Army during the Korean Conflict. This photo was taken in Japan in 1953. (Courtesy of Thomas Livsey.)

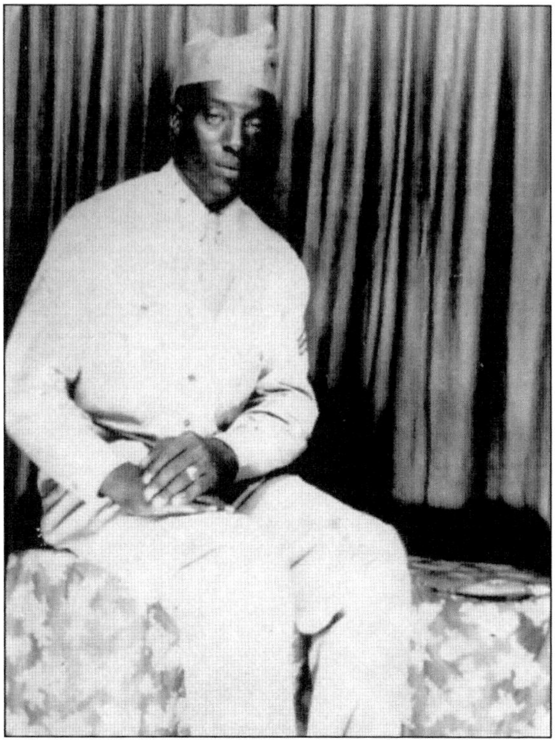

Clyde Everson served during the Korean Conflict. (Courtesy of Gwinnett Historical Society.)

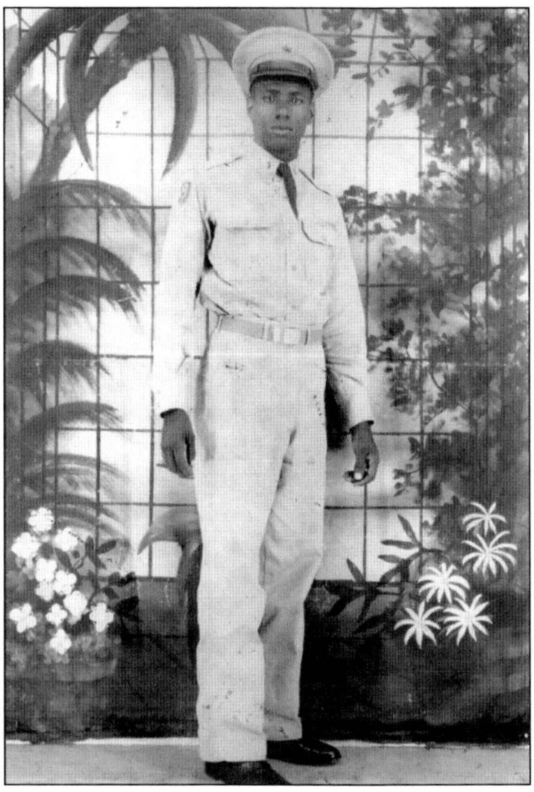

CPL Rufus Dunnigan is pictured in 1953 during the Korean Conflict. He served in the 388th Transportation Company in Manheim, Germany. (Courtesy of Rufus Dunnigan.)

Lt. Roscoe Austin was a pilot in the U.S. Air Force. (Courtesy of Dorethia Livsey.)

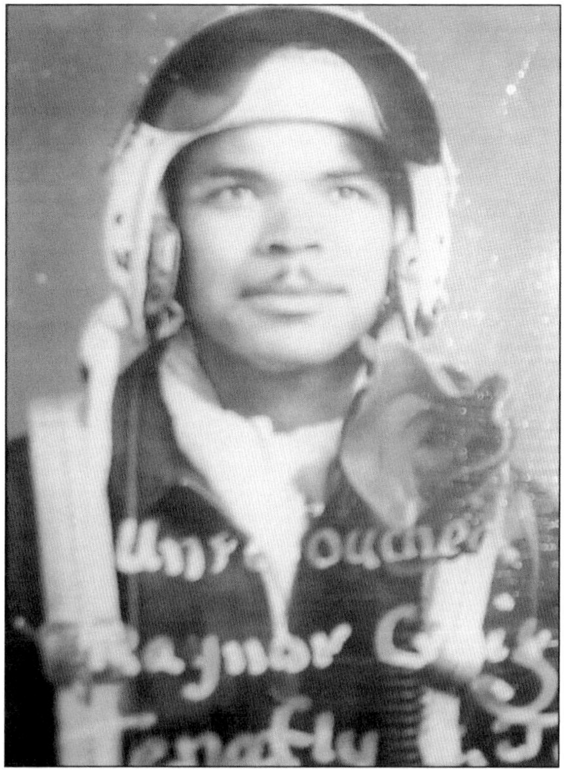

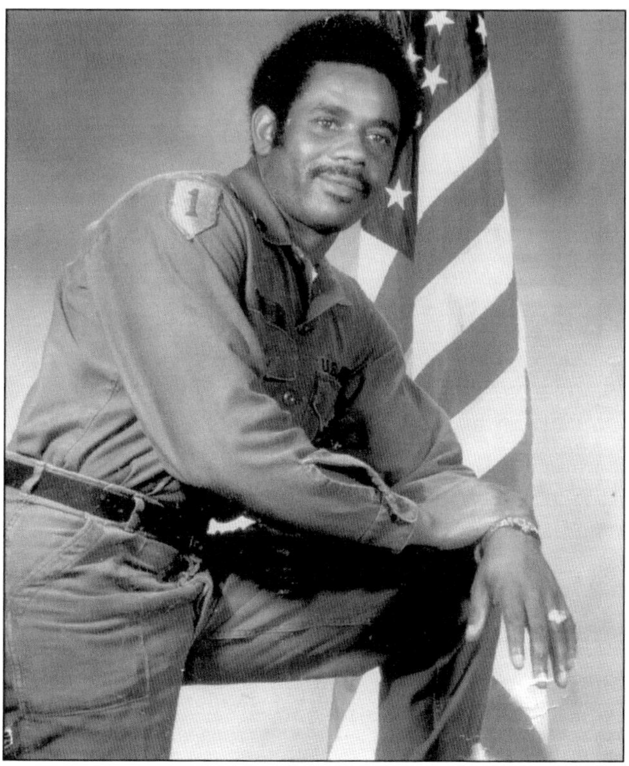

Fred Daniel is seen during the Vietnam War. (Courtesy of Thelma R. Yarbough.)

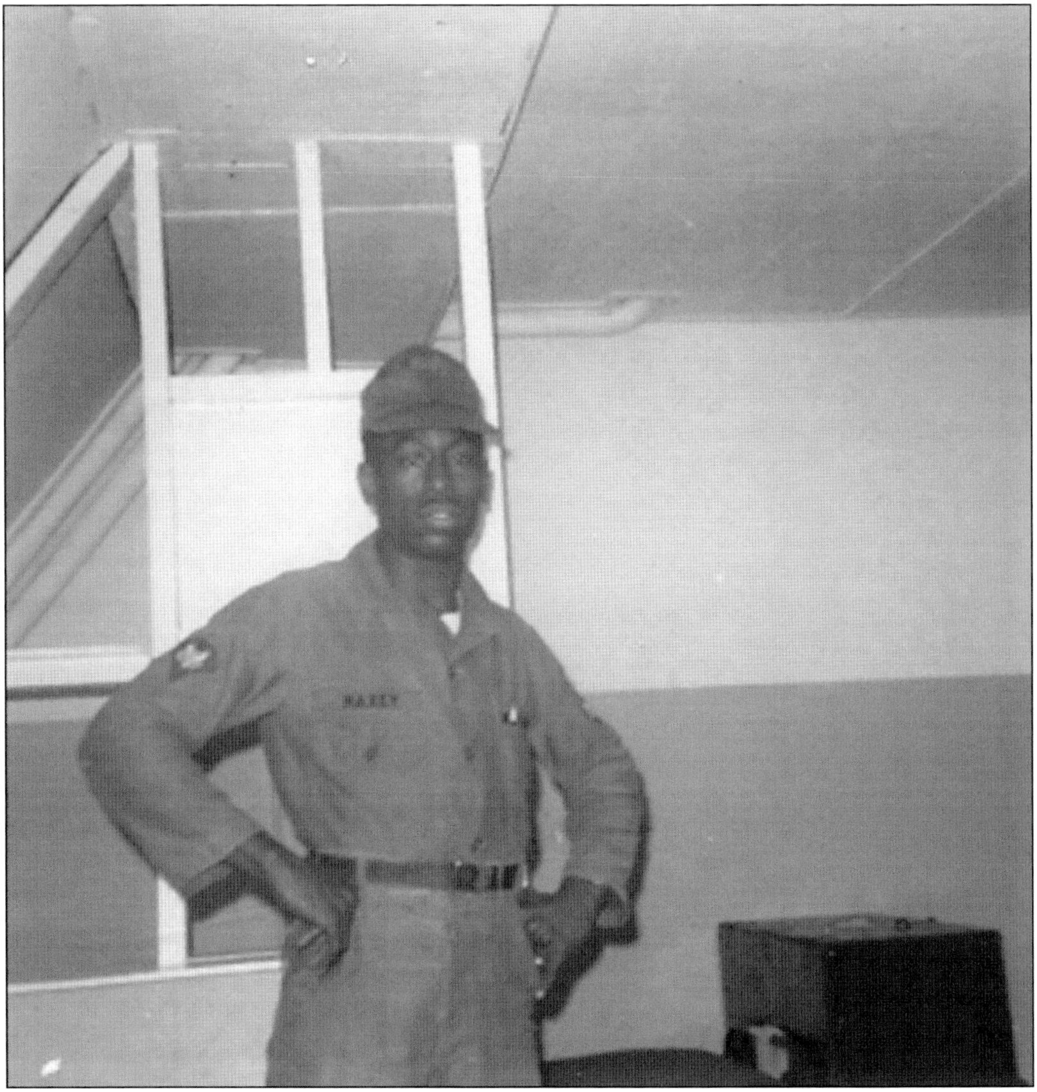

SPC Terry Maxey served in the U.S. Army during Vietnam. (Courtesy of Dorothy Maxey.)

Six

EVERYDAY CITIZENS

I am overwhelmed by the grace and persistence of my people.
——Maya Angelou

Work, church, family gatherings, and social affairs were all a part of daily life in the African-American community. People could be found posing for pictures almost anywhere; it seems a camera was never far from reach for many of these Gwinnett families.

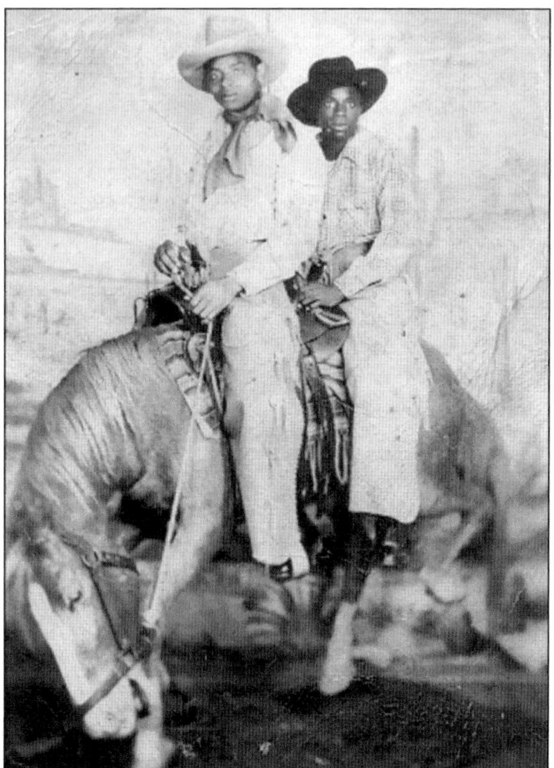

J.D. Yarbough (right) and a friend posed for this photo while serving in the Navy. (Courtesy of Eron and Susan Moore.)

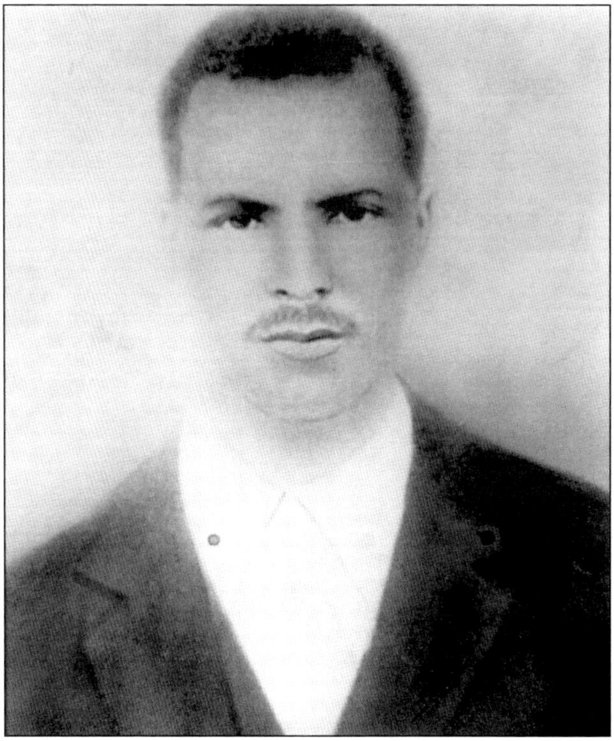

George Moore is pictured in the 1800s. A farmer, Mr. Moore fathered 21 children. (Courtesy of Eron and Susan Moore.)

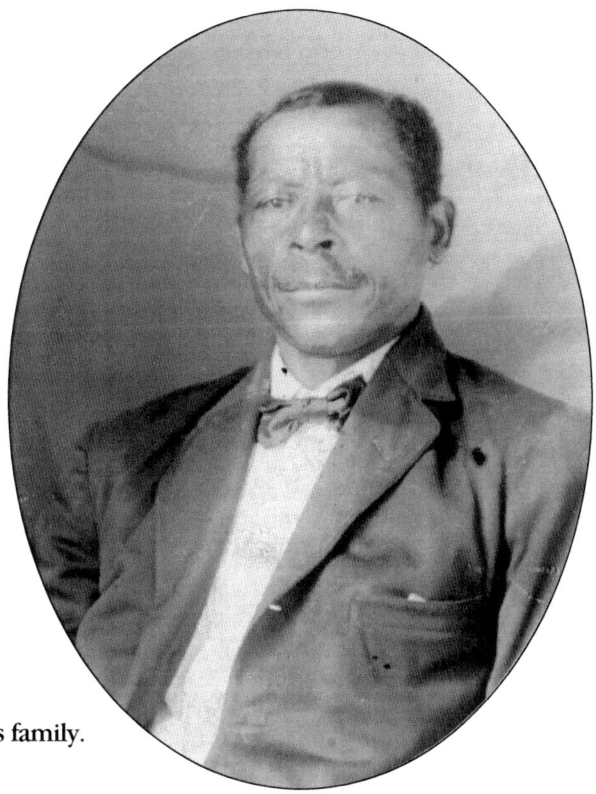

This Snowden family male, seen in the 1800s, farmed in Dacula to support his family. (Courtesy of Ruth Summerour.)

Elizabeth Malcolm Gholston, seen here in her early twenties, died at the age of 33. Her husband Robert is pictured below. (Courtesy of Dorothy Maxey.)

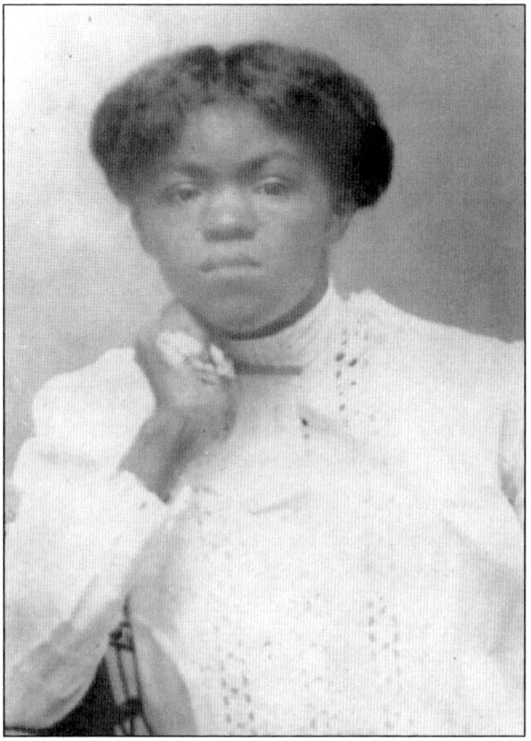

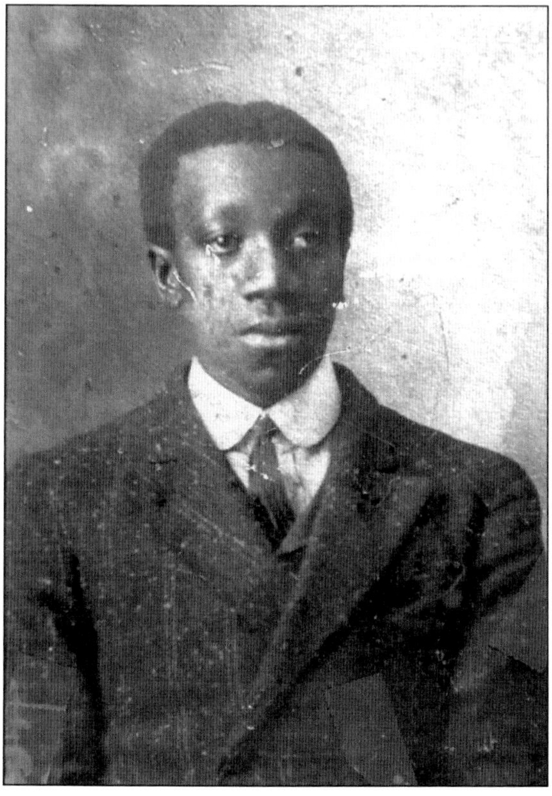

Robert Gholston, pictured at age 19, lived to be 75 years old. He never remarried after his wife Elizabeth (above) passed away. (Courtesy of Dorothy Maxey.)

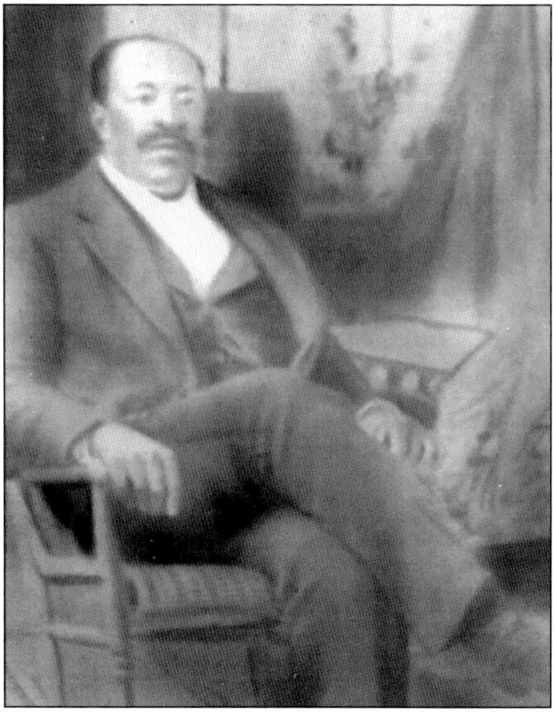

Deacon Scales and his family were active members of the Macedonia Baptist Church for many years. (Courtesy of Thomas Livsey.)

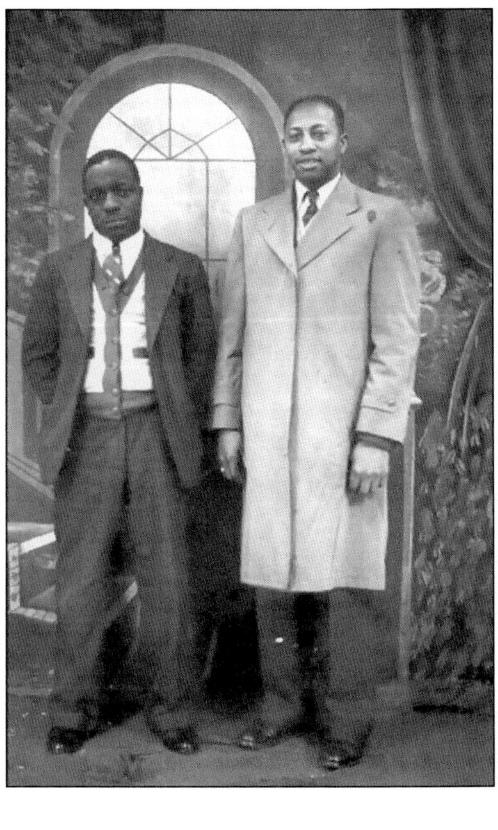

Reverend Lott and Reverend Grogan are pictured in the 1950s. Reverend Grogan was pastor of Pleasant Hill Baptist Church for 40 years. (Courtesy of Dorothy Maxey.)

Mattie Snowden was a midwife in Gwinnett County for many years. She delivered babies of all races all over the county. (Courtesy of Ruth Summerour.)

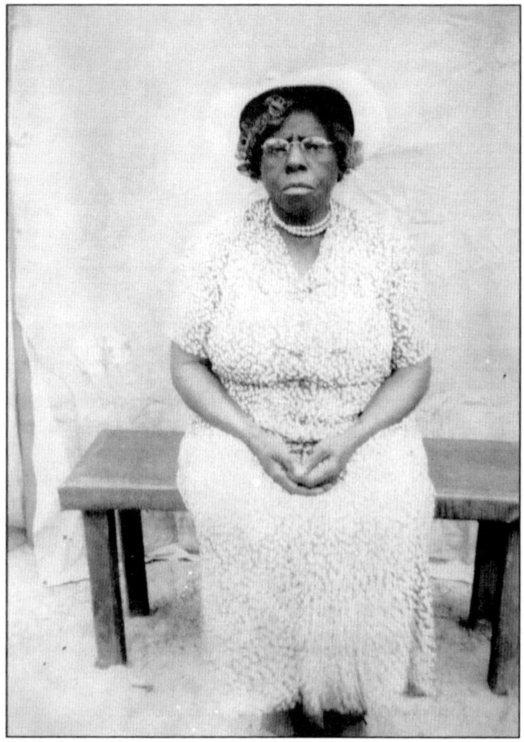

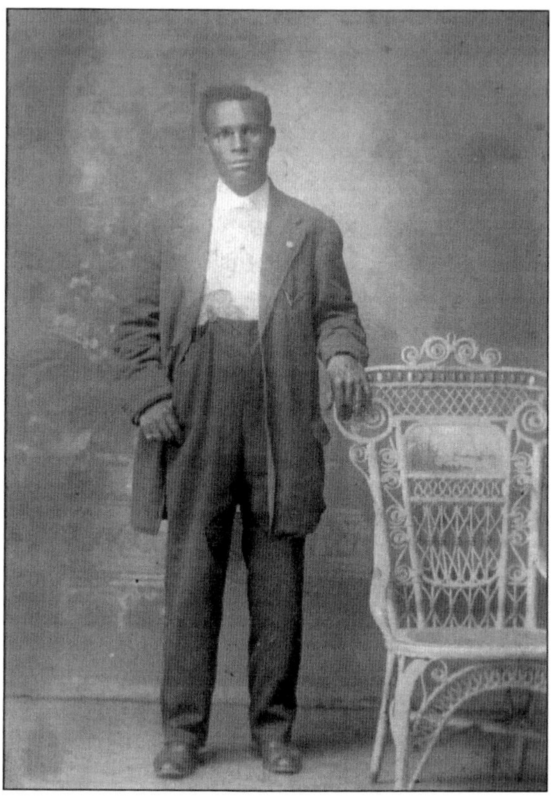

A member of the Snowden family is pictured in the 1800s. He supported his family by farming in Dacula. (Courtesy of Ruth Summerour.)

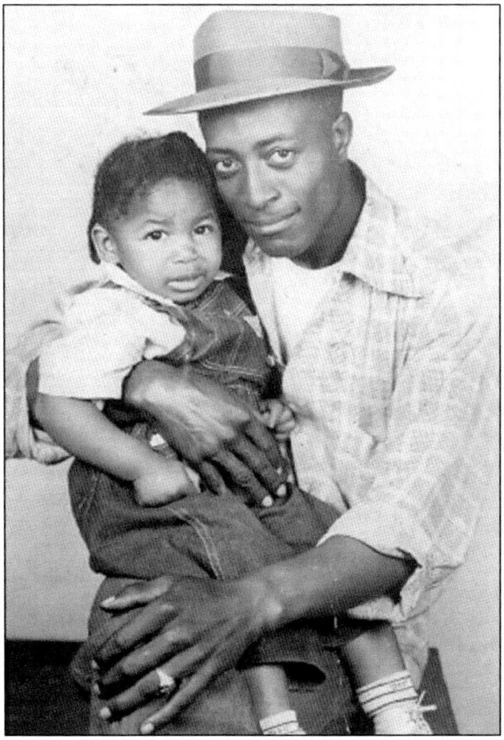

Cliff Maxey Jr. holds his cousin Gracie Mae Moore for a 1940s photo, taken shortly after World War II. (Courtesy of Dorothy Maxey.)

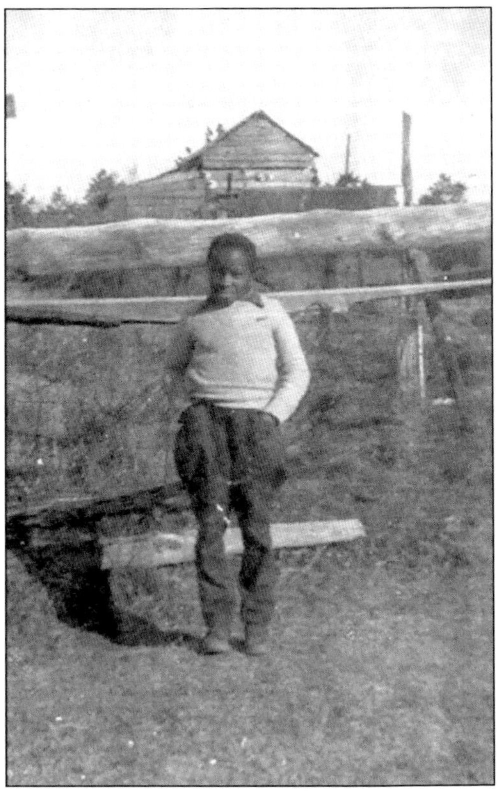

Margaret Lott is pictured in 1950 at the Maxey family home on Honeysuckle Street in Lawrenceville. Notice the old barn and wood fence in the background. (Courtesy of Dorothy Maxey.)

Jurell Austin Lattimore lived in Buford and ran The Lattimore Café. This picture was taken in 1944. (Courtesy of Thomas Livsey.)

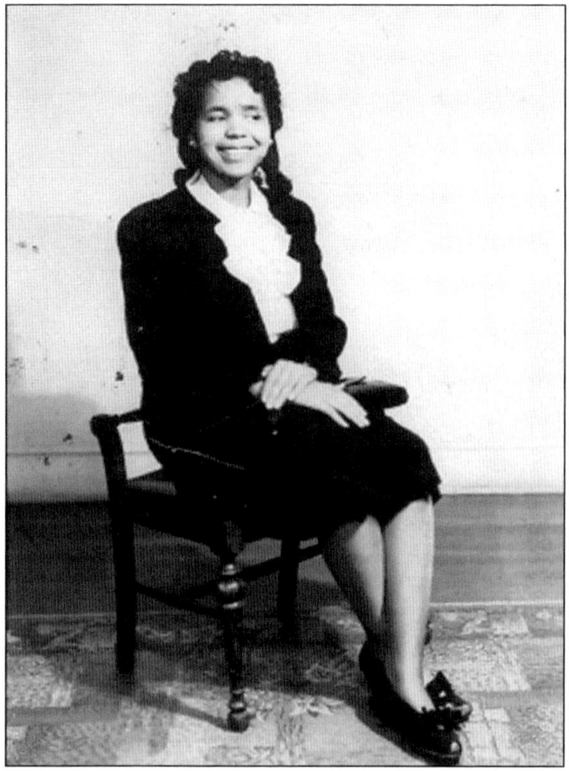

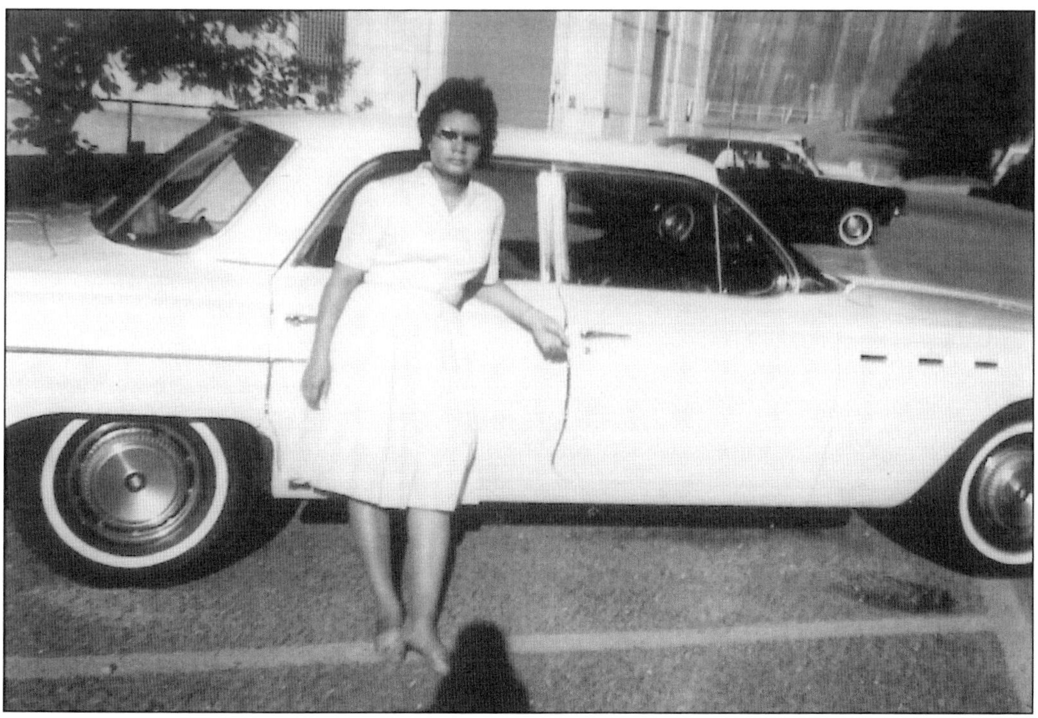

Ruby Mae Williams poses by her car in the early 1970s. (Courtesy of Hattie Peters.)

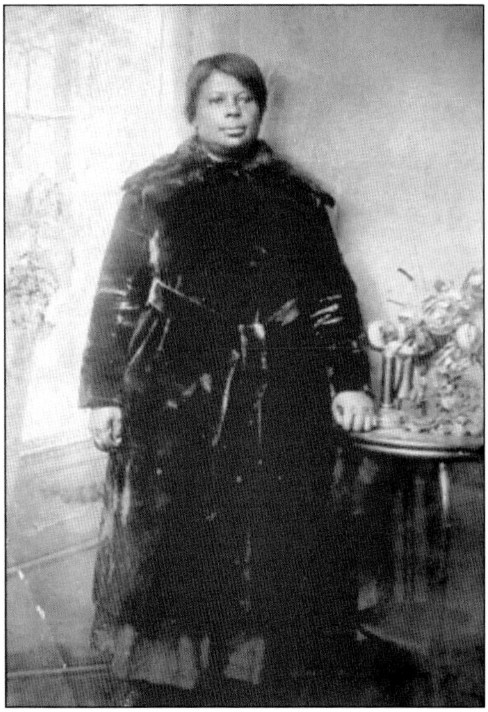

Sara Everson, seen in the 1900s, lived with her family in Dacula. They farmed in the area to make a living. (Courtesy of the Gwinnett Historical Society.)

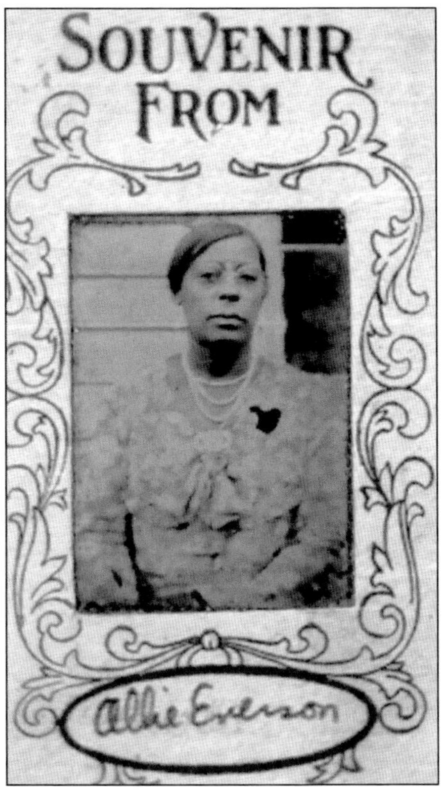

Ollie Everson, pictured in the early 1900s, was a resident of Dacula. (Courtesy of the Gwinnett Historical Society.)

Robert Gholston is seen in the 1940s; he worked as a tenant farmer in Gwinnett County. (Courtesy Dorothy Maxey.)

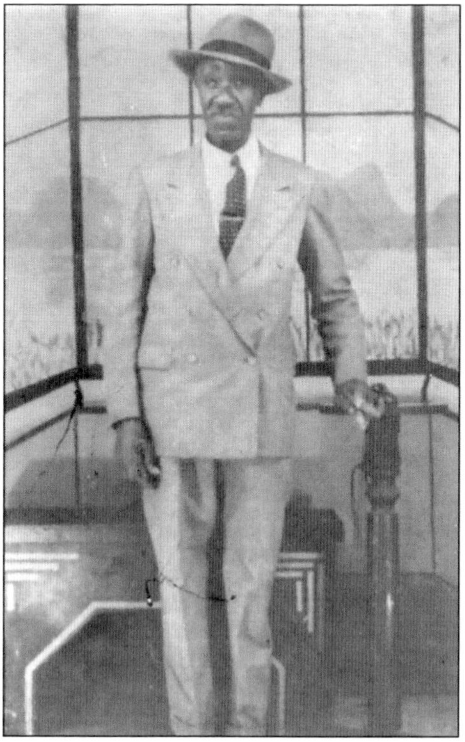

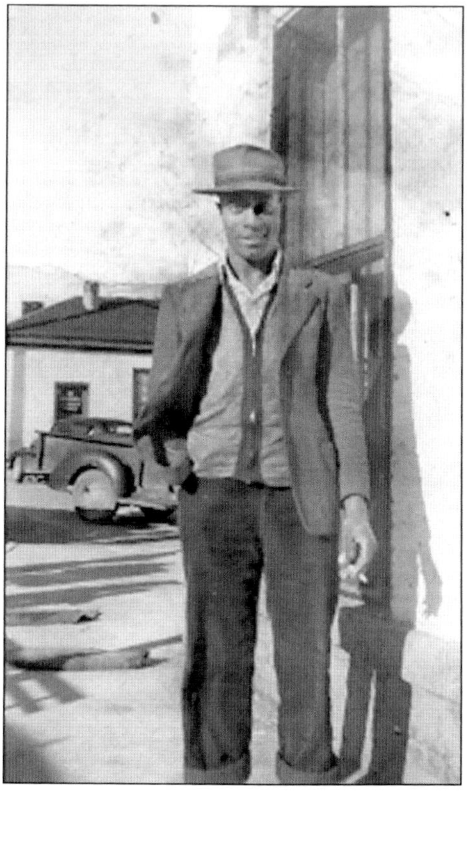

Cliff Maxey is pictured on the square in Lawrenceville in 1940. (Courtesy of Dorothy Maxey.)

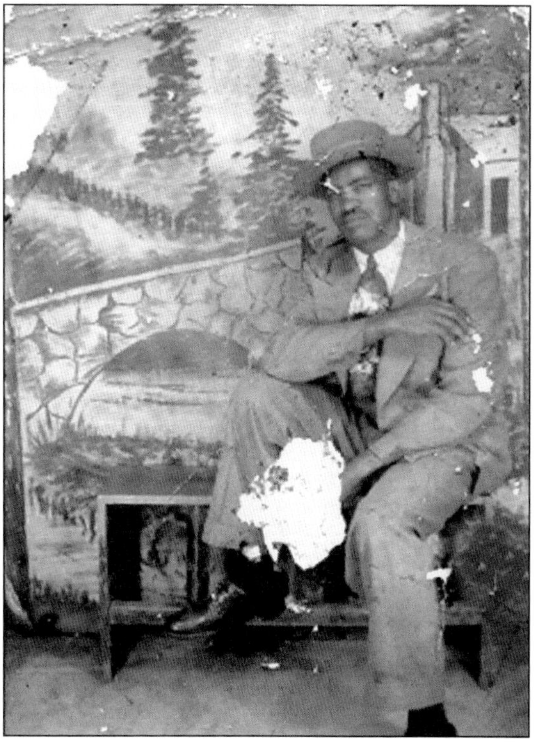

Gene Winder, seen in the 1940s, was married to Clara Winder for 21 years. They resided in Lawrenceville. Mr. Winder worked at the Conseco Shoe Factory for many years and Mrs. Winder was a domestic cook. She still resides in Lawrenceville. (Courtesy of Clara Collins.)

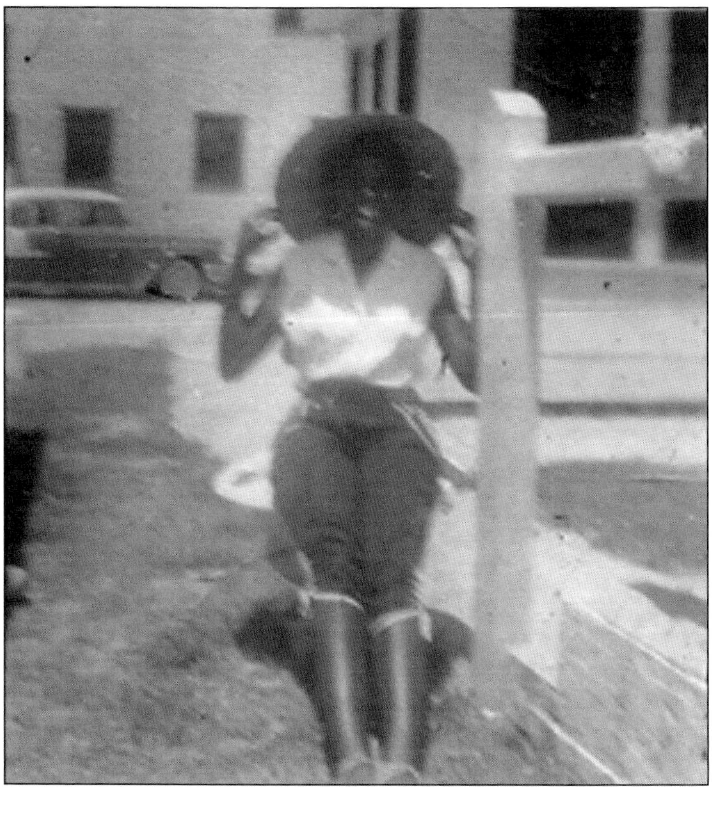

Clara Winder, a domestic worker for 68 years, is seen in the 1960s. She still lives in Gwinnett County at age 80. (Courtesy of Clara Collins.)

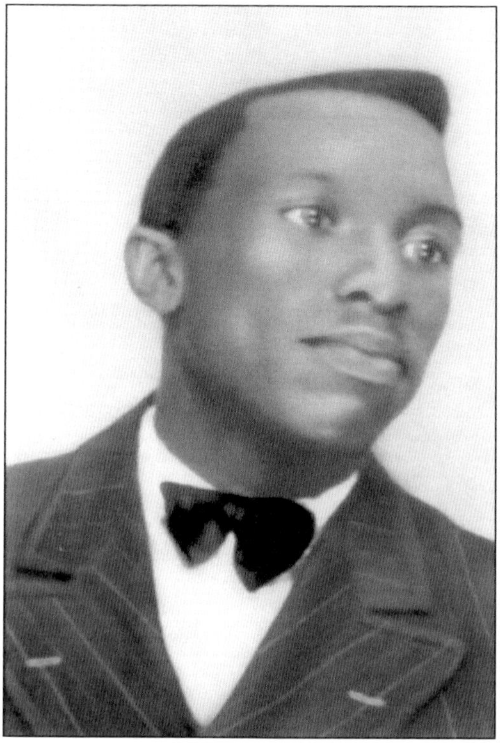

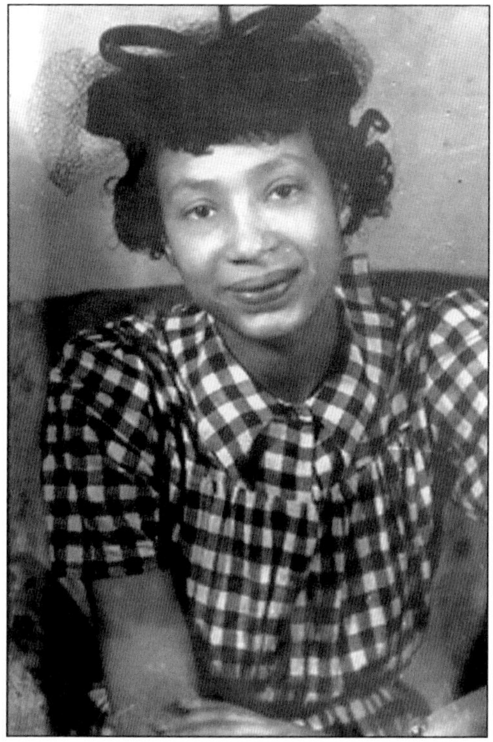

(*above left*) Amos Hutchins is pictured at age 23. He was the caretaker of the Elisha Winn House—the first place of government in Gwinnett in 1818—for over 60 years. (Courtesy of Gwinnett Historical Society.)
(*above right*) Gladys Smith, who currently resides in Lawrenceville, married Henry Smith and had one child. She made her living doing domestic work. (Courtesy of Eron and Susan Moore.)

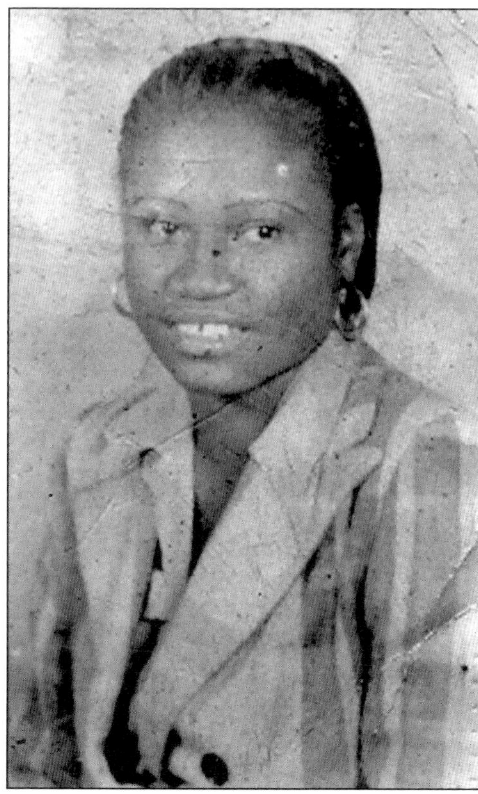

Francis Brown is a homemaker in Gwinnett County, where she continues to reside now in her eighties. (Courtesy of Dorothy Maxey.)

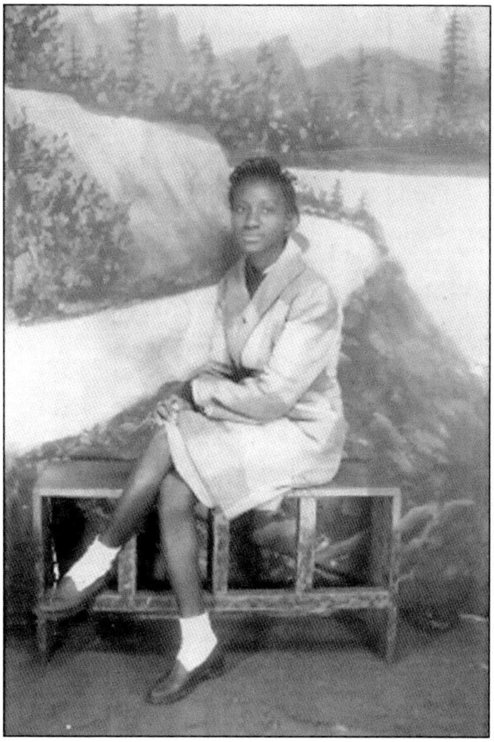

Dorothy Maxey is pictured in 1943. She sent this picture to her husband while he was serving during World War II; he would cover her legs when he showed the picture! (Courtesy of Dorothy Maxey.)

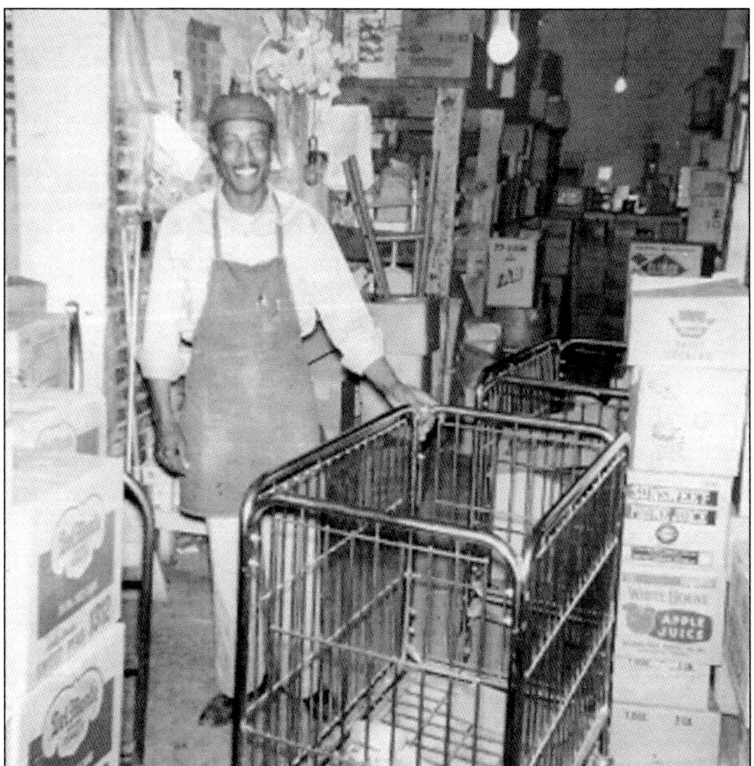

Cliff Maxey is pictured at work in Alford's Grocery Store in Lawrenceville in the 1950s. (Courtesy of Dorothy Maxey.)

Carrene Maxey is pictured as a one-year-old at Pleasant Hill Baptist Church. She still lives in Gwinnett County. (Courtesy of Dorothy Maxey.)

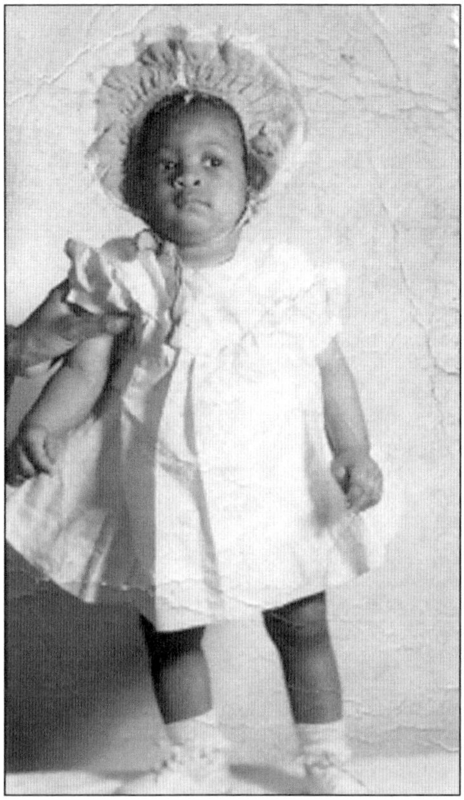

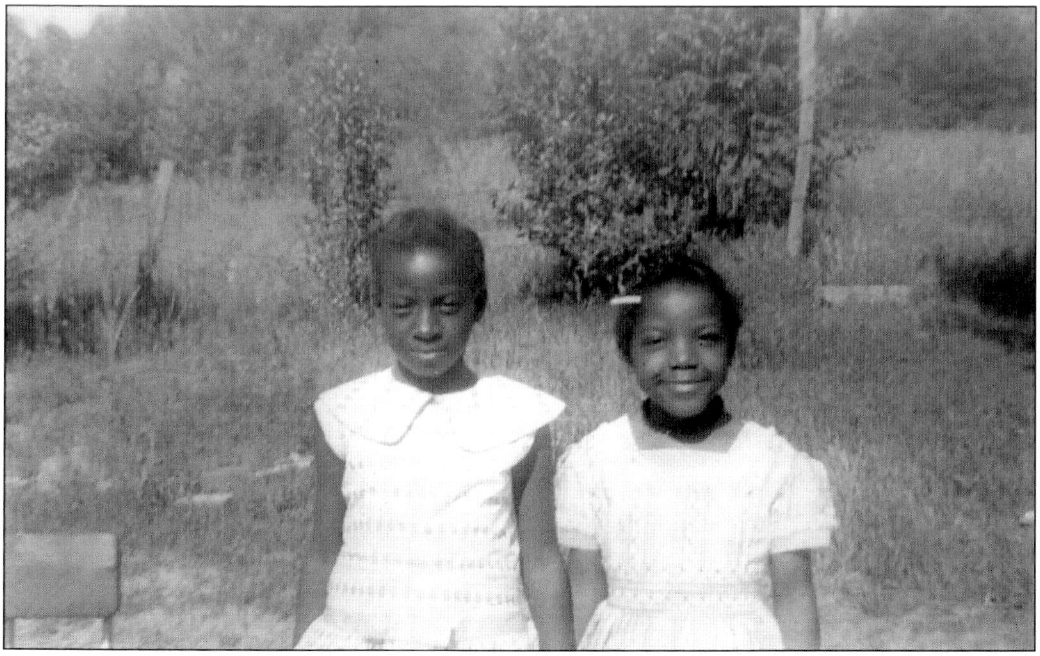

Carolyn Maxey and Carolyn Winn were playmates in the 1950s. Carolyn Maxey still resides in Gwinnett County. (Courtesy of Dorothy Maxey.)

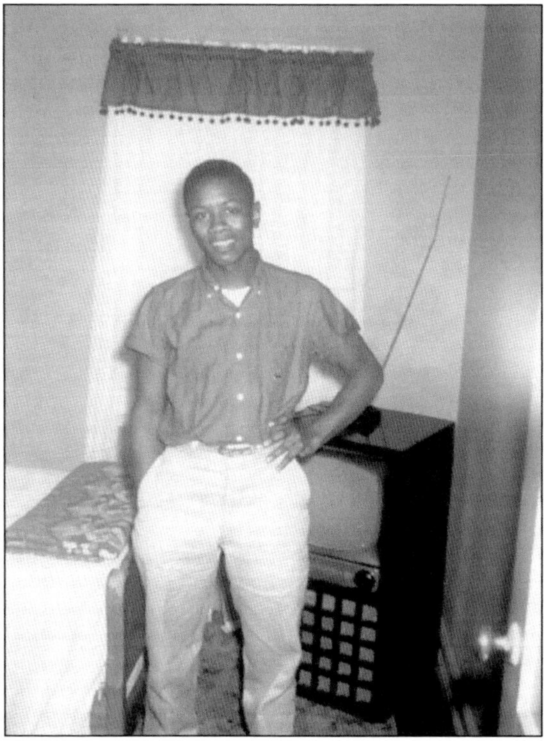

Billy Gholston is seen in 1960. (Courtesy of Dorothy Maxey.)

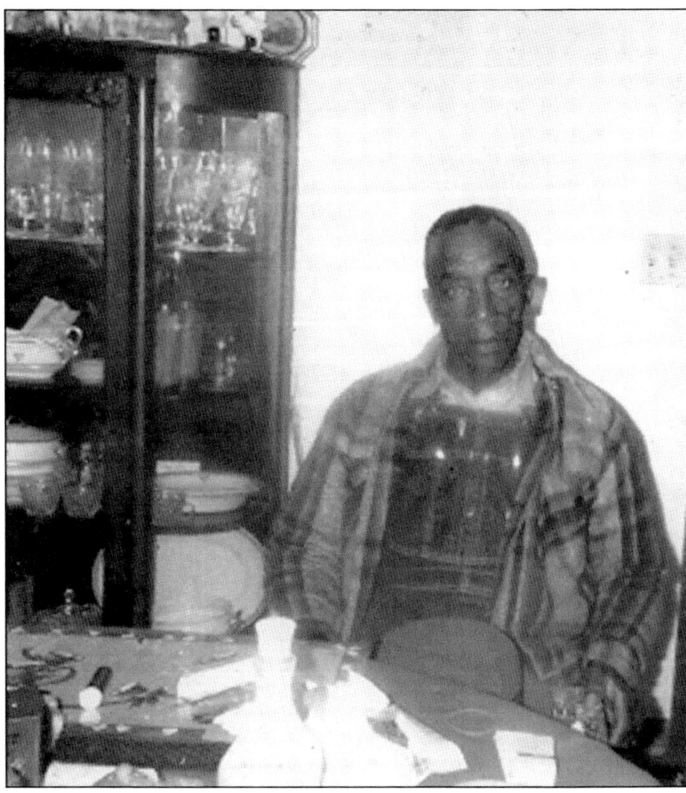

Earl Collins, seen here in the 1970s, was married to Clara Collins and the couple lived in Lawrenceville. (Courtesy of Clara Collins.)

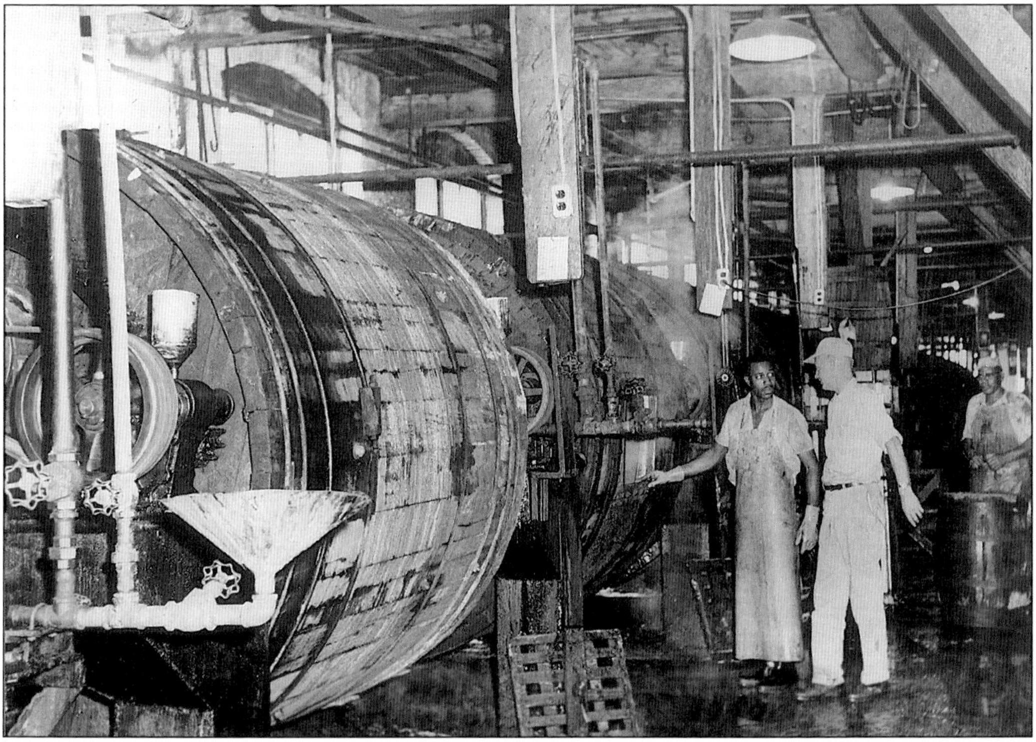

An African-American employee is pictured at the Bona Allen Tannery in Buford in December 1981. (Courtesy of Georgia Department of Archives and History.)

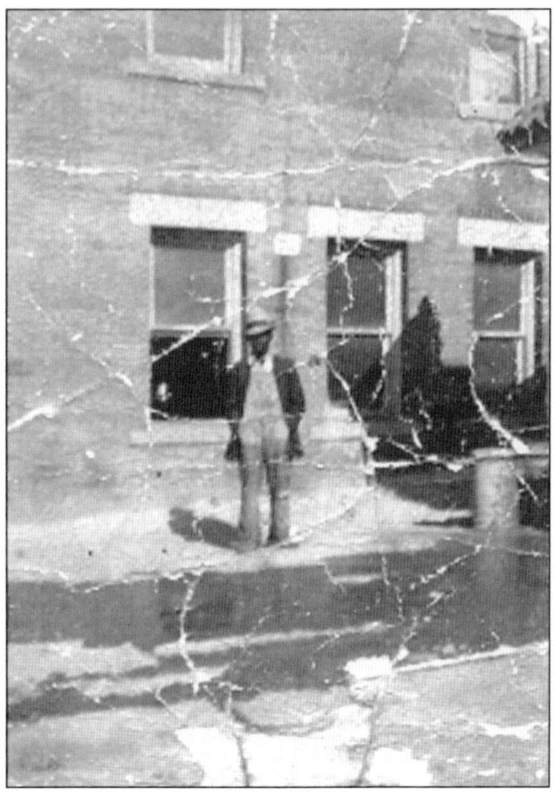

Willie B. Taylor stands in front of the Lawrenceville Fire Department in the 1960s. (Courtesy of Iri Williams.)

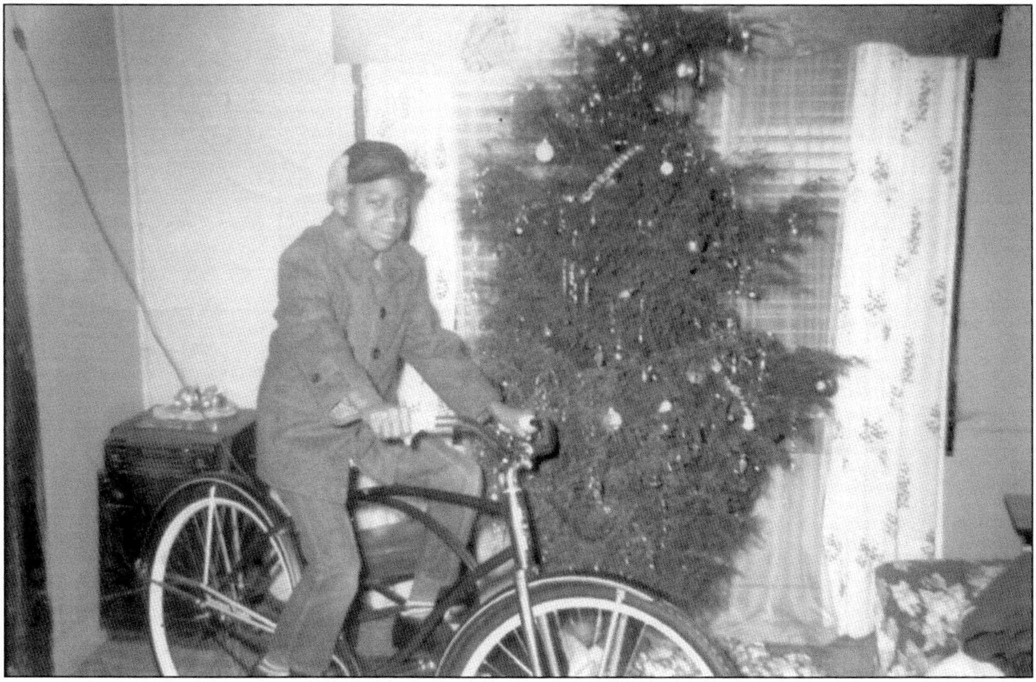

John Maxey was thrilled to receive a bicycle for Christmas in 1959. He was 11 years old. (Courtesy of Dorothy Maxey.)

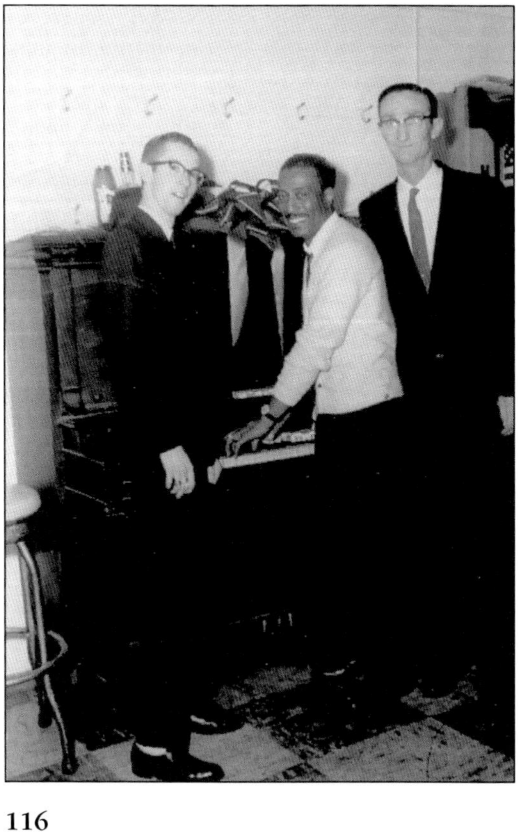

From left to right are Terry Davis, Cliff Maxey (playing piano), and an unidentified individual. (Courtesy of Dorothy Maxey.)

Ruby Williams (left) and Lula Hogshaw (right) posed for this fun picture in Lawrenceville during the 1960s.(Courtesy of Hattie Peters.)

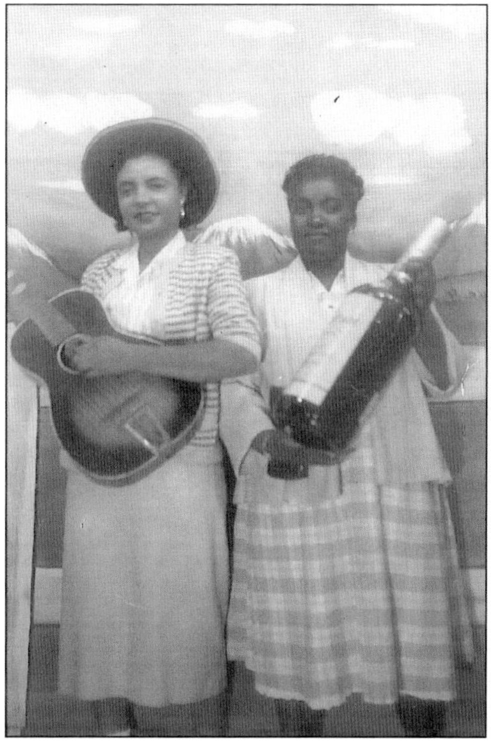

Thomas Livsey is pictured in May 1962. A well-known citizen of Gwinnett County, Mr. Livsey is married to Dorethia Austin Livsey. He was a Department of Family and Children Services board member for 25 years and has always been active in the community. The Thomas Livsey Conference Center is named in his honor. (Courtesy of Thomas Livsey.)

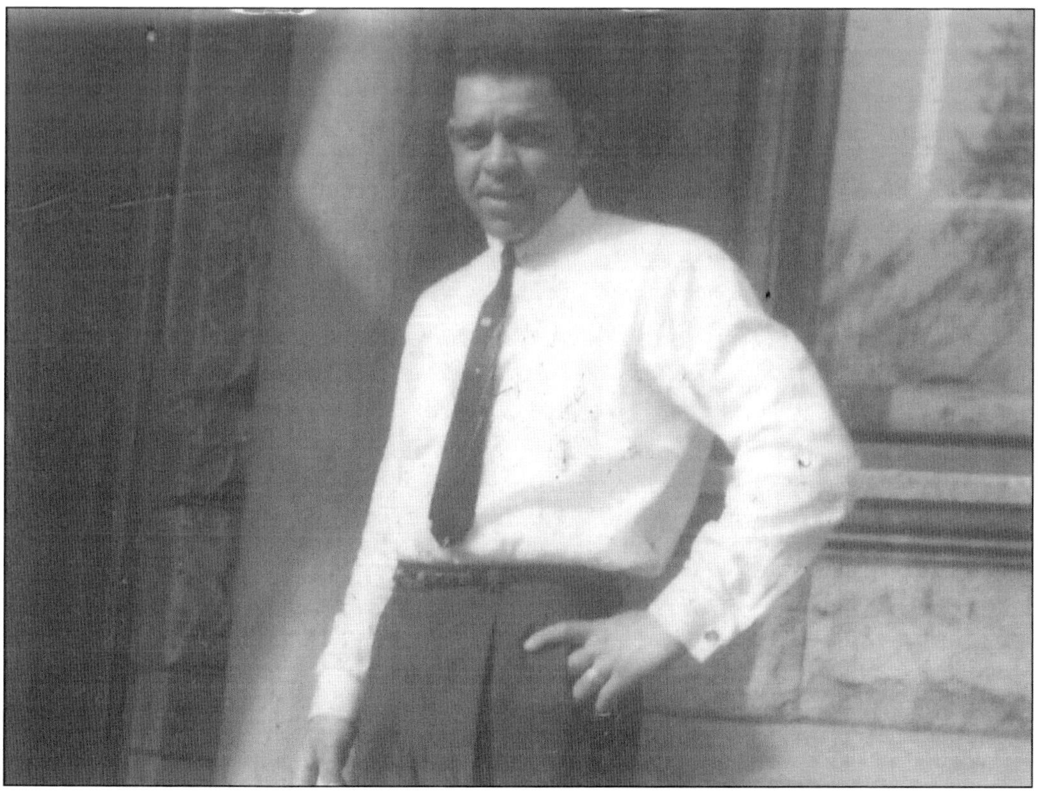

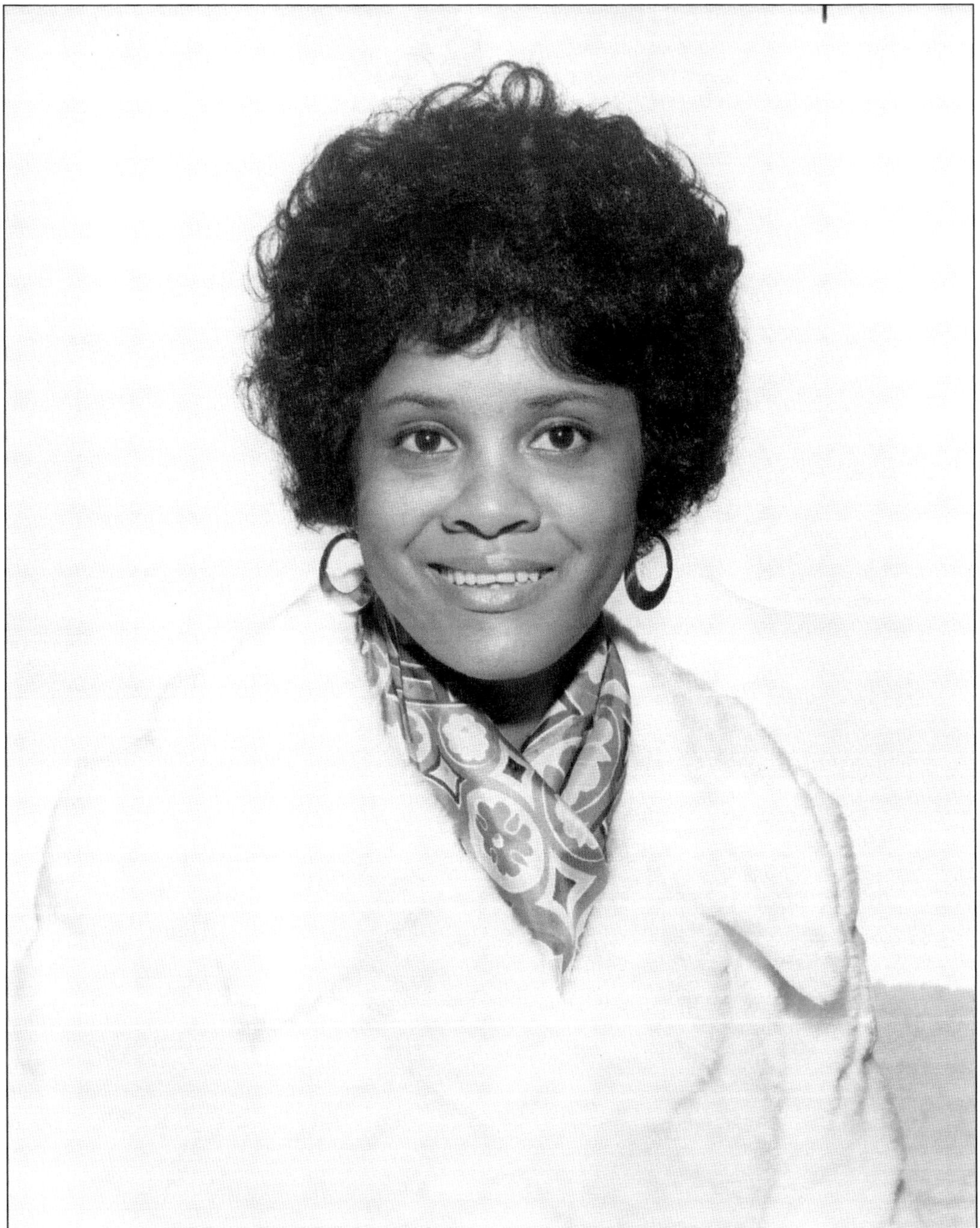

Susan Moore is pictured in 1972 at the Belk Department Store in Lawrenceville. The first black woman to work in the store, she is currently the president of the United Ebony Society in Gwinnett County. (Courtesy of Eron and Susan Moore.)

Seven

Breaking Barriers

Nothing ever comes to one, that is worth having, except as a result of hard work.
——Booker T. Washington

Gwinnett County has many pacesetters in the African-American community. Many people have faced adverse challenges to achieve what was once thought to be impossible; hard work and persistence make people like this stand out in the community. Such barrier breakers are to be applauded and thanked for blazing the trails so many will follow.

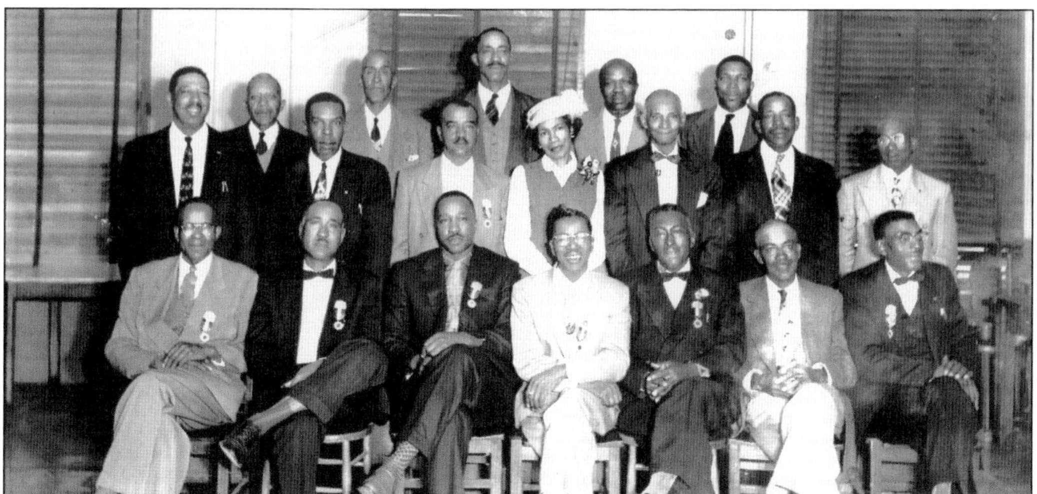

The Brotherhood of Maintenance of Way Employees, American Federation of Labor, and Congress of Industrial organizations held a joint meeting at the Butler Street YMCA. Pictured from left to right are (front row) Rev. N.S. Thompson, chaplain; W.E. Sims, recording secretary; Willie Moses, journalist; Cantrell Hood, secretary and treasurer; Timothy Summerour, president; O.W. Johnson, president Valdosta Local; and James Williams; (middle row) R.L. Barnwell, Luther Davis, J.C. Langston, Sister Geneva Hood, Will Solomon, J.D. Oden, and unidentified; (back row) Maney Barnes, Jim Thomas, Oscar Lee, Joseph Chandler, and Willie Watkins. (Courtesy of Timothy Summerour.)

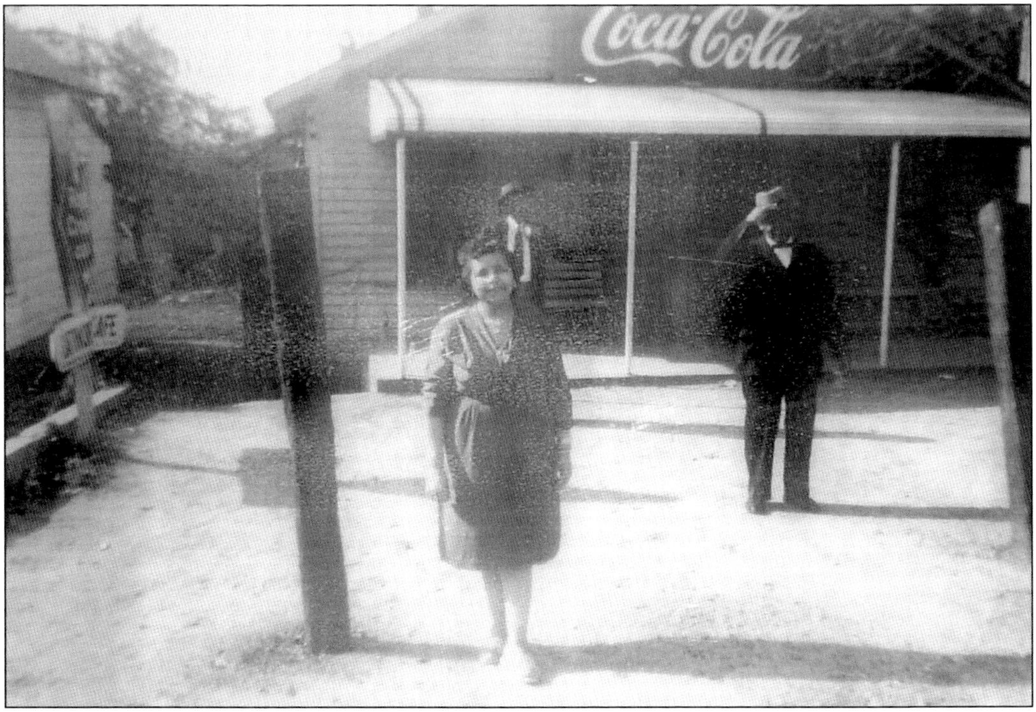

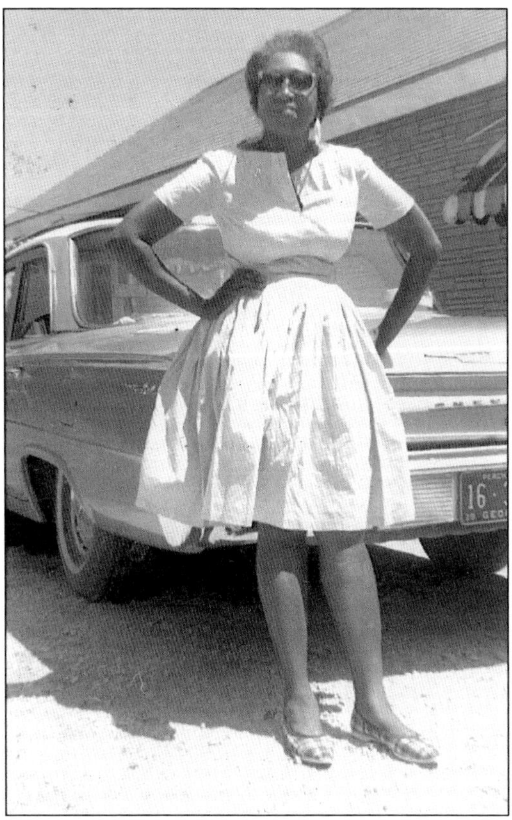

Mrs. Jurell Austin Lattimore is seen in front of her business, The Lattimore Café, in April 1962 in Buford, Georgia. The store was located beside Poplar Hill Baptist Church. Many people would stop by after church for ice cream and other treats. (Courtesy of Dorethia Livsey.)

Mrs. Julia "Soonie" Dunham poses against her car in this July 4, 1966 photo. Mrs. Dunham is one of the oldest African-American citizens living in Gwinnett County today. At the age of 90, she continues to drive and is as sharp and vibrant as any of Gwinnett's younger citizens. (Courtesy of Julia Dunham.)

Beauty P. Baldwin was appointed as the first African-American superintendent of schools in the city of Buford. She served from 1984 to 1994. She continues to serve the community through the educational system as an administrator at the Hopewell Christian Academy. (Courtesy of Beauty Baldwin.)

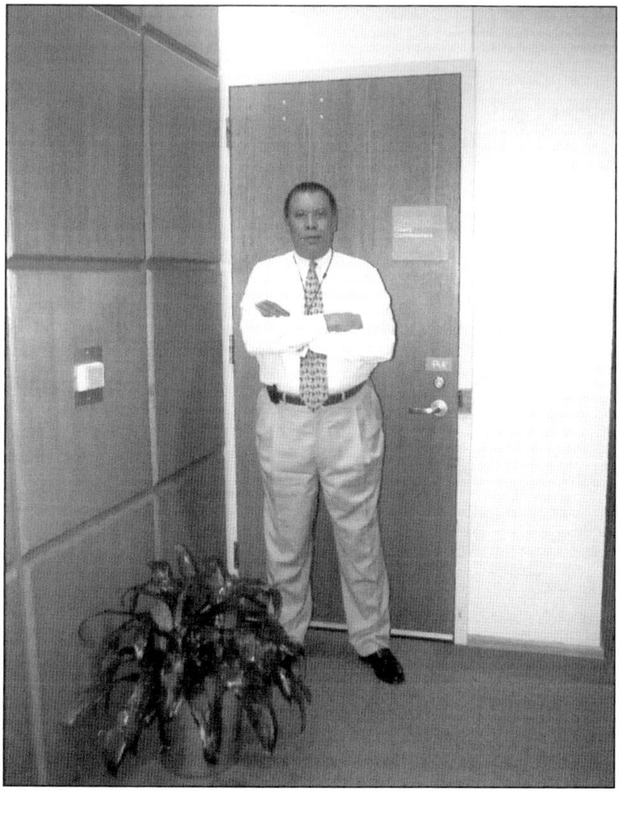

Percy Scott Jr. was elected as the first executive director for the Gwinnett County Human Relations Commission. He is actively involved with the Gwinnett County Schools and the Human Relations Council. (Courtesy of Percy Scott.)

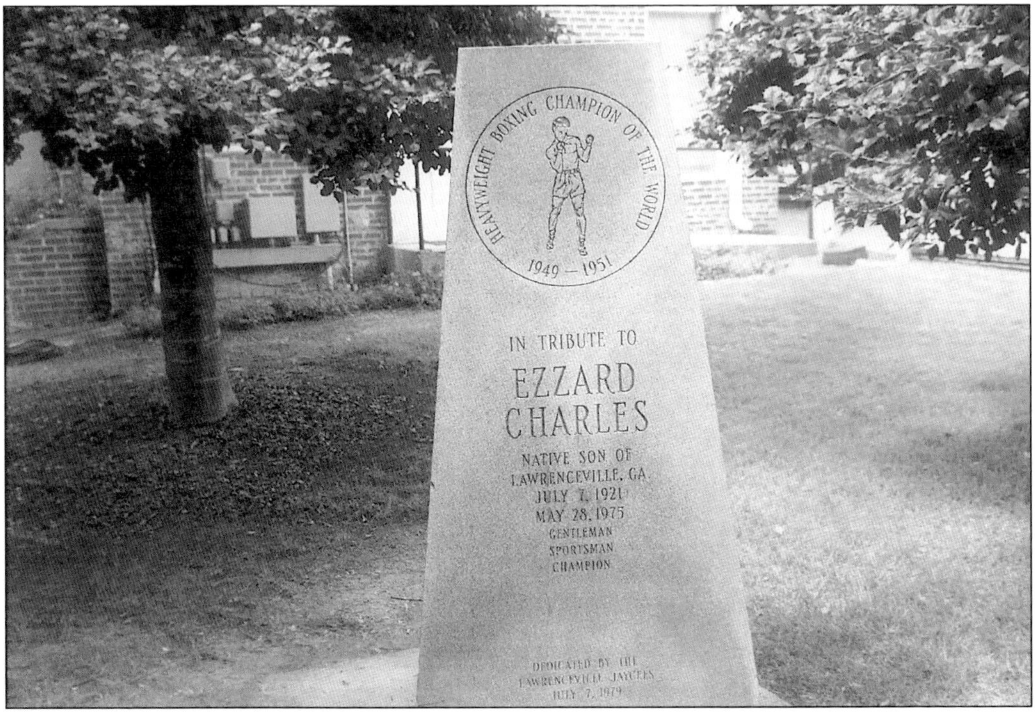

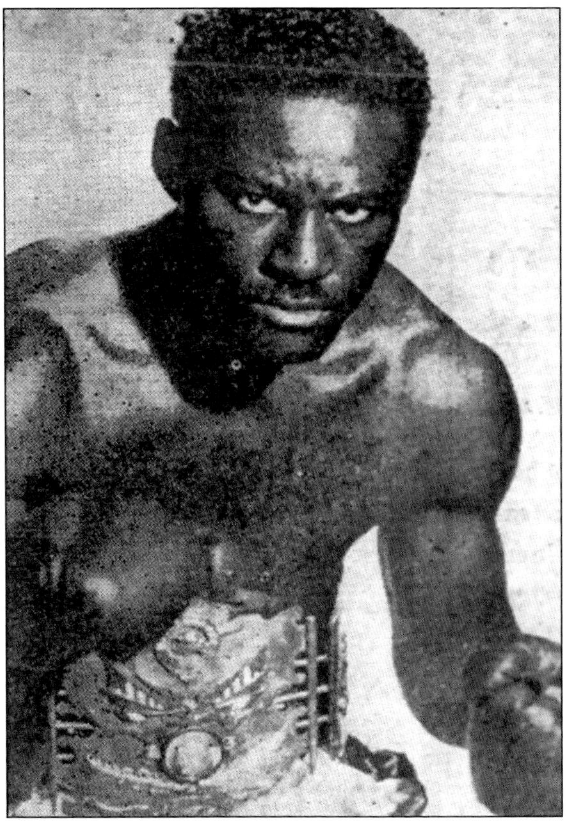

Ezzard Charles was a native of Gwinnett County who became an acclaimed professional boxer. He had 122 professional bouts and 96 wins—58 by knockout. One of Charles's most famous fights was against Rocky Marciano. The monument above stands on the lawn of the Gwinnett Historic Courthouse in Lawrenceville. (Above courtesy of the author; left courtesy of Gwinnett Historical Society.)

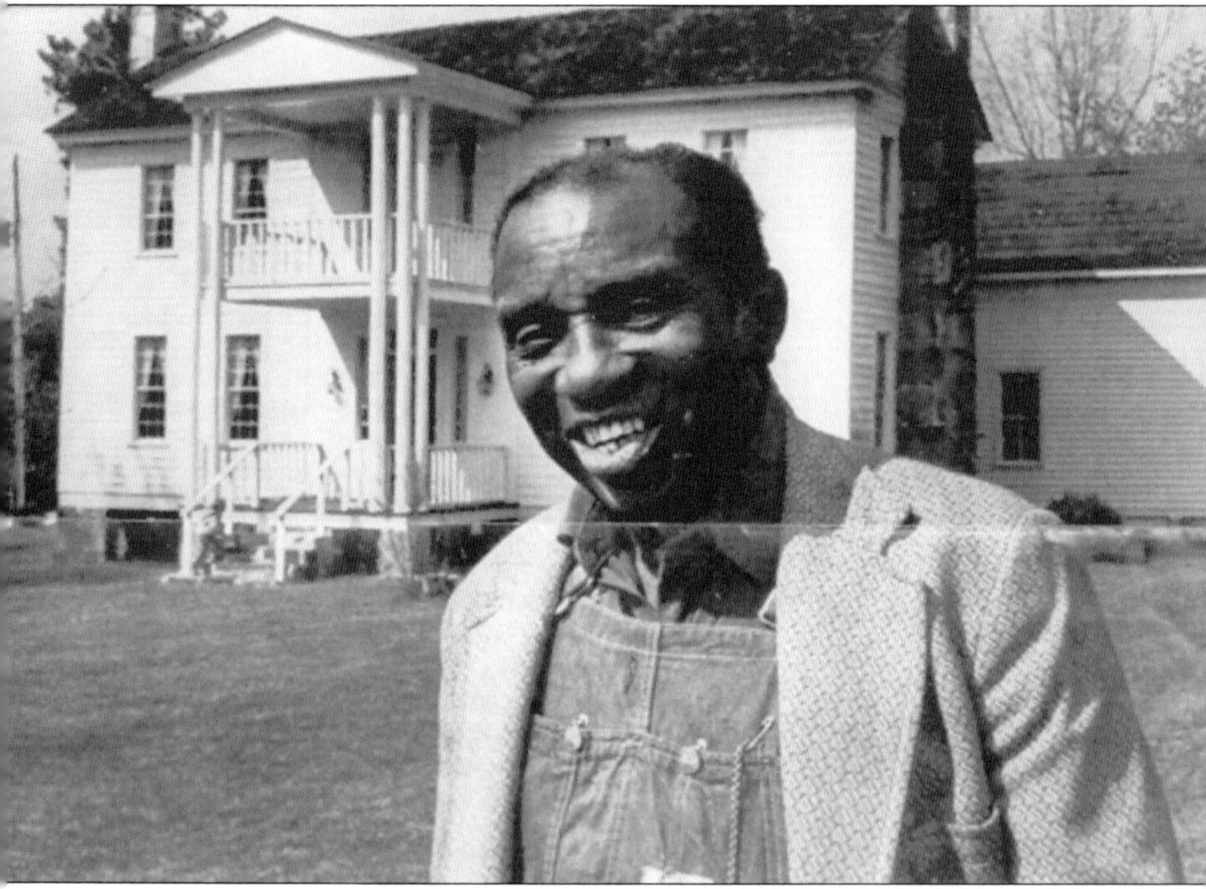

Mr. Amos Hutchins was keeper of the Elisha Winn House in Dacula. The Winn House was the first place of government in the newly formed Gwinnett County in 1818. The house still stands in Gwinnett County today. (Courtesy of the Gwinnett Historical Society.)

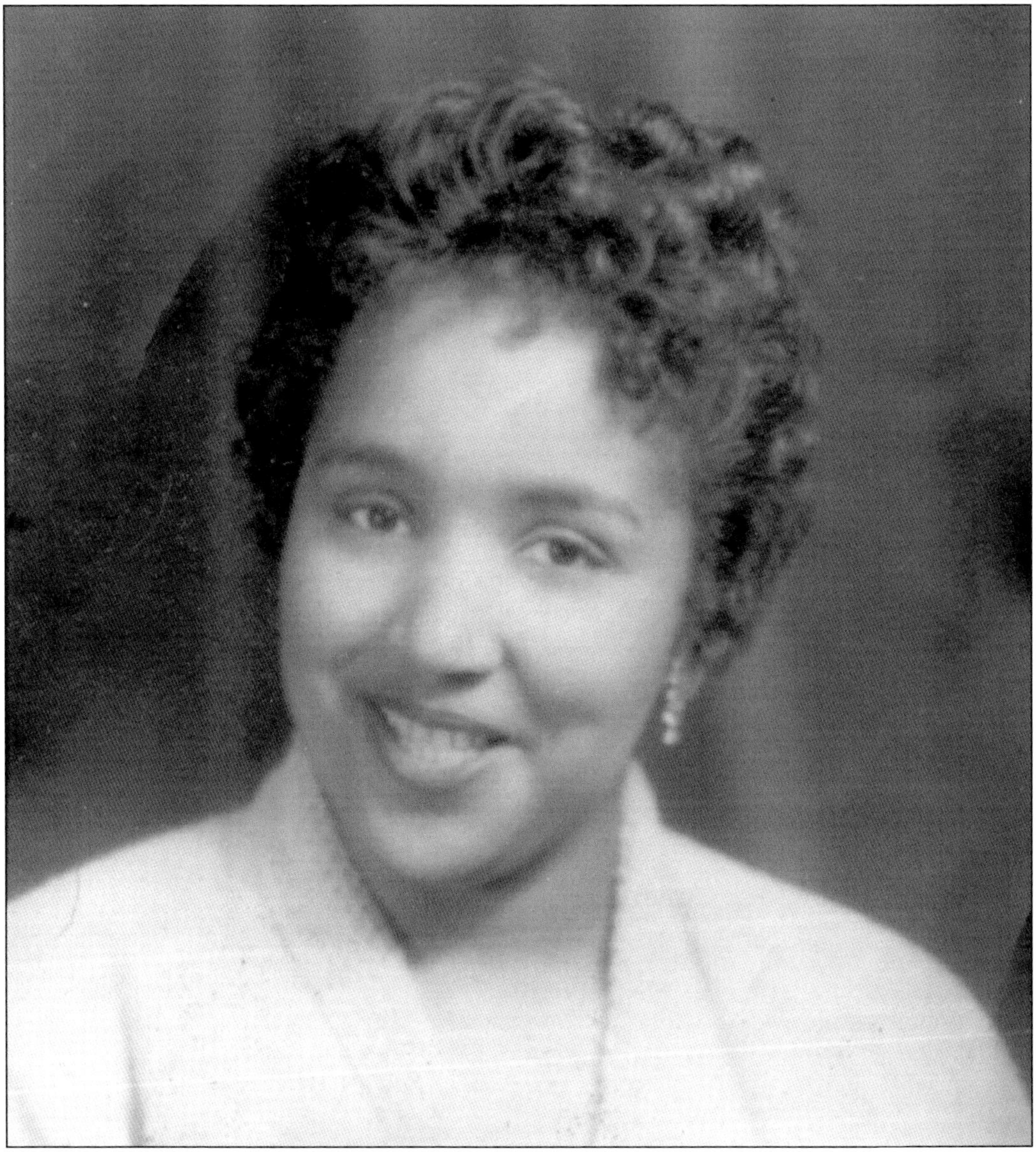

Dorethia Livsey was appointed as the first Black Jury Commissioner in Gwinnett County from 1990 to 1996. (Courtesy of Dorethia Livsey)

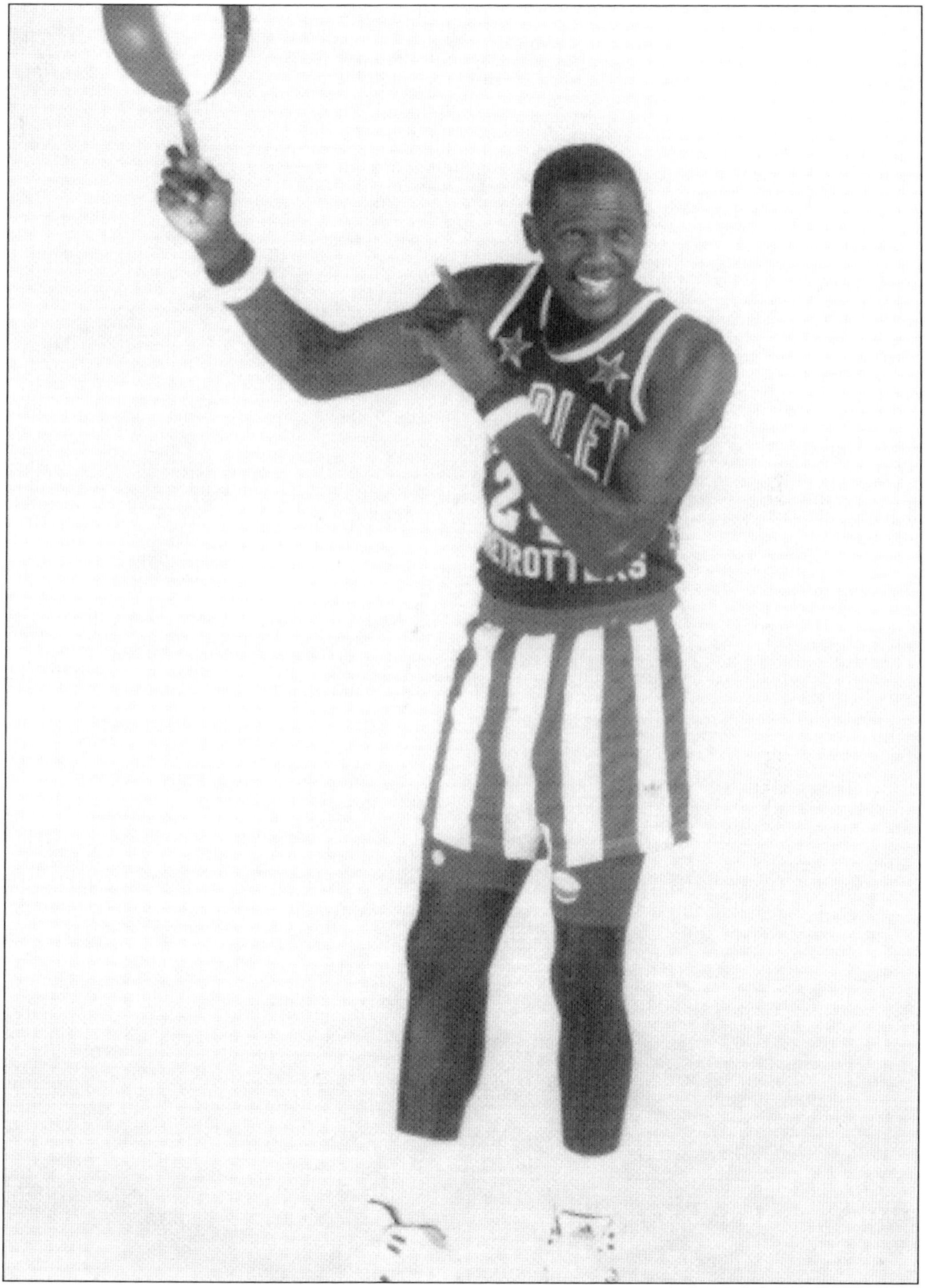

Michael Douglas played basketball with the Harlem Globetrotters from 1986 to 1993. He organized the Michael Douglas Youth Foundation, which is committed to providing positive and educational activities for youth. (Courtesy of Michael Douglas.)

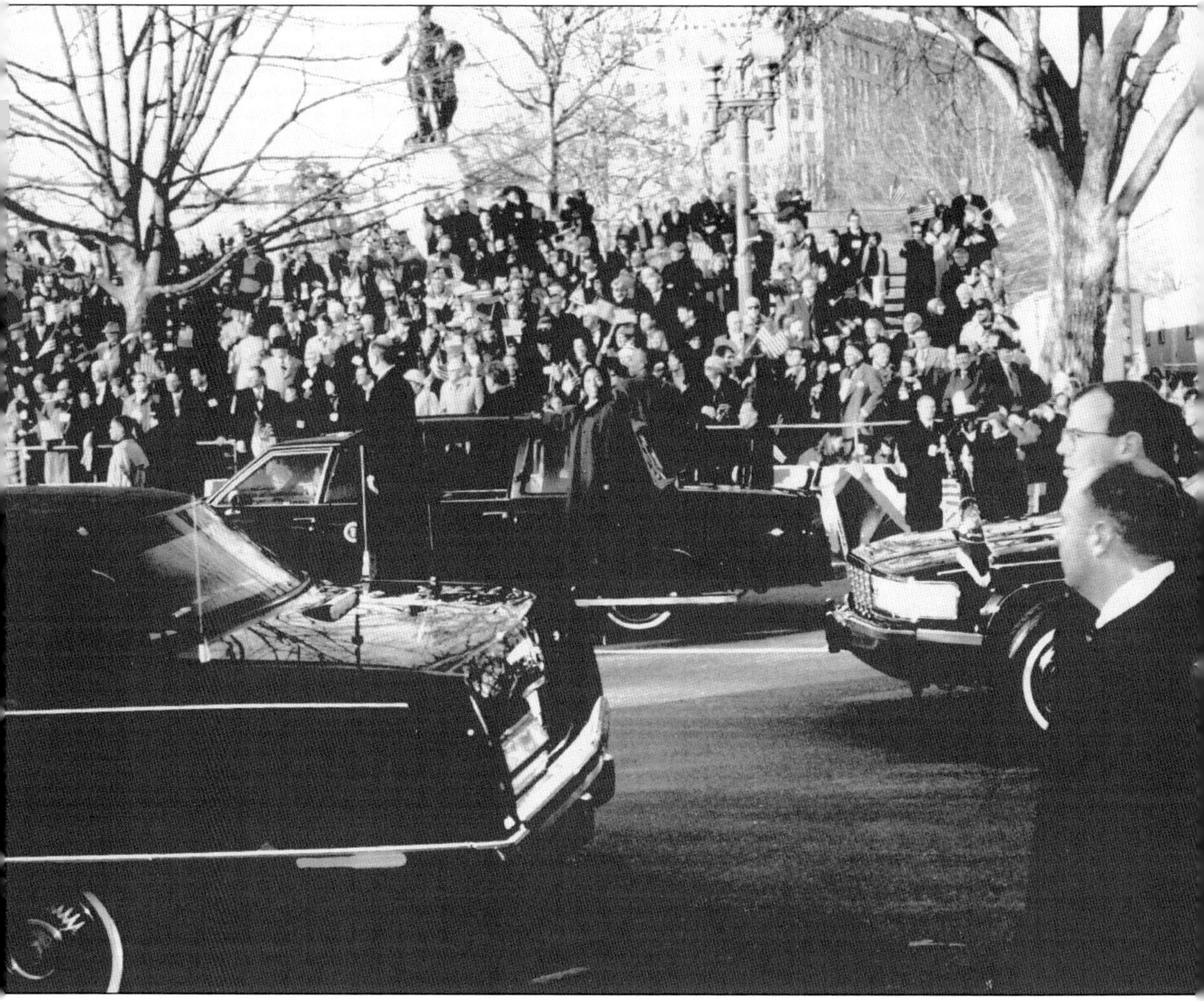

Yvette Summerour is pictured in the Presidential Motorcade of the Clinton Administration in 1992. (Courtesy of Timothy Summerour.)

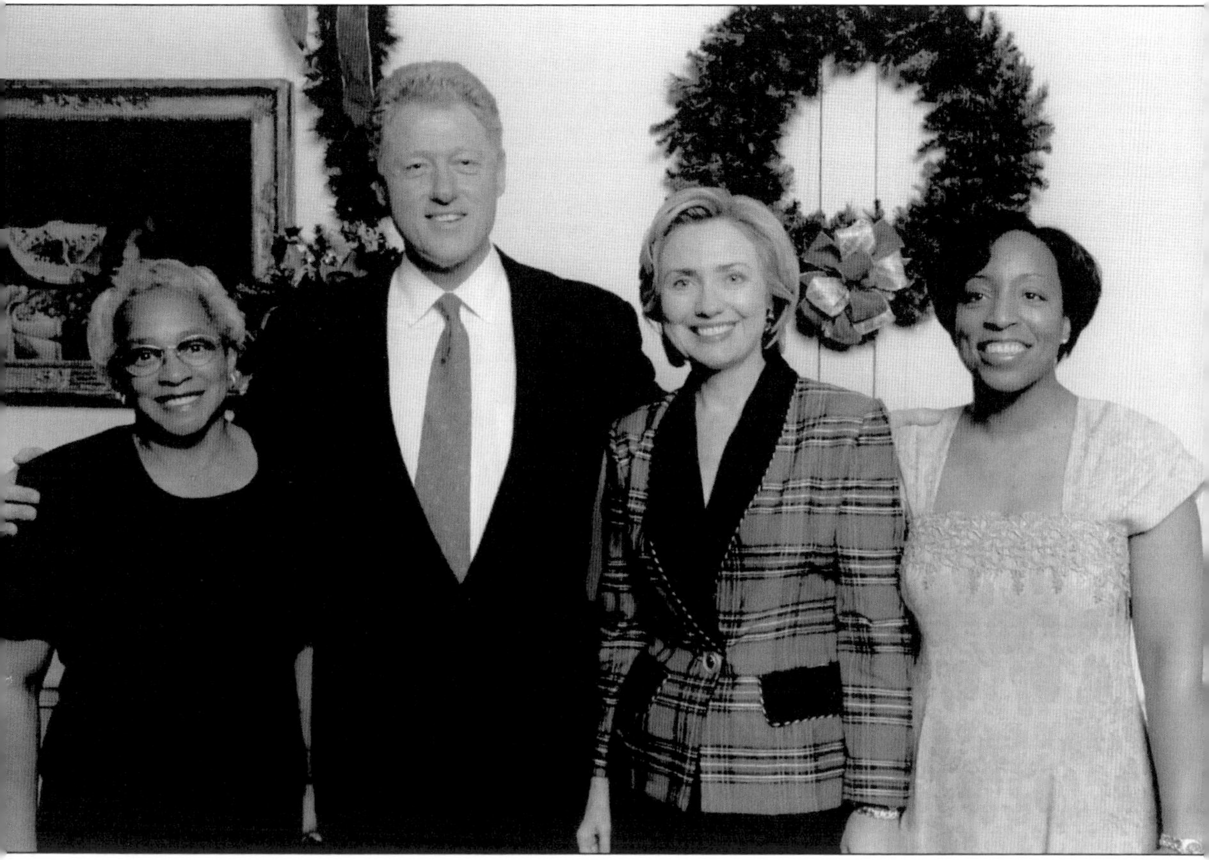

During the winter holidays at the White House this photograph was taken on December 9, 1998. From left to right are Mrs. Ruth Summerour, President William J. Clinton, First Lady Hillary Clinton, and Secret Service Agent Yvette Summerour. Yvette Summerour grew up in Gwinnett County and is currently one of the highest-ranking African Americans in the Secret Service. Yvette started breaking barriers in Gwinnett County long before her days in the Secret Service. She was the first black homecoming queen and the first black captain of the cheerleading team at Central Gwinnett High School. (Courtesy of Timothy Summerour)

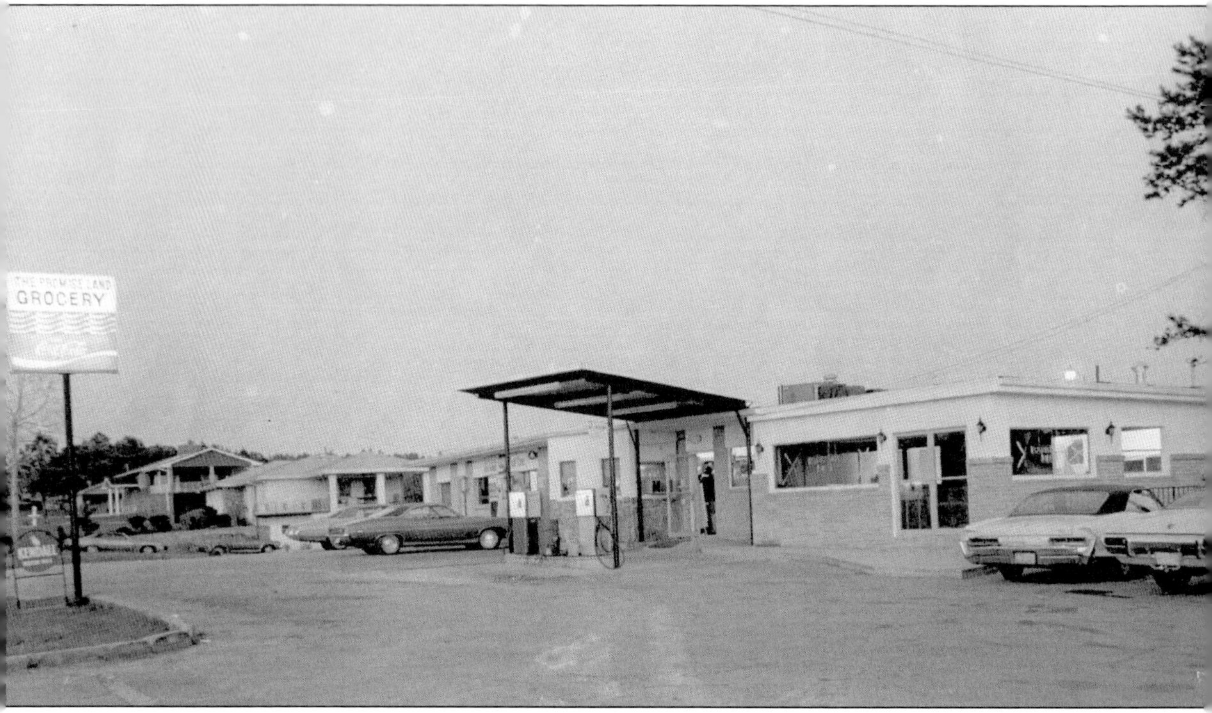

The Promised Land Grocery Store, Gas Station, Barber Shop, Beauty Parlor and Laundry Mat are seen in the 1970s. These businesses are black-owned and located in the southern section of the county. The name "Promised Land" was given to the community in the 1800s by plantation owner Thomas Maguire. The plantation is known for being visited by famous author Margaret Mitchell. She gave many details about the plantation and the surrounding area in her famous book *Gone With the Wind*. (Courtesy of Thomas Livsey.)